BEYOND PROZAC

HEALING MENTAL DISTRESS

DR TERRY LYNCH

FOREWORD BY DOROTHY ROWE

First edition 2001 Marino Books
This edition 2004

PCCS BOOKS
Llangarron
Ross-on-Wye
Herefordshire
HR9 6PT
UK
Tel +44 (0)1989 77 07 07
contact@pccs-books.co.uk
www.pccs-books.co.uk

**Beyond Prozac:
Healing mental distress**

British Library Cataloguing in Publication Data.
A catalogue record for this book is available from the British Library.

ISBN 1 898059 63 2

Cover design by Old Dog Graphics
Printed by Bath Press, Bath, UK

CONTENTS

Author's note

No book can act as a substitute for individualised medical or psychological care. The aim of this book is to promote a broader holistic approach to emotional distress, 'mental illness' and suicide. As it can be dangerous to reduce or stop psychiatric medication, this should only be done with appropriate, ongoing, personal medical guidance and supervision.

Acknowledgements

The author and PCCS Books would like to thank the following publishers and authors for their kind permission to use the following extracts: Dr Fred Baughman for an extract from his letter to the William Glasser website, 2003. BBC's *Panorama* for use of transcripts (2001). BMJ Publishing Group for use of extracts from the *British Medical Journal* listed at the end of the appropriate chapters. Richard Brooks for an extract from his resignation letter to the SSRI review group. Dr William Glasser for an extract from *Warning: Psychiatry Can Be Hazardous to your Mental Health*, New York: Harper Collins (2003). HarperCollins Publishers Ltd © 1997 for extracts from *My Body, My Enemy: My thirteen year battle with anorexia nervosa* by Claire Beekin and Rosanna Street. Excerpt from 'Introduction' by Irvin Yalom, M.D. from Carl R. Rogers, *A Way of Being*. Introduction by Irvin Yalom. Reprinted by kind permission of Houghton Mifflin Company, © 1995 All rights reserved. Dr Nathaniel Lehrman for an extract from his article posted on *RedFlagsDaily* website. Charles Medawar, Social Audit Ltd. David Oaks, Director, MindFreedom, for an extract from the website, www.MindFreedom.org. *Openmind*, for use of extracts as listed at the end of the appropriate chapters. Dorothy Rowe for use of an extract from her foreword to *Against Therapy* by Jeremy Masson (1997) published by HarperCollins Publishing Ltd. STEER for use of extracts from their letters to the *Derry Journal*. Arthur Shafer for an extract from his review of Dr David Healy's *Let Them Eat Prozac*. Fiona Shaw, for use of extracts from *Out of Me: The story of a postnatal breakdown*. (2001), published by Virago Press. Brunner-Routledge for an extract from *Users and Abusers of Psychiatry* by Lucy Johnstone (2000).

Every effort has been made to contact all copyright holders, but if any have been inadvertently omitted, the author and publisher will be pleased to make the necessary changes at the earliest opportunity.

It would therefore behove us well — public and politicians alike — to take an active interest in the welfare of our mentally disturbed compatriots, and not to leave their fate to the sole discretion of the experts. They are very far from being expert. And the figures tell us that there's a more than sporting chance that it will be you, or I, or our mother or our brother or our daughter or our spouse who becomes a victim of their ignorance before too long. Medical paternalism can go too far, and we should beware of giving the medical establishment too much legal power.

(Dr Donald Gould, *The Black and White Medicine Show: How doctors serve and fail their customers*, 1985)

It will generally be found that as soon as the terrors of life reach the point where they outweigh the terrors of death, a man will put an end to his life.

(Arthur Schopenhauer)

And it seems to me perfectly in the cards that there will be within the next generation or so a pharmacological method of making people love their servitude, and producing a kind of painless concentration camp for entire societies, so that people will in fact have their liberties taken away from them but will rather enjoy it, because they will be distracted from any desire to rebel by propaganda, brainwashing, or brainwashing enhanced by pharmacological methods.

(Aldous Huxley, *Brave New World,* 1959)

About the author

For over ten years, Terry Luynch worked as a General Practitioner. During this time, Terry Lynch become increasingly concerned about fundamental issues such as the quality of medical training in mental health, the excessive reliance on medication to treat mental health problems, and the pervasive influence of the pharmaceutical industry on medical practice. In 1997, Dr. Lynch undertook to expand his understanding of mental health problems beyond the narrow medical approach to mental health, culminating in the completion of an MA in Humanistic and Integrative Psychotherapy in 2002 at the University of Limerick. In 2003, he was appointed by the Irish Ministry for Health to the government-appointed Expert Group on Mental Health Policy; the remit of this group is to shape the direction of mental health policy in Ireland over the next two decades.

Terry Lynch passionately believes in the right of every person to live as fulfilled a life as possible. He believes that, in many cases, the current mental health services hinders the individual's ability to live more fully and more productively. In his own life, Dr. Lynch has experienced the pain of losing self-confidence, and the major effect this can have. In his case, he became very anxious as a teenager. The level of distress he experienced did not reach the point where he came in contact with the mental health services. However, his personal experience has given him both an insight into how mental health problems develop, and a passionate desire to see that the mental health services provide the sort of help which is really needed by service users. Terry Lynch believes that it is very difficult to survive in this world if one has very low self-confidence and self-esteem. It is no co-incidence that the majority of mental health service users have little self-confidence and self-belief. Common sense would therefore suggest that society should provide systems and programmes aimed at raising self-confidence, self-esteem and self-belief. Indeed, many of the beliefs and practices which exist within the mental health services might lead one to conclude that the services could do with a rather large dose of common sense.

He believes that, to a considerable degree, the mental health services have lost touch with some of the most basic elements of human interaction and care — respect, listening, communication, support, affirmation, encouragement, empathy, hope, mutuality, working in colloboration with service users, re-integration into society, for example. These are some of the qualities which mental service users repeatedly say mean the most to them. These human qualities need to become the foundation upon which mental health services are built.

FOREWORD

Terry Lynch is a brave man. The medical profession does not forgive renegades, and a renegade is any doctor who criticises the sacred dogma of the profession. A doctor who dares to do this is likely to see career and reputation suffer. Nevertheless, Terry Lynch believes that he must tell the truth about his experience as a doctor, even if this experience contradicts one very important part of medical dogma.

This concerns mental illness, or, as it is now called, mental disorder. The profession of psychiatry is based on the belief that there are such things as mental illnesses, and that these illnesses have a physical cause and a physical cure — drugs and electroconvulsive therapy. Nowadays psychiatrists talk of 'social factors' and 'psychological factors' in mental disorder, and a few psychiatrists see such factors as the prime cause of mental disorder, but for the majority of psychiatrists social and psychological factors merely exacerbate what is for them essentially a physical illness. Such psychiatrists expect general practitioners like Terry Lynch to conform to this belief.

The only way to maintain the belief that mental disorder has a physical cause is steadfastly to refuse to be aware of what is going on and what has gone on in the lives of individual people. Terry Lynch was incapable of doing this. He listened to his patients, and so he came to see that there were direct connections between the form of the patient's distress and the life of the patient. He found too that by listening attentively, encouraging his patients to put into words the teeming mass of thoughts and feelings that brought them pain and confusion, they were able to come to a clear understanding of their situation. Then they could take charge of their lives and create a secure, sustainable way of living.

From his conversations with people who were planning to kill themselves and from his study of the stories of people who had killed themselves Terry Lynch could see that the theory to explain suicide which psychiatrists put forward, that low serotonin levels in the brain led to suicide, was quite inappropriate. Instead he saw in these stories the recurring themes of lovelessness and loneliness. These suicidal people did not love themselves, and, though they might be surrounded by family and friends, they had no one in their life who accepted them as they were and listened to them.

Lovelessness and loneliness cannot be explained by chemical changes in the brain and cured by the ingestion of drugs. Lovelessness and loneliness, like anxiety and depression and all the ways of expressing distress which are called mental disorder, are part of what it is to be human, but a part that can be understood, diminished and banished from our lives simply by caring wisely for ourselves. Terry Lynch understands and cares wisely for us all. His immense warmth and humanity are revealed on every page of this book. It is truly a book for our time and for all time.

Dr Dorothy Rowe

INTRODUCTION

Emotional distress is one of the greatest epidemics of our time. As sometimes happens in epidemics, those afflicted are ostracised. Emotions are a fundamental part of the human condition, but in modern society there is little tolerance of the expression of emotion. When friends or loved ones become angry or tearful, we want them to stop because we do not feel comfortable with painful emotions. The greater the distress, the more uncomfortable we feel. We reach the point where we cannot listen any more. We find ways of repackaging emotional distress to make it more palatable. This allows us to distance ourselves from the epidemic.

The main repackaging process society uses is to classify emotional distress as 'mental illness'. When I refer to 'mental' or 'psychiatric' illness I use inverted commas, but not with the intention of detracting from the real, often excruciating distress experienced by people who have been so labelled. The inverted commas signify my disquiet at the widespread acceptance of these terms without debate about what the terms mean and what might be better words to use.

People turn to the medical profession for help. GPs deal with 90 per cent of the emotional-distress workload and refer most of the remainder to psychiatrists. The medical profession categorises emotional distress into two groups: the psychiatrically ill and the 'worried well'. Drug treatment is the cornerstone of treatment for those categorised as psychiatrically ill, a label which frequently sticks for life. Emotionally distressed people whom doctors decide are not suffering from a 'mental illness' are dismissed as the worried well, needing no treatment. A person's chances of being diagnosed as psychiatrically ill parallels the degree of their emotional distress. Often, neither those labelled as psychiatrically ill nor the worried well receive the help they need from the medical profession, in my opinion.

Medication is by far the most frequent treatment offered to people diagnosed with a so-called 'mental illness', such as depression, manic depression and schizophrenia. In Britain, some people with 'depression' are offered counselling. However, the vast majority of those referred for counselling are also put on medication, and sometimes have to wait up to two years to see a counsellor. I have major reservations about this approach to treatment of so-called 'mental illness'.

I present an alternative view of 'mental illness'. Policies regarding the diagnosis and treatment of medical conditions within modern medicine are dominated by the prevailing views of the medical profession. Where 'mental illness' is concerned, the prevailing views within psychiatry dictate how people in emotional distress are dealt with in society. According to most medical experts, 'mental illness' is caused by a biochemical brain imbalance, a brain abnormality and/or a genetic defect. I do not share this view. I believe that the so-called 'mental illnesses' are understandable expressions of human distress.

Every year, one million people take their own lives worldwide and thirty million people attempt suicide. The prevailing medical belief is that people who end their lives were mentally ill at the time and therefore not in their 'right mind'.

I believe that suicide is a final act of avoidance, which in the context of the person's life always makes sense. We do not need a 'psychiatric illness' explanation for suicide. People who attempt suicide are individuals with unique experiences of life. It is this mosaic of experiences that brings them to a place where suicide seems the only way out of their torment. People who reach the point of suicide all have one thing in common. Overwhelmed with despair, they are desperately trying to put an end to their emotional pain. The tragedy is that in order to do so, they feel they have to kill themselves.

What does it say about our society that such vast numbers of people feel the need to remove themselves from it forever? What sort of help does our society provide for people who fall out of step with the mainstream of society — people who stumble at the hurdles of life and cannot pick themselves up; people whose hopes and dreams have been dashed; those who are labelled by society as different; those who are consumed with insecurity and self-doubt? These are people who have felt hurt so often they cannot take any more: men and women in relationships that initially carried such hopes but which have, over the years, lost their lustre, and those who have experienced far more fear and hurt in their lives than love.

Some people become so despairing that they take their own lives. Many turn to the medical system for help, often being diagnosed as suffering from a 'mental illness', or told that there is nothing wrong with them. The escalating suicide rate is a wake-up call to us all. Concluding that suicide is the result of 'mental illness' may make us feel better, but it is passing the buck. People take their own lives when they reach the point of no hope.

Over the past 20 years, most countries have witnessed their suicide rates increase dramatically. For every suicide, at least 20 people attempt suicide. More than four thousand people take their own lives in Britain each year. In many countries including Britain and Ireland, the increasing suicide rate has been particularly noticeable among young men. The suicide rate in young men under the age of 35 has doubled in Britain over the past 20 years. Suicide in boys and men between 12 and 35 years of age is now up there with road traffic accidents as one of the most common causes of death in that age group. Although reducing the suicide rate in Britain by 15 per cent has been a stated national priority of the British Department of Health since 1992, the British suicide rates remain stubbornly high, showing only marginal overall decline over the past two decades. In 1998, the US Surgeon General stated it was high time that Americans had an honest debate on mental health. I believe such a debate is as urgently necessary in Europe as in America.

Perhaps my personal experience of mental and emotional distress gives me some insight into the distress others experience in their lives. My siblings and I were raised by my grandmother. My parents were both alive and living in America. A decision was made that the children come to Ireland to be raised while our parents remained in America. I was four years of age at that time. This schism in our family had quite an effect on us all. My parents would visit us for about two weeks a year; they were more like a visiting aunt and uncle than our parents.

In my early childhood, I was greatly upset about being separated from my parents. This upset seemed to settle, as I reached a new equilibrium in my life in Ireland. All that changed when I hit the teenage years. Possibly because I did not have the presence of my parents in my life at that time, who were alive and still living in America, I lost my bearings, my confidence and I became quite anxious. I experienced the teenage years as lonely, scary and painful. It took me many years to move on from this. Many aspects of my life were affected, including my ability to study, to interact with others. Even my sporting activities were affected. As a child, I was a very promising young golfer, regularly beating boys many years older than me. For example, when eleven years of age I beat a 16-year-old in a school golf competition. Within three years, that 16-year-old was playing for Ireland, and went on to be one of Ireland's most respected amateur golfers of all time. As my anxiety increased, I lost my fluency, and that special affinity I previously had with that little white ball.

I qualified as a medical doctor in 1982, and worked as a GP until 1997. Having had increasing doubts and concerns for several years regarding many aspects of medical beliefs and practice, I then decided to stop working as a typical GP. I wanted to continue working within the health system, but I felt that the biological focus embraced by my profession was far too narrow, virtually ignoring the emotional, psychological, social and other aspects of the human condition. While this is true of many aspects of health care, it is particularly true in mental health. I felt that a more holistic approach to health care might benefit the public. I set about expanding my understanding of health and illness. I re-trained as a psychotherapist. I tried to get to know and understand myself. I completed an MA in Humanistic and Integrative Psychotherapy at the University of Limerick in 2002, and now work as a GP with a special interest in mental health. In practice, I work primarily as a psychotherapist. I prescribe medication when I believe it is appropriate to do so. A common sentiment expressed to me by clients is that they value the fact that I have a knowledge of the medical approach to mental health and that I work using a broader approach to mental health than the majority of GPs.

The reader may understandably doubt any questioning of medical practice. The public may naturally presume that mental health care is based on best practice, the highest standards, and rigorous science. Throughout history, there have been many areas of life where a combination of vested interests and ignorance has remained unseen and/or unchallenged for years. As explored throughout this book, I believe that mental health is one such area.

1

MEDICAL RESEARCH

During my early years as a medical doctor, I unquestioningly believed that medical research was beyond reproach, the foundation upon which trustworthy scientific medical practice was built. Twenty years later, my views have changed considerably. The calibre of medical research impacts on the quality of medical care. It therefore seems appropriate at the outset to explore the reliability of medical research.

The results of medical research are rarely questioned. People presume that because medical research is supposedly scientific, it must be reliable. This perception of medical research is regularly reinforced by doctors in the media. For instance, psychiatrist Dr Matthew Hotopf, lecturer at the Institute of Psychiatry at London's Maudsley Hospital, explained in *The Guardian* of 7 April 1998 why doctors are sceptical of alternative medicine. He said that all medical treatments have to be carefully evaluated using randomised trials. The implicit assumption in comments such as Dr Hotopf's is that everything doctors do has been researched thoroughly and to a very high standard. Unfortunately, this is not always the case.

According to two scientists who have been auditing trials of new medicines for the past ten years, some clinical trials are so badly flawed that they endanger the health of the patients who take part in them. On 27 July 1999, *The Guardian* reported that scientists Wendy Bohaychuk and Graham Ball were appalled at the poor standards they have consistently found in clinical trials of new drugs. In a third of the trials they reviewed, they found significant under-reporting of side-effects. Dr Ball said that the government has no idea what is going on.

Dr Stephen Penford Lock is a former editor of the prestigious *British Medical Journal*. In an interview published in the *Irish Medical Times* of 15 October 1999, Dr Penford Lock stated that between 10 and 30 per cent of medical research is known to be fraudulent, involving plagiarism and the invention of data. He said that no system exists to deal with suspected cases of fraudulent research. He expressed his concern that large drug trials are often not replicated and can be influenced by pharmaceutical companies. He added that money could act as an incentive, with some trials receiving over £1000 per patient. He also pointed out that some researchers would invent data, having convinced themselves of their findings before they have actually obtained results.

Even in esteemed journals such as the *British Journal of Psychiatry,* it has been estimated that statistical errors occur in 40 per cent of published research, casting serious doubt on the conclusions drawn from these studies. In the *British Medical Journal* of 5 October 1991, editor Richard Smith discussed a presentation given the previous week in Manchester by Dr David Eddy, then professor of Health Policy and Management at Duke University, North Carolina. Dr Eddy told the conference:

Only about 15 per cent of medical interventions are supported by solid scientific evidence. This is partly because only 1 per cent of articles in medical journals are scientifically sound, and partly because many treatments have never been assessed at all. Confident statements in textbooks and medical journals regarding medical treatments have simply been handed down from generation to generation, without having been scientifically assessed.[1]

9

In *Medicine Weekly*, 24 September 1997, psychiatrist Dr Peadar O'Grady expressed his concerns about medical research:

Most medical research is unhelpfully biased, or incompetently or fraudulently constructed, sometimes all of the above. Research is largely funded by pharmaceutical companies, which obviously favour research that will either develop a new drug, or show an old drug to be better than other therapies. Of the research that is done, drug research has an unfair advantage in that advertising from drug companies is what most journals almost entirely run on. Refusing a piece of [drug] research might endanger such revenue, and to publish research showing a drug to be dangerous, useless or less effective than alternatives could be positively suicidal for a journal. The editor of a journal of psychological research once told me that research was biased by funding both of the research itself and of the journals in which it is published.[2]

Similar concerns were expressed by Drs Pat Bracken and Phil Thomas.[3] According to these Bradford-based psychiatrists, the pharmaceutical industry in the United States invests virtually 25 per cent of its total $54.7 billion sales on advertising and other activities designed to promote their products. Pharmaceutical companies give 'educational' material to medical schools without charge, and fund the attendance of doctors at overseas meetings, and directly fund the vast majority of academic meetings. Drs Bracken and Thomas point out that some prominent American academics are raising questions regarding such close ties between doctors and the pharmaceutical industry. They refer to Dr Marcia Angell, editor-in-chief of the prestigious *New England Journal of Medicine*, who speaks of 'a host of financial arrangements' between drug companies and doctors, including academic medicine. According to Dr Angell, these financial arrangements include researchers serving as paid consultants for drug companies whose drugs they are researching, being on advisory boards, speakers' bureaus, patent and royalty agreements, being named as listed authors of ghost-written published articles, promoting products at drug company-sponsored meetings, accepting expensive gifts and trips to lavish, exclusive locations, and having sometimes considerable financial equity interest in drug companies. Dr Angell believes that these extensive financial connections are primarily about marketing and profit.

Drs Bracken and Thomas believe that the influence of the drug industry extends further, into the formation of clinical guidelines for the management of conditions. They point to a 2002 survey published in the *Journal of the American Medical Association* which found that 87 per cent out of 200 authors of clinical guidelines had financial ties with at least one pharmaceutical company, including the companies whose drugs they endorsed. More that 50 per cent of these authors of clinical guidelines have received payments from drug companies to carry out research.

Drs Bracken and Thomas argue that such ties have a major influence in defining how the medical profession interprets emotional distress. They are very concerned that young psychiatrists have a very narrow understanding of human beings, their distress and their problems having been trained within the narrow medical approach, without sufficient regard to alternatives. They call for a full and open debate regarding the influence of the pharmaceutical industry within psychiatry. They ask how much drug industry money is received by the Royal College of Psychiatrists annually. They ask how such monies are spent, and how much drug funding is put into meetings of the Royal College of Psychiatrists.

Drs Bracken and Thomas call on the Royal College of Psychiatrists to create a register of members' interest in pharmaceutical companies, a register which is open to public scrutiny, to which individual psychiatrists are obliged to declare all financial connections with the pharmaceutical industry. These two psychiatrists point out that such a register already exists regarding members of parliament in Britain.

The *British Medical Journal* devoted much of its 31 May 2003 edition to the links between the medical profession and the pharmaceutical industry. Much that was published in this issue is cause for considerable alarm:

Eighty to ninety-five per cent of doctors regularly see drug company representatives despite evidence that their information is overly positive and prescribing habits are less appropriate as a consequence. Many doctors receive multiple gifts from drug companies every year. Most doctors deny that such gifts influence them despite considerable evidence to the contrary. The number of gifts doctors receive correlates with beliefs that drug representatives have no impact on prescribing behaviour. Accepting meals and expenses for travel or accommodation for sponsored educational meetings is common despite evidence that this is associated with an increase in the prescribing of the sponsor's drug. Many professional societies rely heavily on industry sponsorship, just as their medical journals rely on drug company funded trials, company advertisements — despite the obvious conflict of interest. Entanglement between doctors and drug companies is widespread, and evidence shows that interactions with industry influence doctors' behaviour. Evidence is strong and consistent that sponsored research tends to produce favourable results.

An estimated 60 per cent of biomedical research and development in the US is now privately funded, and two thirds of academic institutions have equity ties with outside sponsors. Finding senior medical researchers or clinicians without financial ties to pharmaceutical companies has become exceedingly difficult. Those regarded as 'thought leaders' routinely work as paid members of drug companies' advisory boards despite evidence that the practice is part of industry's promotional machinery.[4]

In the above article by Moynihan, he refers to the concerns of Arnold Relman, a Harvard professor and former editor of the *New England Journal of Medicine*. Professor Relman believes, regarding the practice of medicine, medical research and training, that the medical profession has allowed itself to be bought by the pharmaceutical industry. According to him the medical academic institutions in America have become the 'paid agents' of the drug industry; a practice he describes as 'disgraceful'.

A study by members of the Medical Products Agency in Sweden[5] investigated 42 studies of five antidepressants submitted to the Swedish drug regulatory authority in the process of seeking approval for these drugs in the treatment of depression. Such was the degree of publication bias they found in these drug-company sponsored studies, the researchers concluded that any doctor who relies on these studies to decide which antidepressant to prescribe will be basing their choice on biased evidence.

In another article from the same *British Medical Journal* entitled 'How can research ethics committees protect patients better?' Silvio Garattini and colleagues at the Mario Negri Institute, Milan, Italy commented that 'Clearly there are biases in clinical trials that often tend to favour new drugs'.[6]

Another article in the same journal[7] studied characteristics of GPs who frequently see drug company representatives. In a previous study, the authors had found that frequent GP contact with drug company representatives was strongly and independently associated with higher prescribing costs. In their current study, they found that GPs who have frequent contact with drug company representatives are more likely to prescribe new drugs; to agree to patients' requests for drugs not clinically indicated; to be dissatisfied with consultations ending in advice only without a prescription being issued; and to be more receptive to drugs advertisements and promotional literature from drug companies.

Another study published in the same edition of the *British Medical Journal* had similar findings.[8] The authors point out that it is known that pressure to show that a drug causes a favourable outcome may result in biases in design, outcome and reporting of drug company sponsored research. These researchers found that research funded by drug companies was more likely to produce results favouring the product made by the company sponsoring the research than studies funded by other sources. According to the researchers, these findings apply across a wide range of disease states, drugs, and drug classes, over at least two decades and regardless of the type of research being assessed. They conclude that 'there is some kind of systematic bias to the outcome of published research funded by the pharmaceutical industry'.

In my opinion, medical research into emotional and mental distress should be broadly based, along the following lines:
- *The problem* — 'emotional and mental distress'
- *Possible causes and treatments* — physical, emotional, psychological, spiritual, social, relationships, others
- *Focus of medical research* — research all theories without bias in the search for the cause and the appropriate treatment.

The approach of some scientists would appear to be significantly more narrow:
- *The problem* — 'mental illness'
- *Possible causes and treatments* — physical/biological (genetic, biochemical, brain abnormality)

• *Focus of medical research* — research directed at proving that the cause and treatment of mental illness is
physical/ biological.

Occasionally, medical research is carried out which looks
beyond this narrow focus. Dr Margo Wrigley is a consultant
psychiatrist at the Mater Hospital, Dublin. She assessed the
value of 'pet therapy' in patients with dementia. The study
revealed a statistically significant decrease in abnormal
behaviour and an increase in social behaviour when dogs were
present in the most disturbed groups. Dementia is characterised
by brain cell degeneration. Yet, pets managed to connect with
these patients, significantly improving their well-being. Having
a dog around benefited patients with severe dementia. But
research such as this does not sit well with the medical belief
that 'mental illnesses' are physical illnesses requiring physical
treatments. Dr Wrigley's research raises the possibility that
non-drug treatments which provide love and companionship
may considerably benefit patients. In my experience, research
which goes against the medical grain slips quietly into
obscurity. I do not anticipate a rush within psychiatry to
investigate 'pet therapy' much further.

Most medical research is now funded by pharmaceutical
companies; a fact which clearly influences what type of medical
research is carried out. Usually, when drug companies 'donate'
money for medical research, it is primarily biomedical research
that is funded by this investment. Biomedical research
concentrates on the body as a physical entity and on finding
drug treatments as cures for 'illnesses'. Pharmaceutical
companies are entitled to promote their own industry. However,
in comparison to funding available for research into medication,
little funds are available for research into the emotional,
psychological, social and relationship aspects of 'mental
illness'.

Dr Ernesto Spinelli is a highly regarded British psychotherapist, author and principal lecturer at the School of Psychotherapy and Counselling, Regent's College. In his book *The Interpreted World*, he considers the objectivity of research, cautioning that the assumed objectivity between the data being analysed and the person who analyses the data is questionable given that every person — including researchers — continuously interpret the world through the lens of previous experiences, presumptions and expectations.

Consensus views are often presented to the public as confirmation that psychiatry's beliefs and practices are proper and the best available. However, consensus views are merely a reflection of the prevailing views of the group which hold them. For centuries, people all over the world bought into the consensus view that the world was flat. The medical treatment of depression, schizophrenia and other 'psychiatric illnesses' is based on consensus views rather than scientific proof.

The predominant belief within psychiatry is that the fundamental cause of 'mental illnesses' is a physical defect — a biochemical imbalance, a genetic defect or some other brain abnormality — treatable with drugs, genetic substitution or other medically attractive means. The current reality, however, is the direct opposite; no such cause has been identified for any so-called 'psychiatric illness'. Aspiring as they do to being a scientific profession, doctors would do well to remember that the first prerequisite of any true scientist is an open mind. As surgeon Dr David Marshall wrote in October 1998 in *Medicine Weekly*, rarely do researchers' conclusions differ significantly from their previously held opinions.

Psychiatry itself is in a rather difficult position. Psychiatry's place in health care lies roughly between neurology (the speciality dealing with neurological problems), and counselling/psychotherapy, a largely non-medical discipline. Traditionally, once a health issue is known to have a physical, neurological cause, it falls within the remit of neurology. On the other hand, counselling and psychotherapy deal primarily with emotional distress issues, having no remit to carry out neurological or other medical investigations or to take responsibility for neurological conditions.

Psychiatry's identity is far more tenuous. In an effort both to establish superiority over, and to create an identity distinct from, the counselling professions, psychiatry has for decades emphasised the biological basis of 'mental illness' and the superiority of biological treatments over counselling/ psychotherapy. However, in the event that actual biological abnormalities do ever become identified in people diagnosed as 'mentally ill', the patient will then come under the umbrella of neurology or whatever the relevant medical speciality may be.

For example, occasionally it transpires that a person's symptoms suggestive of 'mental illness' are caused by either under- or over-activity of the thyroid gland — the patient will then come under the care of an endocrinologist. On occasion, patients presenting as being 'mentally ill' will be found to have underlying adrenal gland problems, known as Cushing's syndrome. These patients will also be speedily transferred under the care of an endocrinologist. Occasionally, it transpires that a person's symptoms are caused by pernicious anaemia (vitamin B12 deficiency). These patients will quickly be transferred to the care of a consultant physician, usually a haematologist.

Psychiatric symptoms closely resembling 'mental illnesses' can be caused by several conditions which affect the brain. These include acute intoxication with alcohol and other drugs; head injuries; acute and chronic inflammation of the brain caused by viruses or other unknown causes; dementia. In each case, once an actual physical illness is identified, the appropriate medical — rather than psychiatric — speciality takes over the care of the patient.

If physical abnormalities do become identified for some

'mental illnesses', then psychiatry will lose these patients to the relevant medical speciality. But without the biological approach to mental health problems, what is there to differentiate psychiatry from counselling and psychotherapy? This is quite a tightrope, requiring a delicate balancing act. Actually, there may only be one way for psychiatry to deal with this dilemma — the way in which psychiatry has dealt with it for decades. By persuading themselves and the public to accept the biological hypothesis of causation of mental health problems as if it were an established fact, psychiatry ensures an identity for itself separate and purportedly superior to that of counselling and psychotherapy. And as long as no actual physical causes are precisely identified, psychiatry ensures that patients stay within psychiatry's remit rather than neurology or other medical specialties. This 'in-between' state is the essence of psychiatry's remit within mental health care, though it is rarely publicly identified.

The upshot of walking this psychiatry tightrope is well described by Andrew Scull:

> Biological psychiatry, as always, promises that a medical solution is almost within our grasp. It would be nice if one could believe it. I fear one might as well be waiting for Godot.[9]

For many decades, indeed over a century, psychiatry has assured the public that a medical solution is almost within our grasp, ever so close, just around the corner. This 'bear with us, we are almost there' approach convinces the public of the validity of psychiatry. Biological psychiatry's future depends on maintaining this position.

The concept of neuropsychiatry has been gaining ground within psychiatry as a speciality within psychiatry, a sort-of bridge between neurology and psychiatry. Neuropsychiatry may claim to be the appropriate area of expertise to deal with biological causes of 'mental illness'. To date, however, neuropsychiatry has not identified any such biological causes. The medical profession tends to be very slow to break with tradition. In the event that biological abnormalities are, at some time in the future, found to be associated with brain abnormalities, it will require a remarkable break with tradition to allow psychiatry to be seen as the appropriate expert speciality to treat known physical abnormalities.

Dr Sydney Walker argues that psychiatric symptoms often mask medical disorders.[10] He rightly points to the importance of ensuring that people with psychiatric symptoms are thoroughly checked out for possible underlying physical causes. He also believes that in the future we will have identified physical causes for far more people currently diagnosed as 'mentally ill'. He rightly states that, in the past, some people diagnosed as having a psychiatric illness were in fact suffering from syphilis or other illnesses which at the time had not been identified. He then extrapolates that, since some of the people diagnosed in the past by psychiatrists as 'mentally ill' were subsequently found to be instead suffering from physical illnesses, the likelihood is that the majority of current 'mental illnesses' will in the future be found to be caused by physical disease also.

This is a valid hypothesis, and it is important to be open to the possibility that physical causes may be found for mental health problems in the future. However, it does not seem likely to me that so many people would make a full recovery from serious 'mental illness' problems caused by as yet unrecognised and untreated serious physical diseases. For example, one-third of people diagnosed in modern, westernised countries as having schizophrenia recover; as discussed later, (p. 214) the recovery rate is significantly higher in so-called Third World countries. And while it is theoretically possible, the chances seem slim that they are all suffering from as yet unknown self-limiting physical illnesses from which they recover spontaneously, without treatment; recovery from many of the physical illnesses mentioned by Dr Walker as supporting his case does require specific treatments. Nevertheless, Dr Walker's book is a reminder to doctors not to forget about the importance of a thorough assessment of their patients.

Misinterpretations and omissions regarding medical research can originate from the researchers themselves, from other doctors interpreting the research, or from journalists attempting to interpret medical research. What follows is, in my opinion, an example of serious misinterpretation of medical research which can and does occur with alarming regularity throughout the so-called 'enlightened' countries within the western world.

In the *Irish Examiner* newspaper of 13 May 1999, Dr Patricia Casey, professor of psychiatry at University College, Dublin, was quoted as saying that counselling is a waste of time for treating depression. Journalist Caroline O'Doherty wrote that Professor Casey was speaking following the publication of a study in the *British Medical Journal* which apparently showed that counselling had no benefits for patients with depression. This surprised me, since I have encountered many people with depression who derived considerable benefit from counselling.

I decided to investigate for myself. I phoned Professor Casey's secretary and obtained details of the article, which turned out to be a study on depression by Professor U. Malt of the University of Oslo published in the *British Medical Journal* of 1 May 1999. The only 'counselling' involved in this study was that GPs were asked to be supportive to their patients during the consultation. But since counselling is usually understood to be carried out by a trained therapist, and since few GPs have any training in counselling, supportive words from the GP do not constitute counselling. Indeed, the research paper clearly stated that specific forms of counselling were excluded from the study.

I believe that this inaccuracy was carried further by Professor Casey in an article she wrote for *The Sunday Business Post* of 4 July 1999 with the interesting title 'Counsellor, heal thyself'. In that article, Professor Casey wrote that Professor Malt's study demonstrated that counselling was significantly less effective in the treatment of depressive illness than antidepressants. She did not specifically mention Malt's name, but at my request Professor Casey's secretary confirmed with her that it was Malt's study to which she referred.

In my opinion, people reading those newspaper articles involving a highly influential psychiatrist would erroneously conclude that medical experts had now conclusively established the superiority of antidepressants over counselling in the treatment of depression. Since true counselling was not allowed in this study, such conclusions seem grossly inaccurate.

A week later, Dr Ivor Browne — Professor Casey's predecessor as professor of psychiatry at University College, Dublin — challenged her interpretation of that research study. In *The Sunday Business Post* of 11 July 1999, Dr Browne wrote that the reference to counselling in Professor Malt's study was merely incidental. The central concern of that paper was a comparison of one antidepressant drug with others. Dr Browne pointed out that:

> this study did not involve any significant psychotherapy or counselling input. I can only assume that Prof. Casey was pressed for time when she read this.[11]

I believe that many such misinterpretations of medical research reach the public domain through the medical profession. Consequently, incorrect information is repeatedly given to the public. Rarely is the record subsequently set straight. It is most unusual that one professor should so openly challenge another in the national newspapers. The depth of Dr Ivor Browne's concern is encapsulated in his sentence:

> 'Could it be that orthodox psychiatry has let so many people down?'

Coming from an experienced and highly respected psychiatrist, well known for his human compassion, these are strong words indeed. Dr Browne wrote that there is a well-established body of research demonstrating the effectiveness of counselling and psychotherapy. He expressed surprise that Professor Casey seemed to be unaware of these studies.

In my opinion, Professor Malt's depression study raised more questions than answers. For example, Professor Malt found that almost half of the study participants who were put on placebo (inert sugar pills) recovered from their depression in the course of the six month trial. They were not on any medication, yet their depression lifted. There was not a marked difference between the effectiveness of the sugar pills and the antidepressant drugs used in the trial. Remission occurred in 47 per cent of patients who received the placebo, compared to 54 per cent with one antidepressant and 61 per cent for a second antidepressant. Subsequently, British psychiatrist, Joanna Moncrieff, commented on these findings:

> Although this trial found statistically significant differences between active drugs and placebo, these differences were very small and of doubtful clinical relevance . . . It is arguable that treatment of mild depression in primary care with antidepressants is the worst case of the inappropriate medicalisation of misery and social problems. This may be harmful to the individual concerned by encouraging reliance on physical treatments, and to society by masking the social conditions that are the sources of modern discontent. [12]

Professor Malt did point out a basic flaw in the vast majority of medical research into the treatment of depression and other 'mental illnesses': depression-research trials typically assess patients for five to six weeks, not nearly long enough to come to meaningful conclusions.

The way in which research projects are structured can distort their objectivity. In the above study, patients who had previously failed to respond to the two antidepressants were excluded from the study. So were patients who had severe depression, and those whose depression lasted for more than one year. Had these groups of patients been included in this trial, the antidepressants would have been likely to be even less effective. How can research be truly representative of the whole population when several important groups are excluded from the research?

In many studies, a separate mini-trial — known as 'placebo run-in' — precedes the actual clinical trial, to identify people likely to respond well to the placebo against which the drug on trial will be tested. People who respond well to the placebo are then excluded from the trial. This has serious implications. The trial can no longer be considered to be a broadly based, scientific trial, since one specific group has been excluded. An artificially streamlined pool of people is entered into the trial, which is no longer representative of the broad variety of people who attend doctors every day seeking help. How can the effectiveness of a placebo be properly tested when the study specifically sets out to exclude people who respond well to it? I have never heard of a placebo run-in's corollary — a drug run-in study — being carried out, to remove from studies people who respond exceptionally well to the drug being tested.

In 1972, medical researcher L. E. Hollister described his experiences of what was in effect a placebo run-in trial. All depressed patients who entered the hospital and were candidates for the study were initially placed on a placebo for one week. At the end of the week, 50 per cent of these patients had improved so much that they could no longer be defined as being depressed, so they had to be withdrawn from the trial. Preoccupied with proving that antidepressants work, the medical profession has avoided explaining why so many depressed people get better with placebos alone. Placebo run-in trials have the effect of making the placebo look less effective than it would otherwise be. For example, Professor Malt did not use a placebo run-in prior to his study and the effectiveness of placebo in his study was 46 per cent. This compares to the around 30 per cent in studies involving placebo run-ins.

In *Medicine Weekly*, Professor Patricia Casey wrote an article with the interesting title 'Prozac is now the scapegoat of the ignorant and the cruel'. I found that title interesting because in my opinion, if one has conscientiously held concerns about the current prescribing of Prozac and other antidepressants, it does not automatically mean that one is either ignorant or cruel. In the article Professor Casey wrote that depression is a 'debilitative biological disorder', that 'depressive illness is organic in nature', and she referred to depression as 'biological depression'.

I felt from this article that Professor Casey seemed convinced that depression is an organic, biological illness. But, a biological or organic cause for what doctors diagnose as 'depression' has never been established. Certainly, there are theories suggesting this, but I was not aware that any of these theories had been proven to be true. I therefore wrote the following letter to that journal:

Dear Editor,

I refer to Prof. Casey's article on Prozac in your December 17 edition. On three occasions in this article, Prof. Casey refers to the view that depression is biological in nature. I would be very grateful if, through the pages of your journal, Prof. Casey would outline the research (with references) which proves conclusively that the cause of depression is biological or biochemical.[13]

Professor Casey's reply was brief:

In his letter, Dr Terry Lynch requests that I provide references to substantiate my statements relating to the biological nature of depressive illness. I suggest that he purchase any of the postgraduate textbooks of psychiatry, where he will find a myriad of references to same.[14]

Far from satisfied with this short reply, I wrote the following letter in response :

Dear Editor,

I refer to Prof. Patricia Casey's reply to my letter of 14 January in which I requested Prof. Casey to outline, with references, whatever conclusive proof there is (if any exists) that the cause of depression is biological. Rather than tell me to go off and buy some psychiatry books, I had hoped that Prof. Casey would answer my question.

I am well aware that there are many references in psychiatry books to the view that depression is biological in origin. However, I have not yet come across any article in any journal which constitutes conclusive proof that the cause of depression is biological.

Many articles and much research have linked depression with biochemical changes in the brain. But these are not in themselves proof of a biochemical or biological cause for depression. While these biological changes could point towards a biochemical cause for depression, they could equally be the effect of the depressive state.

What is the current position? Do we have conclusive proof that the cause of depression is biological? If so, then I would love to hear precisely what that proof is. If we do not at this time have conclusive proof that the cause of depression is biological, then our belief in the biological causation of depression is not proven fact; rather, it is a working hypothesis. The thing about a hypothesis is that while it may well be right, it may also be wrong. Which is it? Proven fact, or working hypothesis?[15]

I believe that the question I was asking is profoundly important. Yet neither Professor Casey nor any other doctor replied to my second letter. I rang the journal to make sure that Professor Casey received my second letter, and the editor assured me that she had.

There was no further correspondence or discussion on this issue. Six thousand, five hundred copies of this journal are printed every two weeks. The journal is sent to virtually every doctor in Ireland, including every GP and psychiatrist in the country. Yet, not one doctor wrote to the journal to address the serious issue I had raised. I felt that there was a reluctance within my profession to discuss openly what is a fundamentally important question — what causes depression?

I felt vindicated a year later when the same Professor Casey, in an article, wrote that the exact biochemical underpinnings of mood disorders are not known. And according to British professor of psychiatry Dr C. Thompson, writing in *Medical Dialogue* in December 1997:

For more than 30 years, the dominant hypothesis of the biological basis for depression have been related to noradrenaline and serotonin.[16]

I found it interesting that this professor spoke of the link between serotonin, noradrenaline and depression as being hypotheses, while presuming the biological basis of depression to be factual. This does not surprise me. Presuming that the core basis of depression is biological — rather than emotional, psychological, and or related to life events — is so fundamental to the psychiatric belief system that to even suggest that it is a hypothesis is unthinkable for many psychiatrists. In reality, however, it is as much a hypothesis as the hypothesised link between depression and serotonin.

Much medical research into suicide also seeks to establish a physical, biological cause. As a consequence, other possible contributing factors to suicide do not receive the attention they deserve. Many psychiatrists believe that an imbalance of one brain chemical in particular — serotonin — may be the underlying cause of suicide, just as an imbalance in this same chemical is purported to be the cause of depression.

Although any association between serotonin and depression and suicide is purely speculative, medical experts frequently describe this link with great conviction. As a consequence, journalists unwittingly propagate the misinformation, basing their writings on the statements of the experts. Mary Kenny is an experienced journalist in both Britain and Ireland, and in 1998 she wrote:

> Serotonin is the natural chemical which produces the unmistakable feel-good factor; when you are happy, your serotonin is high. And when you are wretched, your serotonin is low. An unhappy event in your life sends your serotonin level shooting right down. Prozac was developed as a consequence of the discovery of serotonin levels. Prozac makes people feel good by upping their serotonin levels.[17]

Mary Kenny's comments seem reasonable. Unfortunately, not one of these statements is factually correct. As discussed in more detail later, we cannot measure brain serotonin levels. Serotonin has not been proven to produce a feel-good factor. No link has been established between happiness and high serotonin levels, or between unhappiness and low serotonin levels. No evidence exists that unhappy events send serotonin levels 'shooting down'. It is far from established that Prozac makes people feel good by 'upping their serotonin levels', despite all the propaganda.

Mary Kenny can be forgiven for not knowing this, given how freely doctors speak of theories as if they were established facts. Thus, millions of people come to accept as fact something which is no more than a theory. I believe the medical profession has a responsibility to ensure that the public is not misinformed.

References to biochemical abnormalities occur regularly in the media. In an article in the *Irish Examiner* on 14 August 2000 on the over-prescription of antidepressant drugs, journalist Linda McGrory wrote that Prozac and similar antidepressant drugs 'restore levels of the neurotransmitter serotonin in the brain'. While it is worrying that a journalist would express something so inaccurate as this, it is alarming when a medical doctor does so. In this article Dr Robert Daly, professor of Psychiatry at University College, Cork, was quoted as saying that anti-depressants target a brain biochemical deficiency.

In his book *Ronnie*,[18] snooker player Ronnie O'Sullivan discusses his diagnosis of depression and his mainly positive experiences on Prozac. His doctor told Ronnie that if normal people have a serotonin level of ten, his serotonin was about three or four. His doctor told him that Prozac 'makes serotonin, that when you get to level two or three, that is suicidal. I think you are on three or three and a half'. None of this is known to be true. It is pure speculation presented as established fact. As discussed in more detail later in this book, patients never have their serotonin levels checked, because no such tests exist. As was the case with Ronnie O'Sullivan, this biological deficit scenario legitimises the prescription of Prozac, Seroxat and other antidepressants, persuading patients and the general public of the supposed scientific basis for the prescription. Without this legitimacy, it is very unlikely that these drugs would have achieved such widespread acceptance; approximately twenty-six million prescriptions are currently written annually in Britain for antidepressants. It is far more impressive to be told that a drug will balance your brain chemistry than to be told that this is a mood-altering drug which will make you feel 'better than well', will stimulate you, and give you a buzz, some of the main effects experienced by Ronnie O'Sullivan.

In his book, Ronnie O'Sullivan outlines how he had 'grown used to the Prozac' during a tournament. He describes having 'a lot more energy' for snooker. He writes of 'feeling so relaxed it was scary'. He describes how, during the final of a snooker tournament, his psychiatrist rang him. Apparently, his psychiatrist was watching the match on television, and felt that Ronnie was 'starting to nod off a little bit'. The psychiatrist advised Ronnie to take another tablet, advising him that 'in an hour and a half, two hours, you'll come alive again'. Sure enough, Ronnie describes soon feeling 'alive. Awake, buzzy'.

Other sportsmen have also stated that antidepressants have helped them considerably. In my opinion, this begs the question; are the selective serotonin reuptake inhibitors (SSRI) antidepressants in some cases acting as performance-enhancing drugs? The stimulant effect of these drugs is well recognised within the medical profession. If some people feel 'better than well' on these drugs, is it not possible that this is an artificial, drug-induced state similar to that created by other stimulant drugs such as amphetamines, which are banned substances as far as sporting participation is concerned? But because these drugs are widely prescribed for a supposed biochemical deficiency, by a medical profession which the public naturally presume would spot such issues a mile away, the question that these drugs might be performance-enhancing in sport does not even arise.

Not surprisingly therefore, the general public has come to believe that so-called 'mental illnesses' are caused by biochemical deficiencies, brain abnormalities and genetic defects. Most people will by now have heard of serotonin as the underlying chemical responsible for depression. The misinformation has become widely accepted within the caring professions and within the general public.

Meanwhile, as the medical profession searches for a physical cause of 'mental illness' and suicide, real issues are receiving insufficient attention. The social, emotional, psychological and relationship issues — which are usually more than enough to explain why people become distressed and subsequently diagnosed as 'mentally ill', and why people take their lives — are overlooked by modern medicine. Biochemical brain defects may occur; at this time, we simply do not know whether they do or not. In my opinion, the best approach to carrying out research is to keep an open mind, and to research all possible causes with equal enthusiasm. This is not happening at the moment.

In recent years, psychiatry has become quite excited about brain-imaging technology. This research sets out to find abnormalities within areas of the brain, and seeks to identify such abnormalities as proof of biological causation of mental health problems. I believe that this research is potentially valuable. But as with all research, we have to be careful and objective regarding how we interpret the results.

Brain-imaging techniques have found that people with mental health problems do sometimes share certain brain-imaging patterns. Psychiatry tends to claim this research as proof that biology is the primary, fundamental cause of mental health problems. Such conclusions are premature and problematic for a number of reasons. Rather than proving anything regarding cause of mental health problems, these brain-imaging techniques demonstrate something which should not surprise us; that the activity of the brain may well reflect — correlate with — how a person is, emotionally and psychologically.

All human experiences have a corresponding and co-existing physical body reaction to our experiences as we go through our day and our life. For example, when we feel very anxious, our heart beats faster. No one would suggest that the heart beating faster is the cause of the anxiety. The faster heart rate is one of the ways in which anxiety is expressed in our bodies. It is hardly surprising that people who experience certain emotional and psychological states more frequently than others may have relatively similar brain-imaging scans. Such findings prove nothing regarding the cause of anything. Brain-imaging tests on other human experiences will show similar correlations.

For example, brain-imaging tests on people in heightened sexual arousal will equally show these people as having similar brain imaging results to each other. To suggest that this proves that the particular pattern of brain activity observed on brain-imaging scans is the cause of the sexual arousal would be preposterous. Likewise, brain-imaging scans on people in a state of rage will demonstrate similarities to each other, as will any group of people who are experiencing relatively similar emotional and psychological states to each other at the time of the scans. It should not be forgotten that no brain-imaging tests are carried out in the evaluation of people attending doctors prior to the decision on a diagnosis of a psychiatric 'illness'.

I believe that the medical profession's bias towards biological and genetic research — to a far greater degree than emotional, psychological, social research and research focusing on service users' experiences — was well demonstrated in an article in the *Irish Medical Times* of 31 March 2000 by psychiatrist Dr Aiveen Kirley. Dr Kirley wrote that there is currently a debate within medicine on the question of whether or not depression and anxiety are separate entities from genetic, neurobiological and pharmacological standpoints. She did not mention emotional, social or psychological standpoints, and devoted little space to exploring the latter three. Under the heading 'Treatment', Dr Kirley explored the various medication options in great detail. In contrast, psychotherapy and

31

relaxation techniques were briefly discussed in her final paragraph, receiving roughly twenty times less attention than her exploration of drug treatments.

In the event that, at some time in the future, it becomes established that people with so-called 'mental illness', or who take their own lives, did have an imbalance of serotonin, some other brain chemical, or some other physical brain abnormality, an obvious question — which seems to have escaped the medical profession — remains. Is the brain chemical imbalance or physical abnormality the cause of the depression or the suicide, or is the imbalance produced by the long-standing emotional and psychological distress that person has endured, often for many years? Finding a correlation should not be interpreted as having found the cause.

Dr James McCormack, Professor Emeritus at the Department of Community Health and General Practice at Trinity College, Dublin, is known for his scepticism regarding many modern medical treatments. In an interview Dr McCormack said that antibiotics, tonics, cough medicines and tranquillisers are the present-day placebos[19]. I believe that antidepressants should be added to this list.

On 9 December 2003, the *Independent* carried the following story. Speaking at a scientific meeting in London, Allen Roses, worldwide vice-president of genetics with the pharmaceutical company GlaxoSmithKline, said that fewer than half of the patients prescribed some of the most expensive drugs actually derived any benefit from them. His comments came days after it emerged that the NHS drugs bill has soared by nearly 50 per cent in three years. The newspaper reported Dr Roses as saying:

> The reason why [some people don't respond to a particular drug] is because these people have different susceptibilities to the effect of that drug and that's genetic.

Apparently, the idea is to identify 'responders' — people who benefit from the drug — with a simple and cheap genetic test that can be used to eliminate those non-responders who might benefit from another drug. All this sounds like common sense, until one considers that it is far from established that the reason for non-response to medication lies within one's genes. I have major reservations regarding statements which make such authoritative pronouncements, presenting an unproven hypothesis as if it were an established fact. According to the report, Dr Roses maintains that 62 per cent of people taking SSRI antidepressants respond well. The report does not suggest that Dr Roses referred to the fact that up to 50 per cent of people diagnosed as being depressed respond well to a placebo (sugar pill); or to the fact that the difference in effectiveness between these drugs and placebo is a great deal less than 62 per cent.

One of the most promising developments in recent years has been the growing voice of mental health service users. STEER (Support, Training, Education, Employment, Research), a Derry-based mental health association, is one such group. Many of those at the helm of STEER have personal experience of the mental health services. In 2003, STEER responded to Dr Roses' comments, outlining the experience of mental health service users:

In our experience, there is no sound research to show why some drugs work on some and not on others; people with mental health difficulties are routinely lined up and put on the pharmaceutical merry-go-round; where they get off, nobody has a clue. They go up and down, spinning around, constantly disorientated by changing levels of medication, different types and differing combinations of said. It inevitably leaves one with the impression of a lottery or a lucky-dip.

The major difficulty as we see it is the current over-reliance upon the medical model in psychiatry, the

33

dependence on pharmaceutical products is an intrinsic part of that model. This dependence has created a flaw in the delivery of treatment and care of people with mental health difficulties. If the drugs are fallible and have variable levels of success, then psychiatric professionals flounder; it is very difficult for the professionals imbued with this ideology to think of alternatives outside this model.

We recognise from our own experiences, both personally and professionally, that people need a holistic approach, a person has to be treated as a whole, not as a collection of symptoms. This necessarily entails a broad spectrum of services to be made available, and not just jumping on the tailgates of the latest phantasm that is being produced by the pharmaceutical corporations.[20]

According to a report in the *Sunday Herald* of 14 December 2003, all National Health Service employees in Scotland will be obliged to declare any monies they receive from the drug companies as well as shares they hold in pharmaceutical companies, under tough new rules introduced by the Scottish Executive. A register of all such payments is to be created, which will be open to public scrutiny. I welcome this move, which should be extended to include the funding of doctors' groups such as the Royal College of Psychiatrists, the Royal College of General Practitioners, the funding of ongoing medical education and journals, and patient support groups. Such action would be an important step towards identifying the degree of subtle, pervasive influence exerted by the drug industry on health care.

The potential influence of the pharmaceutical industry extends beyond the medical profession. On 5 September 2003, the *New York Times* reported on drug company political contributions. During the 2000 American presidential election, the drug industry contributed $20 million to candidates and parties during the campaign, 79 per cent of it to Republicans. Drug companies bought $50 million in TV commercials and millions more in radio, newspaper and direct-mail ads relating to the presidential election. Pharmaceutical companies contributed a further $26 million in the 2002 Congress elections, again mostly to Republican candidates.

In the *New York Times*, 12 August 2003, Dr Richard Friedman, psychiatrist, director of the Psychopharmacology clinic at Weill Medical College at Cornell University, USA, wrote regarding an important source of imbalance in medical research: the tendency within medical research to favour publishing research supporting a particular drug rather than less favourable research results. Dr Friedman wrote that new drugs tend to be approved based on relatively brief research studies, involving limited numbers of people. Consequently, less common drug adverse effects may not emerge for many years after the drug has become widely prescribed. According to Dr Friedman, pharmaceutical companies can selectively decide which studies to publish, resulting in a publication bias, where studies with results favourable to the drug get published and less favourable studies do not. He maintains that this publication bias has a 'profound effect' on the science of medicine, because doctors receive a biased, distorted, and selective picture regarding the safety and effectiveness of new drugs, making a drug appear far more effective than it is in reality. Dr Friedman believes that such publication bias reduces people's trust in medical research funded by pharmaceutical companies.

This is precisely what happened regarding antidepressants such as Seroxat and Effexor. Research studies yielding unfavourable results remained unpublished for years.

The ghost-writing of medical research was one of the issues raised by psychiatrists Pat Bracken and Phil Thomas. It is estimated that up to 50 per cent of medical research is now ghost-written. This issue was further explored in *The Observer,* 7 December 2003. This report states that doctors are paid considerable sums of money for allowing their names (and therefore their reputations) to be put to research papers, adding to the credibility of these research papers. In general, neither the ghost-writers nor the degree of involvement of drug companies in these research papers are identified. These research papers are then presented to GPs and specialists — in journals and directly by representatives of the drug companies — as independent, objective, reliable, trustworthy research. Many doctors will thus be persuaded to prescribe these products.

Medical research is carried out by human beings, not machines. Researchers too have their hopes and their dreams; their prejudices, blind spots and their biases; their career ambitions; their fallibility and errors of judgement; their indoctrination during medical training. Consequently, I believe the public should be cautious about accepting the findings of medical research on face value, including medical research into 'mental illness' and suicide. The words of Dr Donald Gould, a former professor of physiology and senior medical lecturer at St Bartholemew's Hospital, London, are as relevant and as applicable now as in 1985:

It would therefore behove us well — public and politicians alike — to take an active interest in the welfare of our mentally disturbed compatriots, and not to leave their fate to the sole discretion of the experts. They are very far from being expert. And the figures tell us that there's a more than sporting chance that it will be you, or I, or our mother or our brother or our daughter or our spouse who becomes a victim of their ignorance before too long. Medical paternalism can go too far, and we should beware of giving the medical establishment too much legal power.[21]

Notes

1. Richard Smith (1991) *British Medical Journal*, 5 October.

2. Dr Peadar O'Grady (1997) *Medicine Weekly*, 24 September.

3. Dr Pat Bracken and Dr Phil Thomas (2002) *The Guardian*, 4 March.

4. R. Moynihan (2003) *British Medical Journal*, *326*, 1189–92.

5. H. Melander (2003) *British Medical Journal*, *326*, 1189–92.

6. S. Garattini, et al. (2003) *British Medical Journal, 326*, 1199–201.

7. C. Watkins, et al. (2003) *British Medical Journal*, *326*, 1178–9.

8. J. Lexchin, et al. (2003) Pharmaceutical industry sponsorship and research outcome and quality: systematic review, *British Medical Journal*, 326, 1167–70.

9. A. Scull (1990) Cycles of despair, *Journal of Mind and Behavior, 11*, 301–12.

10. Sydney Walker (1997) *A Dose of Insanity: Mind, medicine and misdiagnosis*. John Wiley and Sons.

11. Dr Ivor Browne (1999) *The Sunday Post*, 11 July.

12. Joanna Moncrieff (2002) *British Journal of Psychiatry, 181,* 531.

13. Dr Terry Lynch (1997) *Medicine Weekly*, 17 December.

14. Dr Terry Lynch (1998) *Medicine Weekly*, 14 January.

15. Dr Terry Lynch (1998) *Medicine Weekly,* 4 February.

16. Dr C. Thompson (1997) *Medical Dialogue*, December.

17. Mary Kenny (1998) *Irish Independent,* December.

18. Ronnie O'Sullivan (2003) *Ronnie: The autobiography of Ronnie O'Sullivan*. London: Orion.

19. Dr James McCormack (1999) *The Examiner*, 8 October.

20. STEER (2003) *Derry Journal,* 12 December.

21. Dr Donald Gould (1985) *The Black and White Medicine Show: How doctors serve and fail their customers*. London: Hamish Hamilton.

2

DOES 'MENTAL ILLNESS' EXIST?

The practice of psychiatry is built around the belief in the existence of 'mental illness'. It is said that approximately 25 per cent of the population suffer from a 'psychiatric illness'. Up to 10 per cent suffer from depression and one per cent from schizophrenia. The remainder 'suffer from conditions' such as manic depression, anxiety, eating disorders, and addiction to drugs and alcohol.

A central feature of 'mental illness' is that the sufferer exhibits features and behaviour deemed by both the medical profession and the public to be abnormal. In depression, the features deemed to be abnormal include the depth of the depression and features such as self-hatred and weight loss. With schizophrenia there are hallucinations, delusions, paranoia, complex thought patterns and withdrawal from life.

Extremes of elation and depression are characteristic of manic depression. Anxiety is considered a psychiatric illness when it is severe enough to disrupt a person's life. The abnormal features in eating disorders are the erratic behaviour around food. In anorexia, the person starves themselves for days on end, often losing so much weight that their life is in danger. Bulimia sufferers control their intake of food obsessively and can go on frenzied food binges, stuffing themselves with more food than many people would eat over days. In the case of addiction to drugs and alcohol, the abnormal behaviours include the extreme desire for the substance and the person's reactions having taken the substance.

According to the prevailing medical view, these behaviours do not fall within the realm of normal, understandable human experience. Hence, they are defined as being 'mental illnesses'. These 'illnesses', the theory goes, are most likely caused by a physical brain defect, a biochemical imbalance in the brain or a genetic defect. Medical treatment for these conditions is built around these beliefs. Antidepressant drugs are advised for 'depression'. Tranquillisers are prescribed for 'anxiety'. 'Schizophrenia' is treated with 'antipsychotics', more accurately described as major tranquillisers. The treatment of choice for 'manic depression' is lithium or another 'mood-stabiliser'. Antidepressants are recommended for eating disorders.

Ninety per cent of the mental health treatment workload dealt with by the medical profession is undertaken by GPs. They refer most of the remainder to psychiatrists. Psychiatry is seen as the speciality with the greatest expertise in emotional distress and 'psychiatric illness'. The views of those who do not always concur with psychiatry — many psychologists, counsellors and psychotherapists, other mental care workers, many service users and their families — are sometimes dismissed by the medical profession as well-meaning but misguided. But cracks appear when the prevailing medical view of 'psychiatric illness' is examined.

Take the medical treatment of 'psychiatric illness'. Regarding health issues, it is universally accepted that prevention is better than cure. No specific medical cure exists for any psychiatric condition, and preventative mental health strategies are conspicuous by their absence. The best that medical treatment can offer is a suppression of symptoms, an approach which is valid but by definition has limited potential. Major tranquilliser drugs used in the treatment of schizophrenia and manic depression are blunt instruments, numbing the person's thought processes. Tranquillisers are prescribed to reduce anxiety. While hailing lithium as a very effective treatment for manic depression, doctors do not know how lithium works. According to MIMS Ireland, the Monthly Index of Medical Specialties, 'The mechanism of action of lithium is unclear'. [1] Like other psychiatric treatments, lithium appears to sedate, numbing the brain's ability to function fully, to feel fully. The numbing effect of lithium and similar drugs does reduce the swings of elation and depression. However, many people taking lithium hate this drug. They feel sedated. They cannot think as clearly; they feel as if parts of their brain have been switched off.

The psychiatric approach to mental health is not unanimously accepted within the mental health professions. Dr Peter Breggin has been an outspoken critic of psychiatry throughout his career and has written extensively about the dangers of psychiatry. He maintains that antidepressant drugs have never been shown to reduce the suicide rate. Indeed, some studies have suggested an increased suicide rate in those prescribed antidepressant drugs. As discussed later, others — including Dr David Healy of the University of Wales — have come to similar conclusions regarding antidepressant drugs. According to Dr Breggin, the threat of being locked away in a mental institution against their will scares many suicidal people away from seeking help when they are in distress. In *Toxic Psychiatry,* Dr Breggin[2] wrote that the reasons why psychiatrists would favour biochemical and genetic theories is no secret. According to Dr Breggin, the entire professional identity of many psychiatrists depends on these beliefs, and for researchers, their funding may be entirely dependent on these beliefs.

Within psychiatry and modern medicine, Dr Breggin is not a popular man. His many books and public statements about the dangers of psychiatry and the need for safer and more humane treatments receive little attention within the medical profession. Why? Because he is rocking the medical boat. He is a threat to the status and position of his psychiatric colleagues. He is questioning that upon which the industry of psychiatry depends; the very existence of 'mental illness'.

Dorothy Rowe is an experienced and outspoken clinical psychologist and author of more than a dozen best-selling books on emotional distress. She has lived and worked in Britain for the past thirty years. In the foreword to Dr Breggin's *Toxic Psychiatry,* she outlines why she thought psychiatrists insist on the existence of 'mental illness':

> If such illnesses exist, then they can be treated by one profession only — psychiatry. But if such illnesses do not exist, if 'illness' is simply a metaphor for the various ways we can feel despair, fear and alienation, then psychiatrists have nothing unique to offer. Anyone who has the necessary wisdom, sympathy and patience — a psychologist, a counsellor, a good friend — could give the help the sufferer needs. Psychiatry would vanish, just as the profession of hangman vanished from Britain once the death penalty was abolished.

While repeatedly stating that biochemical imbalances cause psychiatric illnesses, the behaviour of many doctors does not support this view. When doctors suspect that a person has a biochemical imbalance, they will carry out the appropriate test to check this out. They will compare the test results to well-established guidelines, and decide whether or not the person has a biochemical imbalance. For example, diabetes is diagnosed when the blood sugar level is raised, and thyroid disease is diagnosed when the blood thyroid hormone level is either reduced or excessive. No doctor would dream of presuming that a person had either diabetes or thyroid disease without first carrying out the appropriate blood test. Over time, this blood test is regularly repeated to assess the patient's condition. The treatment dosage is dictated largely by the results of the ongoing, regular blood tests.

However, doctors approach 'mental illness' very differently. In twenty years working as a doctor, I have never heard of any person having a diagnosis of depression, schizophrenia, manic depression or any other psychiatric condition confirmed by a blood test, or any other test. Dosages of psychiatric drugs are not adjusted according to blood test results, as happens with all biochemically-based illnesses. When doctors decide to stop treatment in cases of 'mental illness', no blood test or other biochemical test is done to confirm that the supposed biochemical abnormality has been eradicated. This would not happen with any known biochemical abnormality.

Why no tests? Because no such tests exist. Because no biochemical abnormality has been demonstrated in any psychiatric illness. Does this not raise serious questions about the medical profession's claims that psychiatric illnesses are caused by biochemical abnormalities in the brain? Manic depression is the only psychiatric condition where regular blood tests are carried out. These tests are not done to check the level of any body chemical. Rather, they are done to check the blood levels of the drugs used in the treatment of this 'mental illness', in an attempt to prevent life-threatening toxic effects of the drug.

Similarly, when doctors suspect the presence of a known genetic illness, they will typically confirm the diagnosis with genetic tests, as happens with Down's syndrome, cystic fibrosis and haemophilia, for example. No such genetic tests are ever carried out to confirm a diagnosis of depression, manic depression, schizophrenia or any other 'mental illness'. Whether such confirmatory tests for 'mental illness' will become possible or available in the future is purely speculative. Right now, no genetic tests are carried out on 'mentally ill' patients because no genetic cause has been established and no such tests exist for 'mental illness'.

If brain chemical changes occur during our daily mental activities, these changes are likely to be extremely fast-moving and complex, just as our thoughts and feelings are. The truth is that medical science has virtually no understanding of the extremely complex and delicate brain chemical interactions which occur hundreds of times per second of every day of our lives. The interplay between the brain, the mind, thoughts and feelings is also poorly understood. At regular intervals, research findings purporting to expand our understanding of the human brain and mind are published, often received with much enthusiasm and media fanfare. Frequently, the significance of the findings and their implications are over-stated. For example, as explored earlier, a great deal of research is currently taking place using brain-imaging scans. Researchers make much of observed differences between 'normal' people and those with 'mental illnesses', typically tending to interpret these results as proof that these 'illnesses' are caused by biological brain abnormalities. This is a misguided conclusion. For example, according to a report in *The Guardian,* 17 November 2003, scientists have found that people harbouring racial prejudice share similar findings on brain-imaging scans. These scans merely demonstrate that the brain activity mirrors different states of being. They say nothing about how the state of being came about. A correlation should not be presumed to indicate cause. Brain-imaging research is a valid pursuit. But it behoves us all not to draw conclusions beyond the findings of our research.

Psychologist and author Dr Tony Humphreys has for years been a critic of psychiatry and modern medicine's approach to emotional distress. On many occasions, I have heard Dr Humphreys say the experiences of his clients over many years indicate to him that psychiatry has long outlived its usefulness. He maintains that the medical approach to so-called 'mental illness' is seriously misguided. Dr Humphreys believes that, rather than dismissing symptoms as meaningless, as evidence of 'mental illness' and suppressing them with psychiatric drugs, these symptoms should be made sense of in the overall context of the person's life. He believes that people who experience mental suffering need human understanding and support rather than psychiatric drugs.

Dr Donal Gould is a former professor of physiology and senior medical lecturer at St Bartholemew's Hospital, London. In his book, *The Black and White Medicine Show*, he wrote:

Psychiatry, far from being an exact science, hardly merits description as a scientific discipline at all. We still have small idea of the mechanism of intellectual disorders and deficiencies, and such insights as have been gained within recent years are largely the result of neurophysiologists and other laboratory-based investigators rather than the results of the observations and the acumen of clinical psychiatrists. Good psychiatrists are good not because they know what is actually happening in the computer circuits of the mind and how the nerve cells work, and what is amiss in the brain cells of the mentally ill.

They are good because they are humane, intelligent, empathic, priest-like men and women who understand the problems of their fellow human beings in distress, and can so give the support and encouragement their patients need. Most of the 'special' insights they possess are to be found in the bible and in the works of Shakespeare. Bad psychiatrists are bad because, while sharing their superior colleagues' ignorance of the brain's machinery, they lack their human virtues and intelligence and common sense, and in the absence of a teachable body of proven psychiatric wisdom, they are left without the resources needed for the successful performance of an exceptionally demanding branch of medical practice. [4]

Regarding mental health care, if the welfare of its patients rather than its own survival truly were the medical profession's primary interest, doctors would listen to their critics very carefully. They would look seriously at their own beliefs and practices. They would invite those who conscientiously question the conventional view to meet with modern medicine in a joint and holistic effort to improve the quality of care available to the general public. But this is not happening to a significant degree. On the contrary, in my opinion most mainstream psychiatrists display little interest in developing such an holistic model of mental health.

Both psychiatry and psychology could potentially claim expertise in emotional distress, 'psychiatric illness' and suicide. Each group has its own view about the cause, treatment, research, and other aspects of 'mental illness.' On many issues, there is a vast difference between the views of each group, increasing the likelihood that one might seek to dominate the other. Here is a brief summary of the philosophy and beliefs of each group.

Psychiatry

The perception of psychiatrists as kindly old gentlemen who listen with great compassion and understanding is rapidly dying out. Modern psychiatrists are more likely to see themselves as scientists. Their attention is on forming a diagnosis rather than exploring life issues, problems and feelings with their patients.

Most psychiatrists believe that the cause of mental illness is primarily physical; either a biochemical or other abnormality in the brain, or a genetic defect. The practice of modern psychiatry revolves around this unproven theory. There is a strong alliance between psychiatry and the pharmaceutical industry. Drug companies have a vested interest in promoting psychiatry rather than psychology. The predominant theory of psychiatry is attractive to the pharmaceutical industry: biochemical brain abnormalities can, in theory, be corrected by drugs; genetic defects can, in theory, be corrected by genetic substitution. Either way, there is money to be made.

Psychology, psychotherapy and counselling

While there are differing views within these professions, a predominant belief within psychology, psychotherapy and counselling is that emotional, psychological, social and relationship issues are relevant to any discussion on 'mental illness'. As a general rule, these groups believe that emotional, psychological and social issues are central to any 'treatment' plan.

In the earlier part of the twentieth century, psychiatry was somewhat of a Cinderella within medicine. During the past fifty years, it has managed to become increasingly accepted, both within the medical profession and within the general public. Psychiatry has achieved this respectability by developing itself along the lines of other medical specialties, aspiring to become increasingly scientific.

Filled with a passionate desire to establish psychiatry as a scientific, respectable branch of medicine, the pioneering psychiatrists of the past century made a fundamental error of judgement. They first arrived at their conclusion, and subsequently set up their research to prove that their conclusion was the correct one. Deciding that 'mental illness' was caused by a physical brain defect rather than emotional distress, they designed their research to establish that this was the case. The cart came before the horse.

These zealous doctors needed financial backing to carry out and publish their research. Enter the emerging pharmaceutical industry, which saw the magnitude of their opportunity and took it well. Drug companies began financing medical research and medical journals. Before long, the medical profession — psychiatry included — became enormously financially dependent on the pharmaceutical industry.

46

Through this funding, the pharmaceutical companies subtly increased their control over what type of research was carried out. Indeed, the pharmaceutical industry has shaped the direction of modern medicine much more than is generally realised. He who pays the piper usually gets to call the tune.

The history of psychiatry is far from inspiring. Contrary to the general perception, modern medicine's handling of emotional distress during the past one hundred years is filled with a succession of dangerous and/or addictive 'treatments'. Most of these 'treatments' were discarded twenty to thirty years after they were first introduced. Many were replaced with newer and 'safer' treatments which themselves were subsequently found to be either dangerous, ineffective or addictive. This pattern continues today.

Charles Medawar works with Social Audit UK, the publishing arm of Public Interest Research Centre Ltd, a UK registered charity. The remit of this centre is to assess the quality and value of public services, including health care. He has carried out extensive research on tranquillisers and antidepressants. According to Medawar:

> Over the past 200 years, doctors have prescribed an almost uninterrupted succession of addictive drugs, always in the belief that they would not cause dependence or that patients would be mainly responsible if they did. From alcohol and opium to barbiturates and benzodiazepine tranquillisers [such as diazepam, Valium, Ativan, Xanax, Tranxene, and all other tranquillisers and sleeping tablets currently prescribed by doctors] all of these drugs have been prescribed as sedatives for mental distress.[5]

In his book *Power and Dependence*, Medawar wrote:

> The evidence suggests that the providers of medicine [doctors and the pharmaceutical industry] keep making the same mistakes, mainly because they have been allowed to

deny how badly things have gone wrong. Virtually every anti-anxiety drug and sleeping pill ever prescribed has proved to be a drug of dependence — yet each one has been prescribed, often for many years, as if the risk did not exist. This pattern of error has been established over the past 100 years or more, and continues to this day.[6]

Medawar makes a valid point. Neither the medical profession nor the pharmaceutical industry appear to have learned from the lessons of the past. Alcohol, morphine, heroin, amphetamines, barbiturates, sleeping tablets and tranquillisers were each, in their day, introduced as wonderful, non-addictive treatments. The addictiveness of each of these drugs went unnoticed for decades after they were introduced. Regarding each of these drugs, the medical profession has been slow to accept their addictive potential; the push to have them recognised as addictive came, not from within the medical profession, but from the public. People had great difficulty convincing the medical profession that these drugs were addictive. Throughout history, millions of drug addicts have been created by the 'best' modern medical treatments of the day.

Therefore, when doctors say that antidepressant drugs are not addictive, remember that they said precisely the same thing about a long list of addictive 'treatments'. Based on the experiences of patients taking SSRI antidepressants, for many years I have believed that these drugs are addictive. Contrary to what you hear from psychiatrists and GPs, there is evidence suggesting that the newer antidepressants such as Prozac, Seroxat, Effexor and others may well be addictive. These drugs give an energy buzz, often making people feel better. But so did amphetamines and barbiturates, which were subsequently — many years and millions of patients later — found to be a very addictive group of drugs. I know many people who have had great difficulty coming off these newer antidepressant drugs.

I believe that doctors, faced with patients who are getting withdrawal symptoms from Seroxat, Prozac, Effexor or other newer antidepressants, incorrectly conclude that the underlying depression is not yet healed and the drug prescription is renewed. Doctors made this error of judgement in the past in the case of tranquillisers and other addictive drugs. In my opinion, in the not too distant future, the addictive potential of the SSRI antidepressant drugs will belatedly be recognised by the medical profession. By then, the medical profession may have newer drugs to prescribe which, of course, will definitely not be addictive. I fear that this pattern will continue until the beliefs and practices of the medical profession receive a thorough and independent investigation. Indeed, such an investigation is currently underway into Seroxat. Rather embarrassingly for the UK regulatory authorities, the initial committee formed to assess the safety of Seroxat had to be disbanded when it emerged months later that half of the experts on the committee had links with GlaxoSmithKlein, the manufacturers of the drug.

The drug trials which regulatory bodies (such as the UK Committee on Safety of Medicines) evaluate prior to deciding the effectiveness and safety of medication typically last only 5–8 weeks. In clinical practice however, these drugs quickly become widely prescribed for many months and often for years, without any systematic ongoing surveillance or evaluation. As American psychiatrist Dr Joseph Glenmullen commented, 'Under these circumstances, prescribing an entirely new class of agents [SSRI antidepressants] to millions of people is nothing short of an ongoing human experiment'.[7]

Most of the other treatments used by modern medicine in the treatment of so-called 'mental illness' during the past fifty years have been found to be either dangerous or useless or both. A zealous enthusiasm, a strong desire to help one's fellow man, and a deep conviction that you are right can have

49

disastrous consequences, when coupled to people's desperation for relief of their distress, and the human tendency to use mood-altering substances as coping strategies. As Gabor Gombos, a Hungarian mental health rights activist, put it:

> I remind myself that many of the mistakes in mental health care come from a helping attitude. But they want to help you without asking you, without understanding you, without involving you.[8]

The combination of enthusiasm, desire and conviction when combined can deprive a person of the priceless quality of objectivity: the ability to see the wood from the trees. For example, a central belief of many of the religions which have been involved in religious conflicts down through the centuries is 'thou shalt not kill'. Yet throughout history more people have been murdered in conflicts about religion than for any other single cause.

Similarly in medicine, enthusiasm, desire and conviction are no guarantee that no harm will result from the actions of highly motivated doctors. Here are some of the 'treatments' which medical experts fervently believed in, some of which are still in use, others which were used up to 20 years ago. These treatments caused many problems, including numerous fatalities.

Lobotomy
A lobotomy is a surgical procedure during which part of the brain (usually involving the frontal lobes) is cut. That part of the brain ceases to function properly. This procedure was used as recently as 20–30 years ago for a wide variety of psychological and emotional problems. It is still used occasionally, and there is some evidence that lobotomy is making a comeback. Countless thousands of people who received this treatment suffered serious brain damage. Many

did not survive this assault on their brain and their humanity.

Insulin coma therapy

First introduced in the 1930s and used into the early 1970s, insulin coma therapy quickly gained widespread acceptance as an effective treatment for various forms of emotional distress including schizophrenia. Insulin is a hormone we need to regulate our blood sugar levels. People with diabetes are unable to produce enough insulin in their bodies. Most diabetics need daily insulin injections to regulate their blood sugar. Excessive doses of insulin may reduce blood sugar to such a degree that a coma is induced. The rationale behind insulin coma therapy was to create a coma by dramatically reducing the person's blood sugar level. The coma was somehow expected to cure the person's emotional distress.

It was believed that the best results were obtained by using extremely high doses of insulin, which put schizophrenic patients into life-threatening thirty- to fifty-hour comas. Dramatic results were claimed. It was not until twenty years later, by which time it was widely used, that a thorough study showed that insulin therapy had no therapeutic effect at all. It is now widely recognised within medicine that hypoglycemia (the medical term for low blood sugar) is a medical emergency. Every cell in the body, including brain cells, need a constant supply of sugar to function normally and to survive. If a patient is deprived of glucose for more than two or three minutes, there is a real risk of permanent brain damage. Millions of people around the world treated with insulin coma therapy suffered serious brain damage as a consequence.

It took doctors over twenty years to discover that insulin therapy was neither effective nor safe. Eventually, this treatment was abandoned, but not without strong resistance from many psychiatrists.

51

Electro-convulsive therapy (ECT)

ECT, or 'shock' treatment, first gained popularity within modern medicine due to the notion that epilepsy and schizophrenia were somehow illnesses which were diametrically opposite to each other. The medical logic was that schizophrenia could be cured by its polar opposite — seizures. This theory has never been proven and has been abandoned, though ECT is still a relatively common practice.

There is evidence that certain groups — women, particularly older women, people from ethnic and minority ethnic groups — are more likely to receive ECT, forcible treatment and treatment with drugs.[9] In her book *Out of Me*, Fiona Shaw outlines her experience of severe postnatal depression. In graphic detail, she describes her hospital admissions and major loss of memory due to ECT treatments:

> The loss inflicted in me by ECT went far beyond ordinary forgetting. I lost the language of recollection, the capacity to give narrative shape or continuity to my life. I felt robbed of my autonomy, reliant on other people for material with which to shape any account. So Hugh [her husband] might come to visit me in the evening and I would ask him whom I'd seen that day and what I'd done. But once he'd told me, I was none the wiser. Sometimes I'd feel the faintest echo of recognition but that would be all. There was nothing there with which I could shape my thoughts. If only ECT brought its subjects out in a virulent rash, or made their hair fall out. Maybe then doctors would take its effects more seriously. As it is, most people receive the same kind of brush-off as I did. Queries are not regarded as legitimate doubts about the nature and side-effects of the treatment, but dismissed as the anxious product of the person's depression. All the more reason to get the electrodes on. When I questioned anybody about the possible longer-term effects of ECT on my memory, I was told it would have

none. Yet it left a horrible brand on my mind and memory
for another year and a half, maybe more.[10] (pp. 71–2)

Dr William Sargent was a prominent British psychiatrist at the
time when ECT was first introduced. His enthusiasm for ECT
contrasts sharply with Fiona Shaw's experience of this
treatment. In his autobiography *The Unquiet Mind* published
in 1967, Dr Sargent wrote:

Nowadays, we may only need to prescribe four or five
electric shock treatments, or some new antidepressant drug,
whereupon the patient is himself again, without any need
for elaborate case history or social investigation, still less
the former eternity of talk.[11]

For many years, I have felt that service providers are far more
enthusiastic about ECT than service users. With ECT, as with
other forms of psychiatric treatments, a somewhat different
picture emerges when the views of service users are sought,
something which could be employed more often within mental
health care. A recent study of mental health services in Galway
illustrated the trepidation in which ECT is held by those at the
receiving end of it. Sixty-seven per cent of those who agreed
to ECT felt pressurised into having it. Only 20 per cent said
there were benefits for them from ECT treatment. The study
recommended further research into ECT to justify its continued
use in psychiatric hospitals. According to the report:

The majority of reported feelings about ECT [all these
people had ECT treatment themselves] were quite
disturbing and range from outright terror, helplessness and
apathy, to feelings of coercion.[12]

A client of mine recently told me of her experiences of memory
loss with ECT. Twenty years ago, she sought help from a
psychiatrist for her depression. She had important university

exams coming up a month later. The psychiatrist admitted her to hospital, treated her with eight ECT treatments, then discharged her. Prior to her admission, she was depressed, but her memory was intact. On discharge, her memory was so impaired that her familiarity with her exam subjects was destroyed. Unable to recall the subject material, she decided not to sit the exams.

Is there not the distinct possibility that a treatment which can cause such profound memory loss might also be damaging to the brain? There is research evidence that ECT causes brain damage in animals. An extensive American Psychiatric Association membership survey reported that 41 per cent of the respondents (psychiatrists) agreed with the statement, 'It is likely that ECT produces slight or subtle brain damage'; only 26 per cent disagreed with this statement.[13] While less popular than a few decades ago, ECT is still used, particularly for what psychiatrists call severe or resistant depression. One might expect that a treatment as potentially damaging as ECT would be used only in a scientific way using clear and specific guidelines. Unfortunately this is not always the case.

An audit of electro-convulsive treatment in two British National Health Service regions was published in the *British Journal of Psychiatry* in 1992. This audit, carried out by John Pippard, Mental Health Act Commissioner and Auditor Consultant at the Research Unit of the Royal College of Psychiatrists, uncovered some disturbing findings. He found that patients were twelve times more likely to receive ECT in some parts of England than in others. Patients in some hospitals received four times the seizure-inducing electrical impulse than in other hospitals, the dose given being decided usually 'by habit, rather than rational strategy'. Few consultants were closely involved in the administration of ECT. John Pippard found that little had changed during the previous ten years in the unsatisfactory training and supervision of those who give the treatment.

Since the incidence of conditions for which ECT is used is relatively consistent from one region to another, such a huge variance in the use of ECT has far more to do with the personal beliefs and preferences of the doctors involved than any scientific basis. These disappointing results prompted the study's author to begin his research paper with the quotation: 'In medicine, what may start out as ignorance becomes practice if uncorrected.'

In 2002 William, a client of mine, was admitted to a psychiatric hospital. A man in his fifties, he was going through a great deal of emotional distress, much of which related to relationship issues. He reached a point where he became overwhelmed by it all, and was admitted to his local psychiatric unit. Already on antidepressants prior to his admission, in hospital he was quickly prescribed several drugs. As he remained distraught in spite of the extra medication, his psychiatrist decided that this man needed ECT.

Just prior to his admission, William and I had a discussion. I suggested to him that in the event that ECT was recommended for him, he should refuse it. I did so because I felt that while the effects of short-term drug treatments were reversible, the effects of shock treatment might not be reversible. I knew him well enough to know that he did not need shock treatment. Initially, he did refuse it. However, his spirit was broken from the enormous distress he was going through. Following repeated visits by his psychiatrist and two psychiatric nurses, all of whom insisted that he *had* to have ECT to have any chance of recovering, William consented to the procedure. Shock treatment was scheduled for the following morning.

Later that day, his best friend came to visit him. His friend begged him not to have the shock treatment. That night, William informed the ward staff that he would not have the scheduled shock treatment. Believing that ECT was critically important to William's recovery, his psychiatrist and the nursing staff

55

vigorously tried to change his mind. William had made his mind up. He did not have any shock treatment, then or subsequently.

William made steady progress over the following week. Eight days after the apparently 'vital' ECT was scheduled to take place, William was considered well enough to be discharged from hospital. As part of the routine discharge procedure, the hospital staff discussed his medication with William. 'But I'm not taking any medication', he replied. The hospital staff looked at him incredulously. William told the staff that he had not been given any medication during the previous week. Over a week previously, William's medication had temporarily been stopped in preparation for his scheduled shock treatment. Due to an administration error, William's medication had not been recommenced.

William had improved significantly without the 'vital' ECT and the 'vital' medication. However, when the administration error came to light, William's medication was quickly reinstated, and William was discharged home on 13 tablets a day.

At no time did the hospital doctors discuss or explore William's overwhelming life issues with him. Within days of his admission, his psychiatrists decided that William had bipolar disorder. William was told that this was caused by a biochemical brain abnormality, and that medication would balance this abnormality. Having made this diagnosis, the psychiatrists focused exclusively on the treatment of this 'illness'.

William was informed that since he had a chemical abnormality, it was vital that he continue this medication long-term.

William attended me within days of discharge. He was doped up to his eyeballs — so different from the William I had come to know — to such an extent that he could hardly string a sentence together. Since then, William and I have continued to work closely together. He attributes much of his improvement while in hospital to having found the courage to say 'no' to the shock treatment, to the sense of achievement he subsequently felt through making such an important decision for himself, and to the support of a few close friends.

Within months of leaving the hospital, William stopped attending the local psychiatric clinic. He felt it was a waste of time — consultations lasting less than five minutes, one or two questions asked, medication continued as before, another appointment in four weeks just like the ones before — a pretty meaningless experience for him.

A year later, William and I continue to meet regularly. He attends me both as a counsellor and GP, in which capacity I have gently and gradually reduced his medication. William has worked through many of his personal and life issues, many of which related to coming to terms with major changes in his personal life. From 13 tabs a day on discharge, he is now taking just two tablets a day. William may well be ready to stop these drugs in the coming months. He attributes his recovery to the love, support, affirmation and encouragement he received from a few treasured people in his life, people who accepted him for himself and stood by him when many others ostracised him. It would seem that William's 'biochemical abnormality' — which was never confirmed by any test — has miraculously disappeared. I believe that William's story is representative of thousands who attend the psychiatric services, their distress misinterpreted as illness, caused by imagined biochemical brain abnormalities which are never confirmed with tests.

Prescribing addictive and dangerous drugs
Amphetamines
This group of drugs first became available in the 1950s. They are now known to be highly dangerous and addictive. They fetch a high price on the black market. As has been the case

for over a hundred years with mood-altering drugs, from alcohol (when it was prescription-only) to the SSRI antidepressants, for decades doctors prescribed amphetamines widely and enthusiastically for emotional distress. For instance, 23.3 million prescriptions for amphetamines were written by doctors in 1967 in the USA alone. What short memories we have.

Since they were first introduced as medical treatments for emotional distress, millions of people around the world have become addicted to them. Many have died from their adverse effects. Yet they were easily available as slimming tablets through a doctor's prescription until the mid-1990s. The medical profession was slow to recognise the immense potential of these drugs to do harm. Amphetamine-type drugs and similar stimulant drugs are currently being prescribed to millions of children worldwide labelled as having Attention Deficit Hyperactivity Disorder (ADHD).

Barbiturates, morphine, opium, and alcohol

In their day, each of these drugs was widely used for several decades by the medical profession. They were widely prescribed as effective, safe and non-addictive treatments for a wide variety of conditions, particularly emotional distress, anxiety, and depression. With each drug, doctors were slow to realise how addictive they were. Rather than exercise caution regarding the possibility of addictiveness with each new drug, doctors presumed that each new drug was not addictive. These drugs were widely and enthusiastically prescribed for several decades, leaving millions of drug addicts in their wake.

Tranquillisers and sleeping tablets

For over twenty years after they were introduced in the 1950s, tranquillisers (such as Valium, diazepam, Ativan, and Xanax) and sleeping tablets (such as Dalmane, Mogadon, Rohypnol, and Halcion) were widely prescribed by the medical profession. To this day, tranquillisers are one of the most prescribed groups of drugs worldwide. Doctors largely ignored the lessons which should have been learned from the legacy of addiction created by the over-prescribing of morphine, barbiturates and amphetamine. As a result, the medical profession has created millions of benzodiazepine addicts around the world: people who have become addicted to the treatments prescribed by their doctors, who assured them that these drugs were not addictive.

Even after the addictive potential of these tranquillisers became well recognised in the late 1980s, one such tranquilliser, Xanax, was in the early 1990s heavily promoted by doctors for the treatment of panic attacks. The medical experts recommended that this drug was perfectly safe and free of any risk of addiction. They recommended treatment for several months at a time, even though the accepted guidelines for that group of drugs was for no more than four weeks of continuous treatment. The dosage recommended by the 'experts' was four-five times the previously recommended dosage range.

These experts got it very wrong. Promoting Xanax in this way was a huge marketing success, greatly increasing the use of this tranquilliser. But many people subsequently become addicted to this drug. It has been estimated that by the early 1990s, one and a half million new Xanax addicts were created every year in America alone via the doctor's prescription pad. Many of the people who now attend me have become addicted to Xanax which was prescribed in high doses, with great enthusiasm, by either a psychiatrist or a GP. To this day, I come across people whose doctors have prescribed Xanax for panic attacks, people who have been told by doctors that this drug is specifically designed for panic attacks. This statement is patently untrue.

In *Toxic Psychiatry*, Dr Peter Breggin states that when a

person stops taking tranquillisers, symptoms similar to but more severe than those for which the drug was first prescribed may be experienced. Moreover, Dr Breggin maintains that Upjohn, the company that manufactures Xanax, concealed important information about this tranquilliser. He maintains that Upjohn deliberately misled the public regarding the results of their eight-week research study into Xanax and panic attacks. According to Dr Breggin, Upjohn discarded the results for the second four-week period. When he analysed the original research himself, Dr Breggin was shocked to find that by the end of the eight weeks, the people put on sugar-pills were doing about as well as people put on medication. Actually, the people on sugar-pills were better off, because they did not have to go through the severe withdrawal and rebound reactions experienced by many people in the trial taking Xanax, who experienced an increase of anxiety and phobias, and a 350 per cent greater number of panic attacks, the 'condition' for which Xanax was being prescribed in the first place. He concludes that:

In summary, the FDA [the USA Food and Drug Administration] Xanax study really shows that most patients were better off if they had never taken the drug.[15]

According to Dr Breggin, this dubious research was passed as acceptable by the American Food and Drug Administration (the FDA). Given how quickly Dr Breggin was able to identify serious flaws in this research, how did the FDA accept this research?

For five to ten years, many doctors embraced with great enthusiasm the idea of prescribing high doses of Xanax for people with high anxiety or panic. Towards the end of the 1990s, this trend declined. Few doctors would now prescribe Xanax in such high doses. But the warning signs of tranquilliser addiction and ineffectiveness were there long before this disastrous overprescribing of Xanax for anxiety and panic began.

I clearly recall my own reaction ten years ago to the vigorous pushing of this new 'breakthrough' by the drug company's representatives when they visited me, as they did with all practising GPs. I was not convinced. I was suspicious: how could it be right to prescribe very high doses of tranquillisers for several months and presume they are not addictive? I did not buy into the idea at all. I remember, months later, trying the high-dose Xanax regime reluctantly with one person, whose panic *did* reduce somewhat. But her anxiety reduced because she was so sedated by the tranquillisers. I decided there and then that I would never use high-dose Xanax again.

Many of my medical colleagues — psychiatrists and GPs alike — did accept that high-dose Xanax was a breakthrough in the treatment of anxiety and prescribed it for many years and with great enthusiasm. The medical profession should have known better. Yet the whole debacle has died a quiet death. The medical profession has not been called to account for this grievous error of judgement.

In May 2001, BBC's Panorama TV programme broadcasted *The Tranquilliser Trap,* an investigation into benzodiazepine tranquillisers. Over 20 years before this Panorama exposé in 1980 the British Committee on Safety of Medicines advised prescribing doctors that there is 'little convincing evidence that benzodiazepines were efficacious after four months continuous treatment'. This UK regulatory body recommended that 'patients receiving benzodiazepine therapy be carefully selected and prescriptions limited to short-term use'. In 1988, the UK Committee on Safety of Medicines issued a further warning to every GP in the country. This letter stated clearly and categorically that:

- Benzodiazepines should not be prescribed for longer than four weeks
- They should be given in the lowest possible dose
- They should not be used to treat depression

Clearly, these warnings went largely unheeded and unobserved. Seventeen-and-a-half million benzodiazepine tranquilliser prescriptions were issued by GPs and psychiatrists in Britain in 1999, almost 20 years after the first warning. Most patients are on repeat prescriptions for well over four weeks, and many have been prescribed these drugs for years rather than the recommended four-week maximum duration of 'treatment'. An estimated one million Britons are addicted to these drugs. Broadcaster Esther Rantzen was a presenter of *That's Life*, which in 1984 helped to uncover a major tranquilliser addiction problem in Britain. On the 2001 Panorama programme, she described the reaction of the *That's Life* team from 1984:

> *We were absolutely astonished after we mentioned that problem in one programme that we were deluged with response from our audience, and we suddenly thought this is happening to thousands of people, and this was with harmless prescribed drugs, things that had become household names, Valium, Mogadon.*

That 1984 programme was a key factor in bringing the scale of tranquilliser addiction to public attention. Hardly surprising then that, when informed of the failure of the medical profession and their regulators to address this enormous problem, Esther Rantzen said on the 2001 Panorama programme:

> *How can a serious problem like this, which was revealed to millions of people and the professionals 20 years ago, how can it still be going on?*

When this and other questions were put to psychiatrist Dr Louis Appleby, National Director for Mental Health at the UK Department of Health, the answers were, to say the least, disappointing:

> *It is difficult to defend that we have such a huge problem*

of benzodiazepine prescription and long-term use and therefore dependence.

The following are extracts between this doctor and the programme presenter, Shelly Joffre:

Shelly Joffre: *Because we couldn't get any figures from the Department of Health, we carried out our own survey which shows that over 3 per cent of the population [over one and a half million people in Britain, if the same pattern is repeated across the adult population] have been on benzodiazepines for longer than four months. That shouldn't be happening should it?*

Dr Appleby: *No, no it shouldn't. There's no way of defending that except to say that in order to get people off benzodiazepines you need to have a fairly comprehensive approach to the problem with the provision of alternative treatments so there's no temptation in the first place for people to go on them for anxiety, with treatments for withdrawal, with proper monitoring which I think we haven't had in detail previously. We need to do more than simply tell doctors what to do.*

Joffre: *Undoubtedly. According to our survey, the warnings have been falling on deaf ears. We asked those taking benzodiazepines how long they'd been on them, and remember the guidelines say it should be no more than 4 weeks. 28 per cent said they'd been on them for more than ten years, and it's clear the guidelines continue to be ignored by many doctors. 72 per cent of people said they were prescribed the drugs within the last ten years. Over half were prescribed within the last five years.*

The guidelines that were introduced in 1988 were very clear. They said benzodiazepines shouldn't be prescribed for more than four weeks at a time. Which part do you think doctors didn't understand?

Appleby: *I think the guidelines are completely clear. I don't think there's any problem in understanding them. I think what the*

63

> *problem has been that changing individual prescribing practice requires more than guidelines. It's also necessary for doctors to have a clear idea of what alternative treatments there are, meaning different drug treatments but also in particular meaning psychological therapies for anxiety.*
>
> Joffre: *Isn't that their job to know what sort of treatments are available?*
>
> Appleby: *Yes, yes it is, but prescribing practice changes slowly and I suppose that's one of the lessons of this whole disaster. It's obvious that the cost will be enormous of inappropriate prescribing. These drugs are not particularly expensive but if we have a million or a million and a half of people taking them regularly, then of course we're bound to be spending millions of pounds on drug treatments that aren't needed.*
>
> Joffre: *Can that be justified?*
>
> Appleby: *No, it can't.*

To this day, there is little provision made to help people come off these addictive drugs. Perhaps this is less surprising than might initially seem. To create the level of benzodiazepine withdrawal centres and programmes required to properly deal with over a million medically-created British drug addicts would be seen by the medical profession, the regulators and the pharmaceutical industry as a highly visible public admission of their own incompetence and lack of professionalism. Better to continue to bury heads in the sand and hope the whole problem will just go away than risk that. In any walk of life, when we bury our heads in the sand and do not take appropriate action, we tend to keep making the same mistakes, over and over. This may explain why we are currently in the throes of a more recent, similar debacle with the SSRI antidepressants; and why similar disasters occurred previously with barbiturates and amphetamines and other drugs.

It seems that many doctors do not sufficiently question

what they are told by the drug company representatives, who visit each doctor at regular intervals. As far back as 1989, when I was far more accepting of the medical model than I am now, I routinely questioned drug company sales representatives. As a GP, I might have several such visits every week.

I clearly remember the reaction of one drug company representative to me in 1989. A man in his mid-forties, he had twenty years' experience as a drug rep under his belt, visiting doctors all over the country. After about his third visit to me, I noticed that he seemed nervous, unsettled, shifting in his seat. I asked him why. He replied that no other doctor ever questioned him the way I did. I was intrigued, and I asked him to elaborate. He said that very few doctors question anything that he said, but that I questioned everything. That meeting in 1989 was probably the most informative meeting I have ever had with a representative of the pharmaceutical industry.

In *Confessions of a Medical Heretic*, American doctor Robert Mendlesohn describes a peculiarity regarding the side effects of Valium and other drugs. His comments apply to all commonly prescribed tranquillisers:

> You should be aware of all the drugs for which the side effects are the same as the indications. For example, if you read the list of indications for Valium, and then read the list of side effects, you'll find that the lists are more or less interchangeable! Under the indications you'll find: anxiety, fatigue, depression, acute agitation, tremors, hallucinosis, skeletal muscle spasms. And under the side effects: anxiety, fatigue, depression, acute agitation, tremors, hallucinations, increased muscle spasticity! I admit I don't know how to use a drug like this: what am I supposed to do if I prescribe it and the symptoms continue? Stop the drug or double the dose? What strategy lies behind using drugs like this is a mystery to me.[15]

Doctors speak with confidence about the currently accepted treatments, such as antidepressants like Prozac, Seroxat, Effexor and others. Within the next five to ten years, will the treatments which today's experts speak so highly of have been found out? Will they be found to be useless, harmful or addictive like many of the 'treatments' of the past? According to Charles Medawar, the addictive potential of these newer antidepressant drugs — the SSRIs (selective serotonin reuptake inhibitors) — is a cause for concern. In his previously mentioned article in the February 1998 edition of *What Doctors Don't Tell You*, Medawar wrote:

> The number of Yellow Card reports do suggest a problem. After 17 years of use, the benzodiazepines (tranquillisers) had attracted 28 Yellow Card reports of suspected withdrawal problems, while the numbers of reports relating to SSRIs in less than ten years (as of March 1997) were pushing the 1000 mark and rising.

Alarmingly, it seems that the addictive potential of antidepressants was never systematically researched:

> The authorities are unanimous: with antidepressants, the question of dependence doesn't arise. The Royal Colleges of Psychiatrists and General Practitioners have emphasised there is no risk of dependence, and recommend doctors to reassure their patients about this. The manufacturers of SSRIs clearly also considered such risks remote and did not test their drugs for therapeutic dependence potential, and neither the UK nor USA regulators required such tests to be done. The FDA (but not the CSM/MCA) has required that this be stated on the label — e.g. 'Prozac has not been systematically studied, in animals or humans, for its potential for abuse, tolerance, or physical dependence . . .' (Lilly 1996). This would explain why withdrawal effects came to light only several years after licensing'.[16]

For years, there has been enormous resistance within the medical profession worldwide to the real possibility that antidepressants may be addictive. I experienced this resistance on Irish national radio in November 2001. In an article in the *Independent* of 29 April 2001 entitled 'World Health watchdog warn of addiction risk for Prozac users', Professor Ralph Edwards (of the World Health Organisation's unit monitoring drug adverse effects) had expressed considerable concern that, with regard to the SSRI antidepressants, 'the issue of dependence and withdrawal has become much more serious'.

On Irish national radio in November 2001, I expressed my belief that the SSRI antidepressants are addictive.[17] On air, I read the above statement from Professor Ralph Edwards. Coming from such a reputable source, I would have thought than Professor Edward's warning should be taken very seriously. Dr James Reilly, a prominent Irish GP, then spoke on air on that radio programme. Having listened to what I had said, Dr Reilly said:

> *Can I say one thing very clearly. There is absolutely no evidence that Prozac, SSRIs, that group of drugs are dependency-forming.*

In keeping with a pattern I have repeatedly observed, this prominent GP saw fit to dismiss the concerns of a leading World Health Organisation medical expert. Why would doctors do such a thing? Perhaps because the message is one which the medical does not want to hear; the message is extremely challenging to the medical profession who for years has, just as this GP did on radio, stated with great certainty that antidepressants are definitely not addictive. In keeping with current medical views, Dr Reilly was happy to explain that people coming off antidepressants might certainly experience a 'discontinuation syndrome'. Like the bulk of his medical colleagues, Dr Reilly was certain that this 'discontinuation syndrome' was not evidence of addiction or dependency. This 'discontinuation syndrome' notion is the medical profession's way of acknowledging the presence of problems on cessation of SSRI antidepressants, while at the same time ensuring that the medical beliefs about these drugs — that they are definitely not addictive — remain undisturbed.

In fact, evidence of addiction and withdrawal problems with SSRI antidepressants has been available for many years. Dr David Healy has provided expert witness evidence to two cases in the USA against SSRI manufacturers and so had access to the companies' confidential records of their clinical trials from the 1990s. Dr Healy found that, far from establishing the safety of these products, these trials actually reveal evidence of withdrawal symptoms.[18]

According to an interview with *Health Which?* February 2002, Dr David Healy has said in open court that GlaxoSmithKline (GSK) records reveal that 'there is a withdrawal syndrome from Paxil (USA trade name for Seroxat) including agitation, abnormal dreams and nightmares, that comes through in spades in these healthy volunteer studies', the original studies from the 1990s. Dr Healy says that for GSK to characterise paroxetine (Seroxat) withdrawal reactions as rare, transient, mild and impossible to distinguish from underlying psychiatric illness is 'simply an untenable position'.[19]

In 2002, the British Medicines Controls Agency formulated a list of the top 20 drugs for which withdrawal problems have been reported under the UK's 'Yellow Card' scheme. Alarmingly, five of the top six drugs are SSRI or related antidepressants, a group of drugs which doctors and drug companies insist are definitely not addictive. Paroxetine (Seroxat) alone has attracted more such reports than all other drugs on the UK adverse drug reaction database combined. At that time (2002), the Seroxat patient information leaflet categorically stated that 'remember, you cannot become addicted to Seroxat', and that withdrawal symptoms 'are not common and are not a sign of addiction'.

Drugs which are addictive tend to have a street value. In Seabrook, USA, in 2003, two individuals were charged at Hampton District Court of being in possession of drugs, including Paxil (known as Seroxat in Europe) with intent to sell.

The BBC's Panorama TV programme has produced three programmes on Seroxat in the past two years. The second of these programmes, aired in autumn 2002, provoked the greatest reaction ever received to a Panorama programme, 67,000 calls and 1,400 emails. Commenting on the enormous public reaction to this Panorama programme, journalist Jeremy Lawrence wrote in the *Independent,* 14 May 2003, that while some callers reported positive effects from the drug, the bulk of these calls and emails were from people who had experienced significant problems with Seroxat. In particular, callers reported severe withdrawal reactions, suicidal tendencies and behavioural changes such as aggression on Seroxat. This major public response eerily resembled the public reaction in the early 1980s to an episode of BBC's *That's Life* in which people outlined how hard it was for them to come off benzodiazepine tranquillisers, drugs such as Valium, Librium, Xanax and diazepam. Thousands of people contacted the programme, writing of their own, similar difficulties with these drugs. This major response prompted doctors to take seriously something they had previously been reluctant to acknowledge: that Valium and similar drugs might well be addictive. New advice on prescribing these drugs soon followed from British regulatory authorities, advice which to this day has not been properly implemented.

Concerns regarding suicide and SSRI antidepressants emerged as far back as the 1980s. USA drug licensing procedures required Eli Lilly, the manufacturers of Prozac, to inform the USA Food and Drugs Administration of any concerns about Prozac raised by other national health authorities. However, court records show that Lilly never told the Food and Drugs Administration — or the expert panel set up in 1991 to examine possible links between Prozac and suicide — that as far back as 1985, three years before Prozac received approval by the USA Food and Drug Administration, the German regulatory equivalent of the FDA had such serious reservations about Prozac's safety that it refused to approve Prozac's sale because of concerns over a link with suicide.

In their analysis of Lilly's data, the German authorities said that Prozac seemed to have caused a substantial increase in suicide rates among users, according to court records. Eli Lilly's studies showed that previously non-suicidal patients who took the drug had a five-fold higher rate of suicide and suicide attempts than those on older antidepressants, and a three-fold higher rate than those taking placebos, the latter being eerily similar to the Seroxat studies on adolescents which have recently been coming to light. Eventually, the German authorities approved Prozac, but with a warning that physicians should consider using sedatives for patients at risk of suicide.

In 1990, Dr Martin Teicher of Harvard Medical School reported that he and his colleagues had observed suicidal thoughts in six patients who were taking Prozac. This report was quickly followed over several years by several others expressing similar concerns, as outlined by Dr David Healy.[20] Also in 1990, scientists working for Eli Lilly were pressured by corporate executives to alter records on physicians' experiences with Prozac. Documents which surfaced during legal actions against the manufacturers of Prozac revealed that for years, the company struggled to deal with suicidal actions by people on Prozac in drug trials. One such document — a memo from a top executive within the company — included a request to the company's researchers to alter references to suicide attempts to 'overdose', and suicidal thoughts to 'depression'. A separate memo revealed a company employee's disquiet about these directives:

> I do not think I could explain to the BGA [the German regulatory body] a judge, to a reporter, or even to my family why we would do this especially on the sensitive issue of suicide and suicidal ideation.[21]

In 1991, the USA Food and Drugs Administration set up a committee of experts to examine possible links between Prozac and suicide. Lilly, the manufacturers of Prozac, did not inform this committee about the concerns and actions of the German authorities, as just outlined. When asked why Lilly did not provide this important information to the panel set up to examine a possible link between Prozac and suicide, a Lilly executive stated, 'that was not a question I was asked, so I did not answer that question'(ibid). The committee concluded that there was no link between Prozac and suicide.

Of the ten American specialists who, as members of the FDA panel which assessed the Prozac/suicide risk in 1991, unanimously and formally cleared Prozac of a link to suicide in 1991, seven now say that the 'new' information (discussed shortly, the information regarding increased suicide risk with SSRI antidepressants in the under 18s) would 'prompt them to reconsider that decision, if they were asked'(ibid.). One of that original panel, Dr Jeffrey A. Lieberman, a professor of psychiatry and pharmacology at the University of North Carolina, is quoted as saying that, 'in 1991, we said there wasn't sufficient evidence to support a link between these [SSRI antidepressant] drugs and suicide. Now there is evidence, at least in children, and I wouldn't rule out that it's in adults' (ibid.).

In December 2000, an article appeared in the *British Journal of Psychiatry*, by Dr Stuart Donovan and colleagues; their review of 2,776 patients taking SSRIs who attended the Derbyshire

71

Royal Infirmary over two years. They did not find a link between taking SSRIs and dying from overdosing, which would be in keeping with the prevailing medical view that SSRIs are safer in overdose than the older antidepressants. But they did find a relationship between taking SSRIs and all forms of deliberate self-harm — including overdose, attempted overdose, hanging, gassing, laceration, deliberate road traffic accidents, head banging, swallowing non-medicines — much higher than for the older antidepressants. The relationship is so strong, Dr Donovan says, that he firmly believes promotional material for SSRIs including Seroxat should be changed immediately so that doctors would no longer prescribe them to potentially suicidal patients thinking, mistakenly, that by doing so they are protecting their lives.[22]

A Datamonitor survey carried out in 2002 revealed that many psychiatrists are losing confidence in the effectiveness of the newer antidepressants, such as Prozac and Seroxat. Having embraced these drugs with such enthusiasm for over a decade, psychiatrists and GPs risk public embarrassment and humiliation by acknowledging that they made such a major error of judgement about these drugs. Therefore, you will rarely hear psychiatrists or GPs voice such concerns publicly.

2003 was a particularly difficult year for SSRI anti-depressants. In June, based on data handed over to them just two weeks previously by manufacturers GlaxoSmithKline, the UK Medicines and Healthcare products Regulatory Agency (MRHA) banned the use of Seroxat in people under eighteen years of age. This data consisted of nine separate studies of Seroxat in children and young people commissioned by the drug company, only one of which had been published. Some of the data came from studies completed in the late 1980s. The nine studies revealed a predilection to suicide, aggressive behaviour and psychosis in Seroxat users under 18 years of age. The MRHA took the view that GlaxoSmithKline, the manufacturers of Seroxat, should have drawn its attention much earlier to clinical trials among children which showed that some suffered worrying adverse effects, including agitation, aggression and suicidal tendencies.

Within three months, as the medical profession struggled to come to terms with the implications of this alarming Seroxat development, major problems emerged regarding another antidepressant. On 10 September 2003, Wyeth contacted doctors regarding their antidepressant Effexor. Eerily similar to the belated Seroxat warning three months earlier, the Wyeth letter stated that paediatric studies found 'increased reports of hostility and suicide-related adverse events, such as suicidal ideation and self-harm' among those patients on Effexor. Wyeth stated that Effexor is therefore contraindicated in under-18s.

Drug companies and many doctors have attempted recently to persuade the public that drugs such as Seroxat and Effexor which are unsafe for under eighteens are perfectly safe for those over eighteen. This argument is fundamentally flawed, since there is no evidence that the brain of a 17-year old differs from the brain of a 20- or indeed a 40-year old. As Dr David Healy, director of the North Wales Department of Psychological Medicine at the University if Wales pointed out,[23] if warnings are now being given regarding the safety of SSRI antidepressant drugs for under-18s, clearly warnings should also be issued regarding their use in adults also.

In December 2003, The UK Committee on Safely of Medicines similarly banned the use of all the other SSRI drugs bar Prozac in under-18s. Within days of this announcement, the manufacturers of Prozac themselves issued a directive to doctors not to prescribe Prozac for under-18s. Also in December 2003, the UK Committee on Safety of Medicines initiated an investigation into the safety and effectiveness of these drugs in adults.

In my twenty years' experience in medicine, the current

situation regarding SSRI antidepressants is unique. I know of no other group of drugs, in any medical speciality, which are banned for under-18s while considered safe by the majority of doctors in over-18s.

At a press conference called to announce the Seroxat ban in under-18s in June 2003, Jonathan Chick, a consultant psychiatrist at the Royal Edinburgh Hospital and a member of the Seroxat inquiry panel, admitted that there could be problems with adults too. He said that it always puzzled him why suicide rates in adults taking Seroxat were not lower than among those taking placebo, when he would have expected them to be lower given the (widely presumed) beneficial effect of the drugs on depression.[24]

Also in 2003, Brecon coroner Geraint Williams commented at the inquest of regarding Colin Whitfield, who ended his life two weeks after commencing Seroxat:

> I have grave concerns that this is a dangerous drug that should be withdrawn until at least national studies are undertaken. I am profoundly disturbed by the effect this drug had on Colin Whitfield. It is quite clear that Seroxat has a profound effect on the thinking process of anyone who takes it . . . I have a picture of a kindly, gentle, courteous family man whose primary concern was his wife and children. But on this day he didn't care. He did a deliberate act affected, I have no doubt, by the taking of Seroxat.[25]

At Mr Whitfield's inquest, Brecon coroner Geraint Williams said he would be writing to Health Secretary Alan Milburn to demand the drug be withdrawn for further safety checks. And in June 2002, mental health charity MIND called for:

- An independent review of the safety of Seroxat and the other SSRIs that involves service users and takes full account of the evidence from self-reporting of side and

withdrawal effects.
• Withdrawal of Seroxat (at least for new prescribing) until this has been carried out.
• Improved warnings to prescribers and public.
• Support to enable people to come off safely.[26]

Ironically, at a time when important questions regarding safety and addiction issues remain unanswered, the scope for prescribing Seroxat and other SSRIs is being widened. In January 2003, the USA Food and Drugs Administration — quickly followed by regulatory agencies in many other countries — approved Prozac for prescription to children aged between 7 and 17. In February 2003, the possibilities for prescribing Seroxat were further extended when the drug was approved to treat post traumatic stress disorder (PTSD).

Regarding the safety review of Seroxat set up in May 2003 by the British Medicines and Healthcare Products Regulatory Agency, according to Charles Medawar of Social Audit UK:

. . . the terms of reference of the new review team duck the key issues: could this crisis have been avoided, and how to avoid similar problems in the future? Thus, self-interest still rules. There is abundant evidence that the regulators themselves played a major part in creating the problems now being addressed. This crisis has been looming for years, and the regulatory response was inadequate for these related reasons:
• over-reliance on misleading definitions and on data represented as 'scientific' and reliable.
• endemic secrecy, plus a chronic tendency to dismiss dissenting views
• insufficient, sometimes incompetent analyses of the available data.

Nothing less than a full, independent public enquiry is needed to address these problems. This would be standard practice if the casualties had resulted from, say, an air or rail crash, a sunken ferry or a stadium fire. But there has never been such an enquiry in the UK — not even after thalidomide . . . On the Richter scale of drug disasters — where thalidomide ranks 10 — I would rate the SSRIs somewhere between 7 and 11. The exact number is uncertain, but give it a few years and we shall see'.[27]

There have also been worrying developments regarding Zyban, another SSRI antidepressant, which was licensed in Britain in June 2000 as a safe drug to help people quit smoking. In September 2001, the Canadian department of health issued a warning about Zyban. Health Canada warned doctors that 1,127 adverse reactions in three years had been reported. Since the launch of Zyban, concern has grown in many countries — including Britain, Germany, France and Australia — regarding the safety of this drug.

While drug companies have for years minimised these adverse effects, when it suits them they do not play them down. For example, during its application for a patent for a new version of Prozac, Eli Lilly stated that the new formulation would reduce 'the usual adverse effects' of the original Prozac, including 'nervousness, anxiety, insomnia, inner restlessness (akathisia), suicidal thoughts, self-mutilation, manic behaviour'. I find it interesting that the three alarming adverse effects are placed at the end of the sentence, while the relatively trivial and less alarming ones are at the beginning of the sentence.

The main method used to assess untoward problems with new drugs is the 'Yellow Card' system. Doctors are asked to complete a yellow form if they suspect that a drug has caused side effects. This system is casually implemented. Even in the widely publicised thalidomide disaster of the 1960s, when thousands of newborn babies suffered major limb deformities due to the drug thalidomide, fewer than twenty Yellow Cards regarding this drug were returned by doctors. The public — for whom new drugs are prescribed and recommended by doctors — are the guinea pigs.

As mentioned earlier, drug companies and doctors will not usually downplay a medication unless another medication becomes available as a replacement. Only when the SSRIs became available toward the end of the 1980s — the newer antidepressants such as Prozac and Seroxat — did the medical profession and the pharmaceutical industry begin to fully accept the problems with benzodiazepine tranquillisers. They had a new great hope to turn to. Since then, the SSRIs have become the core of treatment for virtually all the conditions which just 15 years ago were being treated with tranquillisers; anxiety, panic, agoraphobia and other phobias, obsessive-compulsive disorders, eating disorders, and post-traumatic stress. Until the end of the 1980s, tranquillisers were also recommended and widely prescribed for depression.

Since virtually all other long-term medications previously prescribed for these conditions (with the possible exception of the older antidepressants) have been largely discredited, the SSRIs and other newer antidepressant drugs are the only medication the medical profession has to offer. Since no new revolutionary or miracle drug is currently waiting in the wings to replace the SSRIs, the pharmaceutical industry and the medical profession will vehemently stick to their guns regarding the effectiveness, safety and non-addictiveness of these drugs, at least until the patient runs out, and drug company profits are consequently reduced. Whatever the truth about the public needing to take Prozac and its equivalents, the medical profession and drug companies certainly need the public to believe in these drugs, because right now the medical profession have little else to offer.

Medical experts repeatedly tell the public that the psychiatric system works. The public has no way of checking this out for themselves. If a GP or psychiatrist is being interviewed on the radio, and several people phone in to express how the medical treatment of their 'mental illness' did not work for them (and I have heard many such radio shows), the doctor can reply with a statistic which cannot be debated because only the profession has this information. For example, on media programmes about depression, I have heard doctors state that the medical profession knows for sure that antidepressants are 70 per cent effective. The implication is that those who did not respond were therefore part of the other 30 per cent. I used to believe that too, but not any more.

My personal experience of twenty years of working as a medical doctor suggests to me that the effectiveness of antidepressants is significantly less than 70 per cent. In 2002, oven ten years after the launch of SSRI antidepressants, the Royal College of Psychiatrists acknowledged that the effectiveness of these drugs had been overstated. This and other relevant points are referred to in the following article by Bradford psychiatrists Pat Bracken and Phil Thomas in the *Guardian,* 4 March 2002. According to these psychiatrists, the reality on the ground is that many psychiatric service users are unhappy that their 'treatment' consists of one drug after another, a practice which suggests that antidepressants are not as effective as they have been promoted to be. These two psychiatrists point out that while 60 per cent to 70 per cent of people taking an antidepressant drug experience some benefit, between 40 per cent and 50 per cent of people taking a placebo experience significant benefit. They refer to the Royal College of Psychiatrist's action during the previous month to downgrade its claims regarding antidepressant effectiveness, from 60–70 per cent, to 50 per cent. The state that all of this demonstrates that the actual effect of the pharmacological agents in these drugs is at best marginal. They refer to a Datamonitor survey published the previous week, which revealed that many psychiatrists are less confident about the effectiveness Prozac, Seroxat and the other, newer antidepressant drugs. According to Drs Bracken and Thomas, the effectiveness of these drugs may have been over-stated, and there are suggestions that some pharmaceutical companies actually attempted to suppress evidence regarding serious adverse effects which surfaced in their own research. The state that pharmaceutical companies will inevitably interpret the growing questions regarding the effectiveness of antidepressant drugs as justification for further massive investment in the development and publicising of new drugs. Both psychiatrists state their view that this is wrong.

Many researchers raise questions regarding the widely held belief in the effectiveness of antidepressants. For example, in 2002 Irving Kirsch, a psychologist at the University of Connecticut, analysed all the antidepressant drug data on the six most widely used antidepressant drugs approved by the USA Food and Drug Administration between 1987 and 1999.[28] They found that the benefits of the antidepressants are 'clinically negligible' when compared to placebo. Kirsch concluded that 'antidepressants may have no meaningful antidepressant effect at all'.

Long-stay psychiatric inpatients are a particularly vulnerable group. Long forgotten by the outside world, many have become dependent on their carers, and on the institution within which they live. The following comments by a service user, appropriately entitled *Getting hooked within the system of psychiatry: a problem grossly underestimated by the service,* illustrate the conflict between the wish to live independently and the institutionalisation created by the psychiatric system:

> *I feel I became institutionalised at a fairly early age from living in a string of care and foster homes. But I really feel my dependence on institutions started for me at the age of 14 when I entered the psychiatric services. The first place I went to was an adolescent unit in West Sussex. I was reliant*

on the staff and the place for everything, from what I ate to when I ate — even, to an extent, down to the clothes I wore, as we were only allowed a certain amount of clothing. I couldn't always choose who I wanted to visit me or when I wanted them to visit; when I went out, if I went out or where I went to. I had no choice about where I lived, who I lived with or who I shared rooms with; whether I took medication or what I took. And so it went on, down to what time I got up and what time I went to bed. As the years went by, so I became more embroiled in the services, with more and more admissions to psychiatric hospitals throughout the country, until institutions became a dependency.

Because of the high level of dependence that developed in the places I lived, and the staff control of me, at times I developed differing types of dysfunctional behaviour, low self-esteem and also a certain amount of institutionalised anxiety; for example, if the meals did not appear at the given time; if the trolley man did not arrive at 11 o'clock; or even if fish and chips weren't served as normal on a Friday. These structures were at times a crutch for me, and when they were taken away it caused me stress.

In Feb 2001 I left a long-term placement of four-and-a-half years at a medium secure unit and returned to a hostel in the community. Here I had significant problems, not only with my behaviour but also with my inherent institutionalisation. I struggled with the very things that had controlled me but that had also kept me together. Now there was no one to tell me what to do, no structured routine. I could just walk around the shops whenever I pleased without being quizzed, and within reason I could choose and even buy what I wanted to eat. It was utopia. But within three months the very things that I loved became too much for me and I returned to psychiatric intensive care. I think being in hospitals and other types of care for long periods

of time strips people of their identities. I am now 36 years
old, and I and many of the professionals who work with
me do not see me ever living in the community. There are a
lot of Wendy Ifills out there. Where do our futures lie?[29]

I believe that Wendy Ifill is correct when she describes getting
hooked within the system of psychiatry as a problem grossly
underestimated by the mental health services. Many service
users have recounted similar experiences to me over the years.
A sense of personal powerlessness is a feature shared by many
who attend the mental health services, the significance of which
is repeatedly underestimated by the service providers. The
service providers within mental health care frequently fail to
appreciate the degree to which the services increase the sense
of powerlessness already experienced by many service users,
inadvertently setting up many service users to become
dependent on the services. I believe that this tendency could
be reversed if those providing the services continuously bore
in mind the importance of fostering self-empowerment, self-
determination, self-belief and self-confidence in their clients.

Psychiatry now sees itself as a modern scientific medical
speciality, standing proud and tall alongside cardiology,
gastroenterology, neurology, and the other medical specialties.
This position has given psychiatry a respectability and status
which puts it almost above questioning. The counselling
professions have not yet managed to create such status and
position. Psychiatry has therefore firmly established itself as
the field of expertise in mental health and 'mental illness'.

In theory and often in practice, mental health care is
delivered as a multi-disciplinary team. Psychiatrists, GPs,
psychologists, social workers, psychiatric nurses, community
mental health workers apparently working together as part of
the team. This can be somewhat misleading, however. The
psychiatrist is typically seen as the leader of the team, the

principal decision-maker.

This arrangement may suit some members of the multi-disciplinary team by reducing their decision-making responsibility. However, it means that the psychiatric, medical approach to people's mental health problems tend to dominate decision-making and the direction of interventions.

When suicide is discussed in the media, the 'expert' involved in the programme or article is typically a psychiatrist. For instance, RTE's Late Late Show devoted an entire programme to suicide in 1997. During the two-and-a-half hour discussion, two psychiatrists sat alongside presenter Gay Byrne. Throughout the programme, these doctors were portrayed as the acknowledged experts on suicide. Both psychiatrists spoke at length, and the presenter regularly asked them for their opinions.

There was no room for a psychologist on this panel of experts, not even for the President of the Psychological Society of Ireland, Pauline Beegin. She had to be content with sitting in the audience. While the psychiatrists were given freedom to speak frequently and at length during the programme, the president of the Psychological Society of Ireland had only one brief opportunity to speak. In my opinion, hers was one of the most important contributions to the entire two-and-a-half hour programme:

> *Listening to the two psychiatrists, one of the issues I have difficulty with is the whole description of suicide as an illness, or looking at the problems that cause suicide as illnesses, because I believe they are emotional problems that need to be dealt with. One of the things about rural areas [she was responding to the interviewer's question which was about suicide in rural areas] is access to talking to anybody about emotional events that have gotten out of control in your life, that you can't get perspective on, the fear of being labelled as schizophrenic or psychiatrically*

ill puts people off, they can't deal with the stigma, and they don't know who to turn to. The psychologist or psychiatrist is in the local psychiatric hospital which for most people in rural communities is not accessible because they are identified so easily. People are scared that word will get out that they are attending the psychiatrists, that they have a so-called 'psychiatric illness'.

These cautionary words from an experienced psychologist received no further attention during this two-and-a-half hour programme. Gay Byrne quickly moved on to speak to another member of the audience. At no time during the remainder of the programme did Gay Byrne or the two expert psychiatrists refer back to Pauline Beegin's comments. Because psychiatry is seen as the area of expertise in mental health, views which oppose those of psychiatry are easily rebuffed, or as happened on this important TV programme, ignored.

What Pauline Beegin was really objecting to was the medicalisation of suicide. To medicalise a problem means to categorise it as a medical issue. Medical doctors become the experts to whom the public turn for advice and direction. Psychiatry significantly influences government and health departments' initiatives on mental illness.

Others have also expressed concern regarding the medicalisation of life's problems. At a lecture in University College Cork in November 2003, Professor Richard Smith CBE, editor and chief executive officer of the *British Medical Journal*, defined medicalisation as 'the process of defining an increasing number of life's problems as medical problems'. Professor Smith expressed concern that an obsession with finding medical answers to life's problems may mean that we are cultivating a world full of patients. He said that society is in danger of becoming over-medicalised: 'I am not saying that people are not suffering; of course there is a lot of distress and suffering. What I am sceptical about is whether some things are best thought of as medical problems and approached in a medical way.' He cautioned against the process of 'disease-mongering', and referred to a number of forces promoting medicalisation, including patients, pharmaceutical companies and doctors. Regarding the dangers of over-medicalisation, he said that it can have an adverse effect by 'becoming much more of a problem that starts to take over your life. You begin to think of yourself as a helpless victim looking for medical interventions . . . there are dangers with turning everything into a medical problem.' In the *Guardian* of 14 January 2004, Richard Smith was quoted as saying that 'the public is being regularly deceived by the drug trials funded by pharmaceutical companies, loaded to generate the results they need'.

'Social phobia' was one of the examples of medicalisation referred to by Professor Smith during his lecture, according to a report in *Medicine Weekly,* 26 November 2003. 'Social phobia' has now been enthusiastically embraced by GPs and psychiatrists as an "illness" to be treated with SSRI antidepressants. As the following article illustrates, there is a strong case to suggest that the extraordinary rise in the diagnosis and treatment of 'depression' is also an example of medicalisation on a vast scale. What follows is an extract of a review of Dr David Healy's book, *Let Them Eat Prozac.* The review is written by Arthur Schafer, Director, Centre for Professional and Applied Ethics, University of Manitobia, Canada:

> On the face of it, the investigation of possible hazards posed by SSRI [antidepressants] do not seem to have followed the conventional dynamics of science, where anomalies in the data are supposed to spur further investigation. In this case, debate has been closed down rather than opened up...
> Prior to the 1990s, comparatively few people were thought to suffer from depression; approximately 1 in 10,000. With

the discovery of the Prozac group of drugs there came, not coincidentally, an explosive increase in diagnoses of depressive illness. Current estimates claim that one in ten of the population is clinically depressed. A thousand-fold increase. In barely a decade, depression has gone from being a rare disorder to being classed as one of the greatest afflictions of mankind — requiring that millions of comparatively healthy people be treated with powerful medication. An old cliché jumps irresistibly to mind: To the man with a hammer in his hand, everything looks like a nail. There is no nice way of putting this: The drug companies have subordinated patient safety on the altar of blockbuster profits. Aggressive marketing has persuaded the medical profession to prescribe SSRI drugs to people who are simply struggling with mundane anxieties. Unwilling to risk the death of the goose that laid such golden eggs, the companies refuse to sponsor the kind of large-scale scientific research that would map out the true frequency and seriousness of side-effects. Without such research, doctors and patients are unable to make properly informed choices. There may be only 50 ways to leave your lover, but there are at least 150 ways to design drug experiments so that they are skewed in favour of the sponsoring company's products. Want to eliminate evidence of dangerous side effects from your new antidepressant? First, ensure that company scientists design the experiment and tabulate the data before it is turned over to the university scientist whose name will grace the eventual publication. Better yet, when volunteers enrolled in the experiment become agitated (and potentially suicidal or violent), code them as 'failing to respond to treatment'. Amazingly, by this simple sleight of hand, the alarming side effects disappear. What isn't recorded doesn't exist. The respected scientist whose name goes on the ghost-written publication — a widespread practice, as Healy shows — seldom sees the raw data and is happy to collect a generous fee from the company along with the status that comes with having 'his' research published in a prestigious journal. Leading drug industry figures play an unsavoury role in this story, but it cannot be said that either the medical profession or government regulators emerge with armour shining. Those charged with protecting the public from unjustifiable harms seem not yet to have taken on board the central lesson of the 1962 thalidomide tragedy: all drugs are inherently risky. Only honest and well-designed research will tell us which drugs offer which patients the likelihood of more benefit than harm. Because universities and hospitals float on a sea of drug industry money, few seem keen to raise critical questions about unethical research practices.[30]

If 'depression' and other so-called 'psychiatric conditions' are not illnesses; if they are examples of the medicalisation process just discussed, is there an alternative way of understanding these 'conditions'? As explored throughout this book, they can be understood as expressions of human distress, sometimes immense human distress. And unlike the theoretical, uncomfirmable biochemical theories which dominate most doctors' view of these 'conditions', the person's distress is usually palpably obvious, if one is open to seeing it for what it is.

I learned many things from American psychiatrist Dr Peter Breggin's ground-breaking book, *Toxic Psychiatry*. Rather than define mental health problems in terms of 'psychiatric illness', he speaks of 'schizophrenic' overwhelm; 'manic-depressive' overwhelm; 'depressive' overwhelm; 'anxiety' overwhelm. This is an accurate description, illustrating the common experience of overwhelm while simultaneously identifying that some characteristics of this overwhelm vary within the different groups. The concept of overwhelm accurately encapsulates the distress these people are living with, and the coping mechanisms they create to deal with this level of distress. It calls for intervention strategies quite different to those of an illness-based model. It calls for collaborative work between client and service providers, aimed at creating an appropriate, person-centred, flexible, workable recovery process for the person. Such an approach is quite challenging to the medical profession; it is does not fit comfortably into the medical belief system. Doctors tend to approach many mental health problems as illnesses requiring long-term maintenance (primarily with medication) rather than experiences from which recovery is a possible, realistic goal.

In my opinion, a repackaging and a redefining process takes place in the doctor's surgery. The person walking in the door of the surgery tells the doctor of the distress and overwhelm they are experiencing — they may be anxious, panicky, depressed, angry, hurt, or commonly a mixture of these and other feelings and emotions. The GP and psychiatrist then sets out to decide whether these feelings and emotions fit into one of the packages called 'mental illness' that they have been trained to diagnose and treat. In some situations, the overwhelm is experienced and expressed obliquely. To understand this process takes a degree of understanding of the human condition which in my experience is not commonly reached by most GPs and psychiatrists, who have had insufficient training in this area.

In a case which typifies the experience of many patients, a woman was admitted to a leading psychiatric unit, diagnosed as having severe clinical depression. She was admitted under the care of an eminent psychiatrist. During her three-week admission, her contact with her psychiatrist consisted of two brief — less than ten minute — visits per week. These consultations consisted of a short 'Hello, how are you?' and a review of the patient's medication. During these brief meetings, the consultant was accompanied by an entourage of doctors and nurses, a common practice which hardly encourages patients to speak frankly with the psychiatrist.

The medication did not help. Eight weeks after she was discharged home, she remained as depressed as ever despite taking the antidepressants as prescribed. Then her husband became suddenly and seriously ill with asthma. Her depression improved dramatically. Suddenly, she felt needed. Her depression was not and had never been a biological, physical illness. It was an emotional withdrawal reaction. Having no sense of self-worth, one of the few ways she could feel any sense of importance in life was by caring for others. Her children were grown up and had flown the nest. She was in her fifties. She had no one to look after any more. She became depressed because she felt worthless, not because of any brain abnormality. When her husband became ill, she had someone to look after again, and her depression quickly lifted and did not recur.

Medical training is a significant part of the problem. Most medical students tend to come from privileged and stable backgrounds. Most medical students would not have much personal experience of the severe emotional distress they will later encounter in their patients, a point equally applicable to psychology students. In order to study hard enough to achieve the high exam results necessary to enter medical school, many students have led a somewhat closeted teenage existence, a pattern which is continued during the very demanding years at medical school. In this regard, counselling and psychotherapy training courses may be more realistic. Many such training courses insist that the person has more life experience. While I am not aware of relevant statistics, my sense is that the average age of psychotherapy and counselling trainees is significantly higher than that of either medical or psychology students. The extra life experience thus gained may create a more rounded, empathic therapist.

From the moment these teenagers enter medical school, they are indoctrinated into a medical system which places great emphasis on the physical, biological aspects of human existence. For six years, these students learn an enormous amount of information about physical aspects of medicine such as anatomy, physiology, pathology, and drug treatments. Even when students learn about psychiatry, what they learn is not an exploration of the emotional, psychological and social aspects of human existence, nor indeed the daily struggles of relationships and everyday life. Rather, the focus is on psychiatry as a scientific branch of medicine, where people's problems are evaluated in the language of psychiatric illness. The young students emerge as qualified doctors six years later, highly conditioned into the medical, biological approach. Their postgraduate training further cements their preoccupation with the biological aspects of the human being. They believe that they are scientists, but many have already lost a key scientific attribute — open-mindedness. They think they are open-minded, but they look at patients through the tinted glasses of their medical training. The combination of authoritarian teaching and peer competition breeds conforming medical students and doctors.

While psychiatrists might say that they are fully trained in psychotherapy, medication is by far the commonest treatment modality they use. The mere presence of psychotherapy training within psychiatric training does not guarantee that young psychiatrists will become aware of the full potential of psychotherapy and other non-drug treatment interventions.

On several occasions, I have heard psychiatrists state that they are trained in psychotherapy as part of their psychiatry training. However, the presence of some training in psychotherapy within the process of training psychiatrists does not guarantee that psychiatrists are sufficiently open to the potential of 'talk therapy' and other non-drug inter-ventions. The overall thrust of psychiatric training focuses on a biological interpretation of mental health problems. The predominance of this biological approach within psychiatric training may well colour how trainee psychiatrists view interventions which come from a different perspective to that of the biological model.

In 2003, more than twenty mental health service users in the USA went on hunger strike, refusing to eat until they had some answers from the American Psychiatric Association about human rights. Subsequently, there was in interchange of correspondence between the Scientific Panel supporting the hunger strike (a fourteen-person panel of experienced psychiatrists, psychologists, researchers and clinicians) and the American Psychiatric Association. Initially, the American Psychiatric Association was reluctant to engage with the hunger strikers, but the considerable USA publicity forced the APA to respond.

In one of these written exchanges, the American Psychiatric Association admitted the absence of 'discernable pathological lesions or genetic abnormalities' in mental disorders, contradicting an assertion of 'reproducible abnormalities' in the same letter. Further information on these exchanges and the hunger strike can be obtained through the website http://www.MindFreedom.org. The following is an extract from the hunger strikers' Scientific Panel's letter to the American Psychiatric Association of 15 December 2003:

> Psychiatric research is far from showing any reliable connections between mental disorders and biological measurements, much less revealing anything definitive about the nature of mental disorders . . . Given the USA Food and Drug Administration's impotent exercise of its mandate to protect consumers from false advertising, pharmaceutical companies recklessly advertise cartoons

showing neurotransmitter 'imbalances' corrected by drugs. However, in the absence of scientific proof to substantiate such claims, it is ethically and medically reprehensible for doctors to convey such messages to justify prescribing drugs, and for the American Psychiatric Association's own journals to publish such advertisements...Associations devoted to research and treatment of genuine [biological] diseases readily provide consumers with scientific references on the pathological basis of these diseases. The American Psychiatric Association is a 35,000-member organisation, with an annual budget exceeding $38 million. With a handful of allies, it shapes mental health practice and policy in the USA and has convinced taxpayers to spend billions to support its claim that psychiatrists treat 'neurobiological disorders'. The APA should be able to provide a one-page list of published scientific studies to support this claim. Yet, the APA only speculates on future findings: 'Mental disorders will likely be proven to represent disorders of intercellular communication; or disrupted neural [nerve] circuitry'. The hunger strikers asked the APA for the 'evidence base' that justifies the biomedical model's stranglehold on the mental health system. The APA has not supplied any such evidence, which compels this scientific panel to ask one final question: on what basis does society justify the authority granted psychiatrists, as medical doctors, to force psychoactive drugs or electroconvulsive treatment upon unwilling individuals, or to incarcerate persons who may or may not have committed criminal acts? For, clearly, it is solely on the basis of trust in the claim that their professional acts and advice are founded on medical science that society grants psychiatrists such extraordinary authority. We urge members of the public, journalists, advocates and officials reading this exchange to ask for straightforward answers

91

to our questions from the American Psychiatric Association. We also ask [the USA] Congress to investigate the mass deception that the 'diagnosis and treatment of mental disorders,' as promoted by bodies such as the American Psychiatric Association and its powerful allies, represents in America today.

'If only we could give patients more time'

Building up trusting relationships with people requires that the doctor or therapist must be prepared to set aside sufficient time for their clients. GPs' waiting rooms are typically full of people — how could a GP possibly give patients more than ten minutes? I believe it comes down to priorities. I might have forty things I would like to do tomorrow but I will be doing well if I get to twenty of these. I will give attention to what I see as most important. The rest will have to wait for another day.

We all manage to give time to what is most important to us. Doctors say they do not have enough time to give their patients. If doctors have not created a working environment designed to give their patients enough time, it is because giving patients more time is not high enough on the medical profession's priority list. Giving people enough time in the consultation was so important to me that I dramatically changed how I work. I put giving time to people as my first priority. If I can do it, so can other doctors — if it was important enough to them. Where there is a will there is a way.

Giving clients time is a core value of the counselling and psychotherapy professions — hence the standard hour-long consultation. Doctors do not prioritise the duration of the consultation as highly. Hence, patients get eight to ten minutes from GPs. A first consultation with a psychiatrist may last twenty to thirty minutes, further consultations typically last five to ten minutes. Behind plaintive calls of 'if only I had more time to give my patients' lies a reluctance to take the steps necessary to provide people with longer consultations, and a failure to see the importance of giving people more time.

In my opinion, the principal reason why doctors give people so little time relates to their income. Extending the duration of consultations inevitably means seeing fewer patients per day. Doctors would have to reduce their patient list size, reducing their income in the process. A 1993 study funded by the American Psychiatric Association reported that psychiatrists who practise psychotherapy cannot make much more than $100,000 per year, whereas a practice confined to medication and evaluation will yield $300,000 per annum.

There is another possible reason for the short duration of medical consultations. It is easier to remain behind the protective screen of one's role in a short consultation than in a longer one. The engagement with the patient remains at a safe, distant level in a short consultation. Short consultations ensure that the doctor does not have to really connect with the person's distress, their tears, pain, anger, hurt. Short consultations protect doctors from feeling inadequate and/or disturbed when faced with the starkness of the person's distress.

One further reason for short consultations is that, in my opinion, many doctors wouldn't know what to do with the patient in a longer consultation. Having spent many years re-training, in an effort to more clearly understand mental health problems, I have become very aware of how poorly doctors are equipped to deal with mental and emotional distress. I believe this is true of both GPs and the majority of psychiatrists. The public is not aware of this, however, and mistakenly presumes that medical training adequately equips doctors with sufficient expertise in mental health.

In the following two chapters, I present an alternative view of 'mental illness'. This view questions the very existence of 'psychiatric illness'. I explore whether so-called 'psychiatric illness' might instead be an understandable reaction to difficult or intolerable life circumstances. I ask whether life itself, our experiences and our relationships, may trigger the deep emotional distress which is labelled as 'mental illness' by the medical profession.

Issues which are highly relevant to the users of mental health services daily experience, their life and their distress, including the distress of depression, 'schizophrenia' and 'bi-polar disorder', remain unnoticed and unresolved. Issues such as fear, terror, anxiety, stress, powerlessness, overwhelm, hurts; insecurity, identity issues, relationship issues, life changes; unresolved losses and grief; self-esteem, self-confidence, unresolved and unexpressed feelings; lack of assertiveness; abuse, abandonment, rejection, humiliation, ridicule, bullying; being marginalised, displaced, discommoded, disenfranchised; faced with problems, sadness and life situations with seem unresolvable; losing face, loneliness; lack of and fear of love and intimacy, difficult life decisions, self-image issues; fear of failure, fear of success, fear of being invisible to others and for some, fear of being visible; one's own expectations, hopes and dreams and those of others; the gradual accumulation of self-doubt; the angst of having so many choices; the human need to belong, to have purpose; sexuality; issues around sex and relationships; financial issues; the need to find various ways of escaping and withdrawing from the difficulties and challenges of life and indeed from the intensity of one's own feelings; the perceived demands of society that one should pretend, wear a mask, that one should hide one's distress; the anxiety associated with risk-taking in life, especially if one's self-esteem is low; peer pressures; the human need for acceptance, affirmation and reassurance; the human instinctual reaction to protect oneself from overwhelm; the human need for a sense of equilibrium and how this equilibrium gets rocked by various shocks in life; performance anxiety; comparisons between self and others; hopelessness; the human need to trust but fearing being let down if one does trust in people; the challenge of taking responsibility for oneself in a difficult world; understandable but counter-productive habits such as procrastination; fear of being with or around people yet not really wanting to be alone either; ostracisation of various types; isolation; life events; the double-edged sword of wanting to get on with one's life but being terrified to do so.

These are some of the real issues which the users of the mental health services have to grapple with on a daily basis, issues which psychiatry has decided are of little relevance to people's mental health problems and their recovery.

I believe that the degree to which children's' physical, emotional, psychological and social needs are not met has a bearing on their risk of developing distress later in life. This is not to suggest that parents are to blame. I believe that most parents do their level best for their children. But parenting is a tough task. With the best will in the world, important childhood needs can go unnoticed and unmet.

Children frequently suppress their emotional pain because it can be overwhelming. While of course this is not what occurs in all cases, some children grow into adults who try to protect themselves from further hurt and emotional pain. The early years of frightening aloneness make them vulnerable to a major emotional distress reaction if they continue to feel hurt as their adult life unfolds. Relationships with parents do not always improve, sometimes becoming more painful as the years go by.

A study presented to the 1999 winter meeting of the Irish Division of the Royal College of Psychiatrists highlighted how childhood emotional trauma can lead to 'psychiatric illness' later in life. Psychiatrist Professor Anthony Clare and colleagues found that 37 per cent of depressed women attending their GP were sexually abused as children. The likelihood of adult depression paralleled the degree of sexual abuse. More serious sexual abuse involving penetration led to depression in 100 per cent of cases.

I believe that a doctor or therapist should guard against developing set ideas, and applying these ideas to every client. For example, I do not believe that the seeds of all mental health problems necessarily originate from the person's past. Sometimes, current life situations will be sufficient to cause great distress. Sometimes, the past is playing a part in their current distress. A person's past is relevant to their current experience of emotional and mental distress if the past is still alive in the person's present; if there is unfinished business from the past which is influencing the person's current life.

The experiences of three people I am currently working with illustrate this. As with many people I work with, these three people decided to attend me for essentially the same reason. People tell me my being a medical doctor with a broader approach than most other doctors prompted them to attend me. They wanted to attend a person who understood the medical approach to mental health, but who would not rely purely on medication. My being a medical doctor apparently helps people feel that I have a solid training background; clients tell me that my being trained as a psychotherapist in addition to being a GP conveys to them a sense that I am prepared to think 'outside the box', to take a broader, more holistic approach to mental health.

One, a man in his forties, recently mentioned to me that when he becomes insecure regarding his current relationship, he becomes very angry with his partner. As he reflected on a recent row with his current partner whom he loves deeply, a row triggered by his own fears around being abandoned, he recounted that on at least eight occasions during that row, he addressed his partner by the name of his previous partner, a relationship which ended very traumatically for him. The pain of the ending of his previous relationship was still alive in him to such a degree that when he felt very insecure, his communication with his present partner was highly influenced by his experiences with his previous partner, even to the point of looking his present partner in the eye, yet repeatedly calling her by his previous partner's name. While this dramatic example of the past being alive in the present may not be common, more subtle examples are relatively common.

A second person, a woman in her forties, grew up in a home where there was ever-present tension and daily parental outbursts. As a child, in order to minimise her risk of being scolded and in a frantic attempt to minimise the tension in her home, she became very quiet, rarely expressed an opinion, her over-riding aim as a child being the avoidance of conflict. Now in her forties, she continued to relate to the important people in her life with similar passivity, rarely expressing anger or asserting herself.

The third person is a woman in her thirties. She has attended me regularly, and we have a good, trusting relationship. When she attended me recently, she wanted to tell me something she had done but felt great shame around telling anyone. After skirting around the issue for 20 minutes, she finally plucked up the courage. She told me that she had been caught speeding; she was doing 44 miles per hour in a 40 mile an hour zone. I have rarely met a more careful driver. This woman was extremely upset about having 'broken the rules'. She was reared in a family where rules were set and implemented with an iron fist. One dare not break any rules in her home of origin, and she continued to be significantly influenced by this many years later. Minutes after telling me, she needed to check with me if I now saw her in a different light, such was the degree of her ingrained terror of the consequences of breaking any rules.

I recall a twenty-year-old woman who attended me on one occasion. She had suffered from depression for years, had had ECT more than ten times, and a series of antidepressants without improvement. She quickly informed me that she had been to several psychiatrists, and everyone (including herself) was satisfied that there was no identifiable cause for her depression. While she spoke with an air of confidence and assuredness, I sensed fear beneath her words, and she had exhibited a pattern of withdrawal from life over many years. I sensed that she was much more vulnerable that she was prepared to admit to me, and perhaps to herself. While exploring her childhood, she assured me that she came from a happy home. It emerged that she had absolutely no recollection of her childhood up to the age of nine. For any person, this might seem odd, but for a twenty-year-old it was particularly strange to have no recollection of virtually half of her life. I wondered whether she had traumatic childhood experiences which caused her to blank out her whole memory of childhood. There were many people coming and going in her home — many people had access to her besides her parents. I didn't go into this with her, though I suggested that if she was willing, we might explore her childhood further during later consultations. There was also the possibility that her ECT treatments had affected her memory.

She did not make another appointment. Perhaps she did not like or trust me enough to speak to me about this. Perhaps she thought I didn't have a clue, though she did seem to warm to me during the consultation. Or perhaps she did not want her view of her depression threatened. Maybe she really needed to protect herself from pain she may have blanked out for years. According to her, no doctor had been previously struck by her total lack of childhood memories.

Later in life, there are many triggers which may bring suppressed emotional pain closer to the surface. And for many people, life experiences in teenage or adult life are in themselves enough to lead to people becoming distressed to the point of being diagnosed as having a 'mental illness':

bullying; abuse; loss; humiliation; relationships whose passion has faded into monotony as lovers drift apart; mothers at home feeling they are taken for granted; men and women who derive little satisfaction from their work but feel they must stay in that job to pay the bills or maintain their social status; women who would love to have children but cannot, who experience great pain every time their friends talk about their children; bereavements or other life events that generate seismic changes, great insecurity or emotional pain in people's lives. For many people, the world we live in can be a cruel, lonely, cold, judgmental place.

The process by which distress is translated into 'mental illness' is discussed in the following two chapters.

Notes

1. MIMS Ireland, the Monthly Index of Medical Specialties, September 2000, p. 78.

2. Dr Peter Breggin (1993) *Toxic Psychiatry*. London: HarperCollins.

3. Ibid. p. 314.

4. Dr Donald Gould (1985) *The Black and White Medicine Show: How doctors serve and fail their customers*, p. 132. Hamish Hamilton.

5. Charles Medawar (1998) Antidepressants: Hooked on the happy drug. In the newsletter *What Doctors Don't Tell You*, from What Doctors Don't Tell You, 4 Wallace Road, London, N1 2PG.

6. Charles Medawar (1992) *Power and Dependence: Social audit on the safety of medicines*. London: Social Audit.

7. Joseph Glenmullen (2001) *Prozac Backlash,* p. 21. NY: Simon and Schuster.

8. Amnesty International (2002) *Mental Illness: The neglected quarter.* Summary Report.

9. Katy Arscott (1999) ECT: The facts psychiatry declines to mention. In Newnes, C., Holmes, G. and Dunn, C. *This is Madness*, pp.97–118. Ross-on-Wye: PCCS Books.

10. Fiona Shaw (1998) *Out of Me: The story of a postnatal breakdown,* pp. 71–2, London: Penguin.

11. William Sargent (1967) *The Unquiet Mind*, p. 60. London: Heinemann.

12. *The Irish Examiner,* 27 May 2003.

13. American Psychiatric Association Task Force on Electroconvulsive Therapy (1978) *Electroconvulsive Therapy* (Task Force Report 14), Ch. 1.

14. Dr Peter Breggin, op cit., p. 314.

15. Robert Mendlesohn (1990) *Confessions of a Medical Heretic*. p. 42 Contemporary Books.

16. Charles Medawar (2000) The Antidepressant Web, Social Audit UK, 22/9/00

17. The Marian Finucane radio show, Radio One, 19 November 2001.

18. *Mental Health Today,* April 2002.

19. *Health Which?* February 2002.

20. David Healy (2001) The SSRI suicides. In Newnes, C., Holmes, G. and Dunn, C. *This is Madness Too,* pp. 59–70. Ross-on-Wye: PCCS Books.

21. *New York Times,* 7 August 2003.

22. Ed Harriman (2001) *The Guardian,* 17 May.

23. Dr David Healy (2003) quoted in *The Guardian,* Sarah Boseley, 10 and 11 June.

24. *Independent,* 12 June 2003.

25. *The Western Mail,* 13 March 2003.

26. *Mind in Action, 8* June 2003.

27. Charles Medawar (2003) No bridge too far. *Openmind, 123*, Sept/Oct. Permission granted © Mind (National Association for Mental Health).

28. Irving Kirsch (2002) 'The Emperor's new drugs', *Prevention and Treatment*, July.

29. Wendy Ifill (2002) Getting hooked within the system of psychiatry. *Openmind, 118*, Nov/Dec. Permission granted © Mind (National Association for Mental Health). Wendy Ifill is a service user.

30. See http://www.globeanmail.com/servlet/ArticleNews/TPStory/LAC/20031018/BKPROZ18/TPHealth/

3

DEPRESSION

According to the World Health Organisation, depression will become the world's most pervasive serious illness by the year 2020. Currently, depression affects 340 million people worldwide, accounting for one-third of psychiatric hospital admissions. Given the scale of the problem of depression, it behoves the medical profession to investigate depression thoroughly and holistically.

However, the medical profession has become so preoccupied with establishing that depression is caused by a brain abnormality, the possibility that life experiences may cause depression has been neglected. Attracted by the alluring theory that depression may be genetic, the prevailing medical view disregards an obvious possibility. Children growing up in a home where one or both parents have depression may themselves be prone to depression due to the knock-on effects of their family situation on their childhood and later life. It is widely known that if a mother is terrified of lightning and frantically gathers her children under the stairs in a thunderstorm, her children may also come to dread lightning. I have never heard anyone suggest that their increased likelihood of dreading lightning is due to an inherited genetic defect. Similarly, people's political affiliation, career choice and religious beliefs are frequently influenced by the family environment. Yet there is rarely any suggestion that these influences are genetic in origin. It is well known that children who have been physically abused in childhood are at risk of repeating this pattern of abuse with their own children. Again, this repeating of patterns is thought to be due to their previous experiences rather than genetic inheritance. Why then do we presume that the increased incidence of depression in children of depressed parents is genetically determined? No genes for depression have been identified. People who become depressed are not 'mentally ill'. They are trying to cope with living as best they can, often having experienced a considerable degree of stress, hurt, loneliness, loss, rejection and other distressing life experiences.

Diagnosing depression

Psychiatrists the world over look to *The Diagnostic and Statistical Manual of Mental Disorders* (DSM) — put together by panels of psychiatrists convened by the American Psychiatric Association — as *the* guide to diagnosing psychiatric illness. Psychiatrists in Europe may also refer to what is known as the International Classification of Diseases. According to the fourth edition (DSM–IV) a 'Major Depressive Episode' is diagnosed in the presence of nine criteria. In reality, each criteria are merely descriptions of understandable human feelings and behaviours.

Criteria A1 describes the mood in a Major Depressive Episode as 'depressed, sad, hopeless, discouraged', or 'down in the dumps', people feeling 'blah', having no feelings or feeling anxious, increased irritability, bodily complaints such as aches and pains.

Criterion A2 refers to loss of interest or pleasure, loss of interest in hobbies.

Criterion A3 describes changes in eating habits, either an increase or decrease in appetite and/or weight.

Criterion A4 refers to sleep disturbance, most commonly insomnia, less frequently oversleeping.

Criterion A5 describes bodily expressions of distress such as 'agitation, e.g. the inability to sit still . . . or retardation e.g. slowed speech, thinking or body movements'.

Criterion A6 refers to decreased energy, tiredness and fatigue.

Criterion A7 speaks of a 'sense of worthlessness or guilt, unrealistic negative evaluations of one's worth, guilty preoccupations or ruminations' regarding the past.

Criterion A8 describes people's reported 'impaired ability to think, concentrate or make decisions', appearing 'easily distracted' or complaints of 'memory difficulties'.

Criterion A9 refers to 'thoughts of death, suicide ideation, or suicide attempts'.

According to the *DSM*, a formal diagnosis of a Major Depressive Episode can be made when the severity and duration of the person's mood meets criterion A1, and the person also experiences or exhibits four of the remaining eight criteria.

Why did the American Psychiatric Association select five criteria as the magic figure? What is so different between a person who meets six criteria — and is therefore diagnosed as having a Major Depressive Episode and needing antidepressant treatment — and one who meets four criteria, and therefore receives no psychiatric diagnosis or treatment? Why five criteria? Why not three? Or seven? How valid are these criteria?

There is nothing scientific about diagnosing depression. There is no valid scientific means of explaining why five criteria is taken as evidence of 'illness', meriting a diagnosis of a Major Depressive Episode, while the presence of three or four criteria in a person is taken to be 'normal', acceptable, requiring no diagnosis or treatment. Many of the criteria for diagnosing a Major Depressive Episode are understandable human reactions to life as it has unfolded for the person. Individuals complaining of feeling 'blah', children who do not want to play football any more, people looking as though they are about to cry, feeling sad, hopeless, down in the dumps, all of which are specifically mentioned in the criteria — does this sound scientific? Does this sound like evidence of a 'biological disorder', or of human emotional and mental distress? Not for one second do I question the depth of distress. I do question how this distress is interpreted by the medical profession.

These are the official guidelines of the American Psychiatric Association, the best these experts can formulate. Even if doctors stuck faithfully to these guidelines, there is huge scope for misdiagnosis, such is the vagueness of these criteria. But many doctors who prescribe antidepressant drugs every day of the week do not refer to these guidelines when diagnosing depression. It is worth noting that, according to a 1993 USA Rand Corporation study, doctors take an average of three minutes to decide to prescribe antidepressants.

The *DSM* is looked upon within much of modern medicine with the same reverence as the Bible is by Christian religions. Dr William Glasser is an American psychiatrist, internationally known as the creator of Reality Therapy. In his most recent book, he expresses his views on the DSM:

> The *DSM-IV* is the fourth and latest edition of a large book produced by the American Psychiatric Association in which all the known psychological symptoms are described. In it, these symptoms are grouped together into syndromes, each of which is referred to as a mental disorder. The symptoms described are accurate. Grouping them together and calling them mental disorders is wrong.[1]

British psychologist and author Lucy Johnstone also has reservations regarding the *DSM*:

> The *Diagnostic and Statistical Manual of Mental Disorders* (DSM) makes little attempt to hide the fact that the crucial judgements are not medical but social ones . . . A classical example is provided by perhaps the most spectacular instant

cure achieved by modern psychiatry, when homosexuality was dropped as a category of mental illness from the *DSM-III* in 1973 and millions of people thus recovered overnight. Here was a particularly clear example of a social judgement dressed up as a medical one.[2]

Before his untimely death, in his final *Sunday Independent* article on 5 March 2000, the late journalist Jonathan Philbin Bowman described the *DSM* as: 'the book that helps doctors stop thinking, and it certainly helps them stop feeling'.

The confusion within medicine regarding the diagnosis of depression is well illustrated by Charles Medawar. He has researched depression and doctors' antidepressant prescribing habits in great detail. In his excellent *Antidepressant Web* internet site, he concluded:

Perhaps the most unifying definition of 'depression' is that it is a condition to be treated with antidepressant drugs. There may not be a lot to distinguish between the drugs, but there is no end of possibilities for prescribing them.

Contrary to the often-stated scientific basis for the diagnosis and treatment of depression, there is evidence that antidepressant prescribing is quite arbitrary. One study,[3] which set out to assess the appropriateness of antidepressant prescribing, found that as many as 85 per cent of depressed patients treated in an out-patient setting would be excluded from the typical study to determine whether an antidepressant would work. Psychiatrist Dr Mark Zimmerman, the study's lead researcher, commented that 'no one knows for sure whether antidepressants are effective for most of the patients we treat'.

In addition to 'depression', these drugs are now used to 'treat' many other supposed medical 'conditions'; from shyness to 'social phobia'; from 'general anxiety disorder' to post-traumatic stress. This situation is eerily similar to the medical enthusiasm for prescribing benzodiazepine tranquillisers twenty years ago. While the medical profession does not appear to have learned from past debacles in mental health prescribing, the pharmaceutical industry certainly has learned from the past. In the late 1960s, the drug company Sandoz produced Serentil, a new tranquilliser which was aimed at people who felt nervous in social situations. Serentil, according to their ad, could ease 'the anxiety that comes from not fitting in'. But Sandoz was prevented from tapping into this potentially enormous market by the USA Food and Drug Administration, which forced the company to withdraw the drug and issue a statement to the effect that Serentil was useful only for 'certain disease states' and was not intended for use in everyday, anxiety-provoking situations.

Over the past forty years, the drug companies have learned their lesson well. They have skilfully adapted to the requirements of the international regulatory authorities. Together, the pharmaceutical industry and the medical profession have medicalised human experiences such as fear, anxiety, shyness, blushing, sadness, loneliness, unexpressed grief, under the guise of 'diagnoses' or 'disorders', such as 'social phobia', 'general anxiety disorder' and 'depression'. For the pharmaceutical companies, the key is to convince the medical profession that certain everyday, anxiety-, stress- and distress-provoking situations are 'disorders' or 'disease states', true medical conditions, which can be treated with medication. Once convinced of this, doctors will convince their patients and the public of the validity of the medication. The drug companies have learned that, in order to sell a drug, they first need to convince doctors of the existence of a 'disease' or 'syndrome'. The drug will then sell itself, and the prescriptions and profits will follow in due course.

Research has shown that the first one or two episodes of depression are usually stress-induced. As mentioned earlier, brain-imaging techniques are currently creating great excitement within psychiatry as a possible way of establishing a biological — brain abnormality — cause for 'mental illness'. One such study, using brain-imaging techniques to assess brain areas activated under specific circumstances, found that:

the area activated in depressive patients by negative thoughts was the part of the brain known as the amygdala, a region associated with fear.[4]

A study published in *Science*[5] looked at brain-imaging techniques in shy adults. Using functional MRI scans, researchers from Harvard Medical School and Massachusetts General Hospital assessed responses to two groups of photo images; people known to them, and people they had never seen before. They found an unusually high activity in the amygdala of shy adults when shown photos of people unknown to them. The amygdala is a part of the brain involved in regulating emotion and basic instincts such as fear, the part of the brain activated in depressed people in the previous study mentioned. How interesting that the brains of shy people react similarly to the brains of people diagnosed as 'depressed'. These results should not surprise us, since fear is a virtually ever-present feature in people experiencing any form of emotional and psychological distress.

One of the commonest patterns I have observed in people who have a long history of depression is that it is strongly linked with fear. Andrew's story is one such case; every aspect of his case I have heard over and over, from many clients diagnosed as having 'depression'. A forty-nine year old single man currently attending me, Andrew has been diagnosed as having 'clinical depression' for over twenty-five years. He has been on antidepressants for most of this time. He says that being on medication has not helped him get his life back on track. But they do numb his distress, making it more bearable, and less likely that he will work his way out of his life problems and issues.

For as long as he can remember, his contact with the mental health services — GP and psychiatric services — has consisted of brief meetings where his medication is the central focus of attention, preceded by a question or two regarding his mood. Throughout his long history of contact with the mental health services, it has gone unnoticed that feeling unsafe, absent self-esteem and self-confidence, his tendency to avoid challenge and responsibility through fear, are ever-present experiences for Andrew.

Not surprisingly, having been unnoticed, these issues have remained unresolved for over twenty years. This is a great pity. The degree of fear, insecurity, and social awkwardness that Andrew has experienced goes right back to his childhood, escalating as he encountered the considerable challenges of the teenage years. By the time he left school at eighteen years of age, his patterns of fear, avoidance and withdrawal were already well established, patterns which he has maintained throughout his life. Always too afraid of the risks inherent in entering a relationship, Andrew has never had a long-term relationship, and very few short-term relationships. His life revolves around a safe, small, predictable circle of people and things. He lives with and cares for his mother, and spends most of his time thinking about his mother and aimlessly watching television. He has not worked for over ten years. When he did work, he always picked jobs which involved very little responsibility and risk. Even then, after a few weeks he would leave the job, usually because he felt very awkward around other people. Andrew has become so entrenched in this way of living that he recreates these patterns daily, without being aware that he is doing so. It is as if through fear, as a child, he began weaving a pattern of avoidance and withdrawal from people, risk and responsibility, as a way of coping with his enormous sense of fear, insecurity and self-doubt. He continued to weave this pattern throughout his teenage years, his twenties and thirties, through to his current life. The original purpose of the weaving is to create a safe place, secure from the risks and hazards of life. This is understandable, and in its own way appropriate and protective. However, the longer one weaves such a cocoon, the thicker and more solid it becomes. Eventually, one can become imprisoned within this cocoon, the predictable consequence of years of withdrawal and avoidance. Mesmerised by seductive biological theories, GPs and psychiatrists regularly fail to notice such patterns and their significance. Consequently, they remain unidentified and unresolved.

A recent study from Rotman Research Institute and the University of Toronto used brain-imaging techniques to assess how the brains of people diagnosed as being depressed responded to cognitive behavioural therapy and the antidepressant Seroxat.[6] To their surprise, the researchers found a significant difference in the brain's response to these treatments. They found that antidepressants reduce activity in the brain's emotion centres, the limbic system. In contrast, cognitive-behavioural therapy reduced activity in a different region or the brain — the cortex. Commenting on these findings in the *Wall Street Journal*,[7] psychology professor Steven Hollon of Vanderbilt University explained that these findings make sense. He outlined that antidepressant drugs dampen the lower limbic areas of the brain, which are concerned with emotions However, following cognitive-behavioural therapy, activity in the cortex is more settled. This has a more lasting effect; the cortex is a far more advanced part of the human brain than the more primitive limbic systems. These brain scan images showing a healthier response following cognitive-behavioural therapy, reflecting the person's greater sense of autonomy, self-determination as opposed to dampening one's feelings with antidepressants.

These results support the findings of a 2001 study, funded by the Rotman Research Institute, the University of Toronto and the Canadian Institute for Health Research. This study found that cognitive therapy works better than antidepressants. After a year, the relapse rate after cognitive therapy was 25 per cent, compared to 80 per cent relapse rate on SSRI antidepressants.

In other words, even the results of scans are suggesting that psychological factors such as fear are very relevant to depression. Yet the medical profession has chosen to focus almost entirely on drug treatments at the expense of a proper assessment of the role played by fear and stress in the creation of mental health problems, and a full and proper assessment of all possible interventions.

'Do you want something for it?'

The diagnosis of depression is often based on a casual exchange between doctor and patient, as Patricia experienced when she visited her GP:

GP: *Patricia, do you think you might be depressed?*

Rachel: *Yes, I suppose I could be.*

GP: *Would you like to take a course of antidepressants for a while?*

Rachel: *No, I'd prefer to get over this without medication if at all possible.*

This type of casual negotiation is a common occurrence in the GP's surgery. The conversation has an innocent, friendly quality about it, but this is deceptive. Patricia refused the offer of antidepressant drugs so there was no more said about it. Had she accepted the medication, this casual chat would soon become a definite psychiatric diagnosis. Six months later, the fact that the GP offered the antidepressants as one might offer someone a cup of tea would be long forgotten. Had Rachel taken the antidepressants, this would in the future be taken as evidence that Rachel suffered from depression, a 'mental illness'. After all, why would a patient take antidepressants if she did not have 'depression'? Her notes would state that she has depression, which may affect her life in many ways.

This 'diagnosis' might reduce her chances of future employment or insurance cover. A prospective relationship partner might shy away if he found out she has been diagnosed as having a 'mental illness'. If Rachel found herself in the GP's surgery three years later with complaints that even vaguely suggested that she was depressed, the GP would quickly recall that Rachel had previously needed antidepressants, and so conclude that this was obviously a recurrence of her known depressive illness. Had Rachel taken the antidepressants, she would possibly have been labelled for life. Rachel's problems largely related to a very troubled relationship with her mother, who demanded that Rachel be always at her beck and call, and gave thirty-five-year-old Rachel no freedom to separate from her mother and create an independent life for herself. As often happens, her GP did not take the time to seek to identify what stresses might be going on in Rachel's life.

Diagnosis and treatment based on subtle negotiation also regularly takes place with patients who come to the doctor because of stress and anxiety. Pauline was going through a tough patch in her life. After years of marital disharmony, she finally decided that enough was enough. The time had come to leave her husband. For twelve months she was under intense stress, striving to create a life for herself and looking after her two children on her own. One day, while attending her GP with one of her children, the doctor asked her how she was coping. Pauline said that things were tough, but she was getting through it. Her GP asked Pauline if she wanted something to help her cope with the stress.

That 'something' was a tranquilliser, which Pauline wisely

refused. Pauline was coping. Pauline needed her wits about her now more than at any other time in her life. Many's the person who when asked 'do you want something for your anxiety?, said 'yes' and ended up addicted to tranquillisers, worse off than before they took them — an addiction created by the medical profession. Tranquillisers — like other mood-altering psychiatric drugs — have their place. But these drugs should be used as infrequently as possible, in as low a dose as possible, for the shortest time possible.

A friend related the following story to me. A middle-aged woman friend of hers became quite emotionally distressed due to stressful events in her life, events which were also affecting her husband's emotional well-being. She attended her GP for help. The doctor quickly prescribed Prozac for her. On hearing that her husband was also upset, the doctor prescribed Prozac for him too, without even talking to the man. Shocked at this doctor's casual attitude towards the prescription of Prozac, neither of them took the tablets. That GP lost two patients from his practice that day.

'Clinical' depression

'Clinical' depression is a term which has gained popularity with both the medical profession and the public. As illustrated by a leading British psychiatrist's description of 'clinical depression', this term has no specific definition:

> Human beings, to live with themselves, have a natural infusion of positive perspectives on things that enable us to keep going in life. When that's taken away, its called 'depression'. Clinical depression is simply a depression bad enough to need medication.[8]

'Clinical depression' is widely accepted in the public domain as having a far more specific and scientific meaning than that candidly acknowledged above by psychiatrist Dr Patrick

McKeon. The term 'clinical depression' is usually understood to mean that the person in question is sufficiently depressed to ensure that the diagnosis is definite, unquestionable; a real, biological illness. The term 'clinical' conjures up images of doctors, hospitals and clinics. The medical profession is known to approach health in a 'clinical' fashion. The phrase 'clinical depression' instantly labels the sufferer as having a medical problem, a definite 'mental illness'. People who question the medical profession's approach to depression are easily rebuffed. Now that depression is 'clinical', how can non-medical people challenge the views of medical clinicians in their own field of expertise, clinical medicine? Yet, as I mentioned earlier, no tests are carried out to confirm this 'clinical' diagnosis, because no such tests exist.

Patients and their relatives are more likely to acquiesce to taking antidepressant drugs once they are told that their depression is 'clinical'. This term implies that the patient really cannot understand what is going on since it is a clinical, medical problem. The patient should really just keep taking the tablets and leave the rest to the experts. Power shifts from the patient to the doctor, decreasing the patient's understanding of what is going on for them. Their input into their own recovery is reduced. Psychiatrist Dr Nathaniel S. Lehrman is former Clinical Director of the Kingston Psychiatric Centre in New York. Regarding 'clinical depression', he holds a significantly different view from that of Dr McKeon above. The following is an extract from his article on 'depression', which is posted on *RedFlagsDaily*, Nicholas Regush's excellent on-line publication:

> The current medical treatment of depression, and especially the prescription of drugs for it, represens one of the greatest fallacies in the history of medicine. Depression is not a disease, like pneumonia or malaria. It is a reaction — of both body and mind, like fever. But while fever is a physiological response to a biological disease process

within the body, depression is usually a psycho-physiological reaction to an individual's current psychosocial interactions. Depressive reactions are also seen in animals exposed to continuing levels of stress from which they cannot escape. Today's psychiatrists listen less to patients' problems, focus more on their reactions (anxiety, depression, disorganization), and then, on the basis of those reactions, 'diagnose' — and medicate — much more quickly. But while these drugs may make patients feel better (too often they have the opposite effect), they will not help the patients in the long run unless they produce more effective energy in the patients so they can then solve their problems better. And this is quite rare.

Whether a depressed patient improves with drug treatment is completely unrelated to the medication. Reduction or removal of the pressures upon him, as often occurs when one is 'sick,' can alone produce temporary improvement. Sometimes improvement follows other changed circumstances, of which the drug-prescribing doctor is unaware. Whether such changes in circumstance cause permanent improvement is a different question, which is rarely asked because drug studies usually run only for a limited number of weeks.

Depression has become very big. Feelings of 'helplessness, loss of hope, sadness, crying, sleep or appetite disturbances, or difficulty concentrating, for at least two straight weeks' is sufficient for the very common diagnosis of 'clinical depression'. Over the past half century, hospitalizations for depression have increased almost thirty times, from 9.8 per 100,000 in 1943 (in New York, which had more per capita than any other state) to an estimated 280 per 100,000 (nationally) in 1994.

And that's only the beginning. Scientists estimated in 1997 that 18 million Americans suffer severe depression each year, with one in five of us experiencing a depressive episode during his or her lifetime (that's 20,000 per 100,000). One researcher says 10 to 30 percent of depressives and manic-depressives kill themselves. All this has evoked intense alarm from the Surgeon General, who views it almost as an epidemic. These views of depression, based on today's drug-oriented approach to treatment, conflict almost totally with the experience of many, including myself, who treated depressions successfully before the drug era.

It is estimated that 28 million Americans now take prescribed (doctor-controlled) antidepressant medications. Production of these drugs has consequently become a huge business, with 'global sales estimated at $6 billion a year and rising'. Prozac sales alone amounted to more than $1.7 billion in 1999 — a third of the Eli Lilly and Company's total business — while prescriptions for its major current competitors, Zoloft [Lustral] and Paxil [Seroxat], also continue to rise rapidly. Despite the side-effects experienced by a quarter of Prozac users, Lilly recently spent $15 million to advertise the drug directly to the public — to increase patients' demand for it from their physicians. And at a time that our churches, moral guides to the nation, face many grave financial problems, the major funder of the new Public Broadcasting System 'Religion and Ethics Newsweekly' is the Lilly Foundation.

As Dr Nathanial Lehrman mentions, some people experience a sense of relief when diagnosed with a 'psychiatric illness'. It legitimises the person's distress. A diagnosis can immediately result in a lifting of pressure and expectations, from oneself and others. Being so diagnosed can result in an immediate response of sympathy and caring from important people in their lives. This says more about the values of our society than about the inherent validity of psychiatric diagnoses. For some people, the resulting breathing space can be enough for the person to turn things around in their life. Unfortunately, for many people struggling to cope in a world they find very difficult, living within the role of being 'ill' can become an attractive option. The 'sick role' can become a socially legitimate reason to continue living within the sometimes major limitations created by one's fears and insecurities. This only happens in a minority of those so diagnosed. In my opinion, the lack of a structured, flexible vision of empowerment, recovery and reintegration into society increases the likelihood of this reaction. The views of a leading Irish psychologist concur with Dr Lehrman's views:

> The number of diagnoses of depression has markedly increased since the SSRIs [the newer antidepressants such as Prozac, Seroxat] were launched [in the late 1980s]. The medical profession tends to diagnose according to whatever treatment is available. Before, you diagnose someone with agoraphobia but there was nothing you could prescribe. Now you can diagnose them with depression and treat them with Prozac. The drugs don't cure you but they give you a buzz.[9]

Rather than being a 'mental illness', what is called 'clinical depression' is more accurately described as a great degree of emotional and psychological distress, as in the following case histories.

Four cases of 'clinical' depression
Jim took early retirement from work at fifty-five years of age. Always used to being busy, he did not know how to occupy all his new-found free time. He soon became depressed and anxious, withdrawing into himself. He became irritable with his family. Jim's GP diagnosed that Jim was clinically depressed

and antidepressants were prescribed. These drugs numbed Jim's feelings. Two months later, Jim felt less anxious but his depression remained. In an effort to overcome his depression, he then came to see me for a second opinion, in my capacity as a GP with a broader approach to mental health problems than his own GP.

It quickly emerged that Jim tended to become depressed when confronted with major life changes. Insecure since his childhood, Jim needed a great deal of security and predictability in his life. On several occasions over the course of his lifetime, major life changes increased his sense of insecurity, resulting in Jim becoming depressed. I felt there was nothing 'clinical' about Jim's depression. Jim's retirement closed the door on his working life. I felt he needed to create new meaning and purpose in this new phase of his life. We discussed various possibilities. Jim decided to become involved in several community activities.

As is usually the case when one's self-esteem and self-confidence is low, trying new things and meeting new people was initially very scary for Jim. I and his family supported, reassured and encouraged him as he tentatively opened these new doors in his life. After several weeks, the anxiety created by these new situations decreased, as he settled into these new activities and realised he could survive in them. He made many new friends and now has a busy, vibrant life. Off all medication and no longer depressed, Jim has a renewed sense of security, self-esteem and self-confidence.

Twenty-year old Paul was coming to the end of his second year at university. Having sailed through the first year, Paul did not anticipate any hitches. All went well until the week before the exams, when Paul became very uptight. He could not sleep and was too nervous to eat. Paul sat the exams but was extremely anxious throughout. He performed far worse than he would have expected and ended up failing. Then his personality seemed to change. Paul became withdrawn, even from his closest friends. He stayed in bed until late afternoon, having no interest in anything. He blamed himself over and over again for being such a fool: for screwing up the exams, his life and his family.

In Dublin he was referred to a psychiatrist, who concluded that Paul was suffering from clinical depression, for which he needed antidepressant drugs. These drugs were the only treatment the psychiatrist recommended. In a letter to me, the psychiatrist wrote: 'Because of his clinical depression I have put him on an antidepressant.' A repeat appointment was arranged for three weeks later, at which the psychiatrist briefly asked Paul more about the tablets than about himself. The next appointment was scheduled for three months later.

As often happens, the psychiatrist misread the situation. Paul did not feel comfortable with the psychiatrist, who asked a list of leading questions, questions which did not invite Paul to open up, or create an interaction which might assist Paul to open up. Consequently, the 'expert' doctor did not even get a glimpse of how distressed Paul really was. Because of how he approached Paul, the psychiatrist did not grasp that Paul was suicidal. At the time when Paul was at his lowest ebb, the psychiatrist decided that Paul did not need to attend him again for three months.

Paul decided to travel the 120-mile journey to attend me at frequent intervals. He came to see me in my capacity as a GP, knowing I have a particular interest in mental health. I had been Paul's GP when he was younger. He felt he could trust me. The psychiatrist was on his doorstep, but Paul had no desire to return to see him again.

We built up a trusting relationship. I soon realised that Paul's exam crisis had nothing to do with 'clinical' depression. He had experienced a performance anxiety reaction, a severe anxiety reaction engendered by an intense fear of not performing well in his exams. Performance-related anxiety is quite common. It occurs in people who have had reason at some time in their lives to seriously doubt their ability to perform, to get it right. Paul's performance-related anxiety went right back to his early school days, when he had major difficulties for three years dealing with one very authoritarian teacher. His confidence in his own ability to perform suffered hugely as a result. Throughout his childhood, Paul compensated by putting twice as much effort into his schoolwork rather than experience the humiliation he felt at the hands of that teacher.

By trying so hard, Paul got by in school. His parents understandably thought that his childhood experiences were over and done with. But, under the surface, Paul had always remained terrified of failing. This fear rebounded on him in his second year at college. Paul did not need antidepressant drugs. He needed a great deal of support and compassion to help him come to his own understanding of the experience. Only then could he see that there was light at the end of the tunnel. Nine months later, the crisis was over. Paul passed the repeat examinations and has returned to college. He has received a great deal of support from his family and from me.

Paul did not take the antidepressants, which according to the psychiatrist were essential. But he has recovered. Having overcome the shock of failing his exams, Paul has re-established contact with many of the friends from whom he had withdrawn. He now believes that his unique worth as a human being cannot be erased by the results of one exam.

The psychiatrist incorrectly interpreted Paul's behaviour as signs of 'clinical' depression. This medical expert missed the point. Yes, Paul was depressed. But his feeling of depression was one of many emotions he was going through. Paul withdrew from people not because he was mentally ill, but because he felt humiliated and overwhelmed. Paul believed that he had lost face in the eyes of his friends so he could not bring himself to meet them. All his friends passed the exams. They were all cheerfully planning their summer holidays. The only thing Paul had to look forward to was repeating his exams. It is hardly surprising — and certainly not a sign of a 'mental illness' — that he felt the need to withdraw from his friends and from life.

Living involves a continuous interplay between mind and body. Our bodies continuously respond to our minute-by-minute emotional state. I have known several previously healthy people who died suddenly as a result of over-whelmingly sad news, such was the effect of their shock. It is true that depression can be accompanied by a slowing down of bodily activity and functions. But it does not follow that depression is caused by a clinical, physical illness.

Fifty-five-year-old Elaine began attending me eighteen months ago, at two-to-three week intervals. She decided to meet me having read the Irish edition of this book, liking the idea of working with a GP who believes that there was more to the treatment of depression than medication. She had lived with a diagnosis of clinical depression for thirty years, and had been on antidepressant medication for over thirty years — Molipaxin being the antidepressant she was taking for fifteen of them. Her 'clinical depression' was primarily managed by her GP over the years. She had on two occasions attended a leading psychiatrist, who agreed with the diagnosis of clinical depression and recommended life-long medication. No other intervention other than medication was suggested by either the GP or psychiatrist. It quickly became obvious to me that from an early age, several issues and relationships had contributed to Elaine becoming fearful, withdrawn, unexpressive and unassertive. She totally lost her confidence at a very early age, and never regained it. These very obvious characteristics had not been picked up either by her GP or psychiatrist. Through her work with me, Elaine began to risk communicating more assertively. Elaine was in a loving relationship. Her partner enthusiastically embraced the idea of raising Elaine's self-esteem and assertiveness. Early in our work, Elaine expressed the wish to come off her antidepressant. Previous attempts to do so had failed. After several months working together, I felt she was ready to begin the process of medication reduction. Since she was on Molipaxin for 15 years, I felt that reductions must be small and unhurried. I embarked on this process in a way which I believe few doctors would have done. Most doctors simplistically believe that one can stop an antidepressant — particularly an older-type anti-depressant such as Molipaxin — suddenly, without much support. Most doctors naively believe that if the person then struggles, this is evidence of a recurrence of the person's 'condition'. They recommence treatment, frequently recommending to the person that they clearly need the medication for years, if not for life. I switched Elaine to the liquid form of Molipaxin, since this allowed for very gradual reductions. I was not surprised to hear that this was the first time that Elaine's chemist ever received a doctor's prescription for Molipaxin liquid for an adult. Gradually, over many months working together, we reduced Elaine's Molipaxin, ten mgs every 6–8 weeks, while simultaneously working to enhance her self-esteem, self-expression and assertiveness. Having become institutionalised to being on medication, at various stages in this process Elaine doubted whether she could do it. Our mutually agreed plan was flexible, allowing for her to increase medication again if she felt she needed to, though in Elaine's case she did not increase the dose at any stage. In my opinion, doctors grossly underestimate the psychological dependence which being on mood-altering medication creates. Elaine needed reductions to be small and gradual. This approach allowed her time to get used to being and coping on smaller doses than she had been taking for decades. Elaine is now, at the time of writing, on 20 mgs of Molipaxin, less than one-fifth of her dose when we first met. She is delighted with herself, feeling much more self-reliant and self-empowered. Like most older antidepressant drugs, Molipaxin is a sedating mood-altering substance. Elaine now feels far less sedated than previously. We both feel that Elaine will be able to continue this process of reduction over the coming months, as she continues the process of reclaiming her assertiveness, her identity, becoming empowered and in control of her life.

When reducing SSRI antidepressants, I also reduce them gradually, over many months. Typically, I switch people to the liquid form of the drug, if one is available. I then decrease in small increments. Few doctors see the need to reduce antidepressants in very small increments.

In January 2004, I received an urgent call from Emer, a forty-year old woman. Emer had attended me twice previously with a view to reducing her antidepressant medication. She initially decided to see me when, in response to her desire to come off her drug, the psychotherapist she was attending privately mentioned my name to her as a doctor who was more than willing to wean people off antidepressants. Our last meeting had been five months previously. The therapist Emer attended intermittently was on vacation, and she was due to attend the psychiatric clinic the following day. Emer was extremely upset, so we scheduled a meeting for the following day. On the phone, Emer spoke of the possibility of increasing her antidepressant medication from Effexor 75mgs to 150 mgs. Her psychiatrist had previously told her that 150 mgs was the 'therapeutic dose' she should be taking long-term. At the outset of our meeting, Emer said that her life was out of control, and that it might be best if she doubled her antidepressant medication, to 150mgs. During that hour, we explored the various stresses and strains which were overwhelming Emer at this time in her life. Emer cried for at least 30 minutes of our meeting. At other times she was angry, overwhelmed, sad. More than once, we laughed together during that hour. We explored possible ways for Emer to regain control of various aspects of her life which were overwhelming her. As our meeting drew to its conclusion, I asked Emer how she felt, and how she felt about increasing her Effexor medication from 75mgs to 150 mgs. She replied that she felt a great deal better, lighter, relieved, stronger. Having initially resigned herself to doubling the dose of her antidepressant to 150mgs Effexor, Emer and I agreed to increase her antidepressant by a lesser degree, to 112.5 mgs (Effexor comes in 37.5, 75 and 150mgs strengths only. No liquid form of Effexor is currently available.) Emer decided not to attend the psychiatric clinic that day. From previous experience, Emer felt that at that clinic, nothing other that an increased dosage would be recommended, especially if she burst into tears as she did with me. Emer felt that her medication would quickly be increased to 150 mgs by her psychiatrist, along with a metaphorical slap on the wrist for not following his advice all along. Her psychiatrist — whom she attended intermittently for three years — never explored the stresses in her life, even though she had five children under ten whilst trying to run a business, and various other stresses. When Emer attended me a week later, she reported feeling a great deal better, more in control, on top of things. She had felt that way since our meeting. She did not notice any benefit from increasing the medication dose slightly the day after our meeting. She felt that she could probably have got by without increasing the dose. I felt that at the end of our first consultation, but I didn't want to push it. Increasing her dose by half of what the psychiatrists were recommending seemed a reasonable compromise. A week later, Emer wanted to reduce the dose back to 75 mgs. We did so, and a week later Emer continued to feel more in control, more calm. She still has work to do regarding her assertiveness and her self-confidence. But by approaching her distress the way we did, I believe that Emer is more — rather than less — hopeful and empowered. Over the coming months at Emer's request, we will explore ways to increase her confidence, self-esteem, assertiveness, self-expression, self-empowerment, whilst simultaneously considering the possibility of gradually stopping her drug. Had she attended the psychiatric clinic that day, we both feel that the psychiatric alternative would have resulted in a much higher dose of medication for more that six months, and little exploration or resolution of the real issues which were triggering Emer's distress and overwhelm in the first instance. I believe that every day thousands of people experiencing similar overwhelm to Emer's are typically receiving 'therapeutic doses' of medication from GPs and psychiatrists after brief consultations which frequently neither explore nor address the key issues in their lives.

Some years ago, I referred a fifteen-year-old girl to a psychiatrist. Her parents brought her to me in my capacity as a GP knowing I have an interest in mental health. She was going through an emotional crisis. At the first consultation, the psychiatrist diagnosed depression. He put the girl, Claire, on two medications: an antidepressant and a tranquilliser. She attended the psychiatrist five times. Each follow-up consultation focused more on the drug treatment than on her. The psychiatrist commented in a letter to me that Claire was 'extremely self-critical and had self-esteem difficulties which mainly relate to weight problems. She is quite sensitive to teasing, and this seems to be happening to some extent at school at present'.

In these two sentences, the psychiatrist described the kernel of Claire's problem: extremely low self-esteem, severe self-criticism, a very negative self-image and extreme sensitivity to the opinions of others. However, the psychiatrist did nothing about these important issues. Four months later, Claire attended me in a state. Sedated by the medication, she could not function properly. Over the next few months, I weaned her off all medication. She felt a lot better off medication. I then referred her and her family to a psychotherapist. Three years later, she has finished school and created an independent life for herself.

Elderly people in nursing homes are particularly at risk of depression. There is a tendency within medicine to attribute this to elderly patients being more likely to have physical problems or dementia. But there are other obvious emotional, psychological and social reasons why the elderly in nursing homes are more likely to become depressed. They have been removed from their home and familiar surroundings. They may be separated from family and loved ones. And in some nursing homes at least, patients have little to do to occupy their time. While it is certainly not true in every case, some elderly people see a nursing home as a place to wait to die.

In my opinion, the medical profession's downplaying of emotional, psychological and social causes of depression in comparison to physical causes is a serious oversight.

Questioning the medical view

Most doctors conduct their consultations with the clear understanding that the doctor is the expert. The doctor will tell the patient what is wrong with them and what treatment they need, because doctor knows best. He listens to the patient all right, but as he listens, he is preoccupied by what he sees as his main priority in the consultation — to make a 'diagnosis' so he can commence 'treatment' — which typically means drug treatment.

For decades, the medical profession has believed that antidepressant drugs are 70 per cent effective in treating depression. In 1980, when I was studying psychiatry in medical school, this 70 per cent cure rate was accepted as gospel — an established fact. Yet according to highly respected psychiatry textbooks at the time antidepressant drugs were first introduced (the late 1950s), depression had a spontaneous recovery rate of 70–80 per cent without any drug treatment.

Doctors believe that the case for using antidepressant drugs is very strong: 70 percent effectiveness compared to 30 per cent using a placebo. Some medical experts — most notably Dr Peter Breggin[10] — are concerned that the research which has 'proved' that antidepressants are 70 per cent effective may not be nearly as reliable as the medical profession believes. In his book *Talking Back to Prozac*,[11] Dr Breggin points out that in the Prozac studies submitted to the USA Food and Drug Administration in the 1990s, as many as between 30 and 50 per cent of the people taking Prozac dropped out of the studies, either due to side effects or lack of effectiveness. A simple mathematical calculation shows that a 70 per cent improvement rate is impossible. Dr Breggin contacted one of these researchers, who had claimed these studies demonstrated a 60 to 70 per cent success rate with Prozac. The researcher admitted to Dr Breggin that he did not include the one third of his patients who had dropped out of the study in his calculations. Including these study drop-outs — as they obviously should have been — only 47 per cent of people on Prozac improved — a far cry from a 70 per cent success rate widely and repeatedly claimed for these drugs for over ten years by both drug companies and the pharmaceutical industry.

Results from the aforementioned 1999 study by Professor Malt — lauded by psychiatrists — do not suggest a major difference in effectiveness between antidepressant drugs and placebo. Remission occurred in 47 per cent of patients who received the placebo, compared to 54 per cent with one antidepressant and 61 per cent for a second antidepressant. Medical research suggests that antidepressants are only 50 per cent effective in adolescents. This is barely distinguishable from the effects of placebo, and should raise serious questions

126

about our approach to depression in young people. In their book *From Placebo to Panacea*, Fisher and Greenberg[12] discuss how difficult it is to demonstrate real benefits for psychiatric drugs when compared to placebos.

According to the respected Cochrane Review, 'the difference between antidepressants and active placebos is small'. The Hypericum (St John's Wort) Depression Trial Study Group compared the effectiveness of St. John's Wort and sertraline (a frequently prescribed SSRI antidepressant, trade name Lustral) to placebo. Neither drug fared significantly better than placebo in reducing depression severity, disability or overall improvement:

> On the two primary outcome measures, neither sertraline nor St John's Wort was significantly better than placebo. Full response occurred in 31.9 per cent of the placebo-treated patients versus 23.9 per cent of the St Johns Wort-treated patients and 24.8 per cent of sertraline [trade name Lustral]-treated patients.[13]

Doctors believe that 70 per cent of suicides are the result of untreated or poorly treated depression. It should therefore be relatively easy to prove that antidepressants are as effective in reducing the suicide rate as they are in depression. Yet numerous studies have failed to prove that antidepressants reduce the suicide rate at all. An analysis of suicide published by Herman van Praag in the *World Journal of Biological Psychiatry*[14] found that suicide rates are remaining stubbornly high. Praag outlined that over several decades the suicide rate remains largely unchanged, and the rate of suicide attempts may have increased. He stated that to completely replace psychotherapy with antidepressants was wrong, since these drugs cannot be expected to deal effectively with distressed people and their worries.

Some research has indicated that these drugs may increase

the likelihood of suicide, an issue discussed in detail by Dr David Healy.[15] As mentioned earlier, since December 2003 all SSRI antidepressants bar Prozac have been banned for use in under-18s, and a week later the manufacturers of Prozac advised doctors not to prescribe Prozac for under-18s. The UK regulators took this action based on evidence from research studies which were completed by 1996, yet which were not published or acted upon for years. For example, the first major drug trial of Seroxat in children was completed by 1996. However, the results were only published in 2001. Antidepressant drug trials that produce unfavourable results were not published, nor were the UK or other international regulators made aware of the existence of these unfavourable results. Frequently, drug regulatory agencies do not see the actual data from drug trials. Instead, they are sent a summary of drug trials. This summary is put together by the drug companies themselves, for the purposes of obtaining a license for the drug. The SSRI review group, which studied the safety of SSRIs on children and advised the UK authorities to ban these drugs for under-18s, are now examining the effectiveness and safety of SSRI antidepressants in adults. In March 2004, Richard Brook, chief executive of the independent UK charity Mind, resigned from the SSRI review group. The only lay member of the SSRI review group, Richard Brook stated that the British drugs regulatory authority were negligent. He resigned having been subjected to months of sustained pressure not to reveal the review group's findings that for years Seroxat has been prescribed by doctors in unsafe doses, and that evidence of this was with the regulators for over ten years. Having for months unsuccessfully requested the UK Committee on Safety of Medicines to inform the public of this, Richard Brook felt he had no choice but to inform the public himself, given the risks involved for people taking the drug. In response, he received a letter from the UK authorities warning him that by doing do, Richard Brook may be prosecuted under the Medicines Act of 1968, which legally protects the confidentiality of data and information from drug research trials. In 2003 alone, 17,000 people in Britain were prescribed such higher doses. In his letter of resignation in March 2004, Richard Brook wrote:

> The nature of the announcement fails to make public the fact that the clinical trial data you issued was available to the regulator for over a decade . . . Despite four major regulatory reviews during this period and considerable consumer reporting and disquiet, the Committee on Safety of Medicines failed either to identify or communicate these key facts. As far as I am aware, the Medicines and Healthcare Products Regulatory Agency has not seen fit to acknowledge or address what in my view appears to be extreme negligence . . . I believe my continuation on the expert working group without a frank and open admission of these important facts has become impossible. Consumers are entitled to full information both about medicines and how the regulator operates.

According to Mind, the UK mental health charity of which Richard Brook is chief executive, an independent investigation of the process of drug regulation is required. This view is shared by Charles Medawar of Social Audit UK, who I believe knows more about SSRI antidepressants that the vast majority of doctors. Responding to Richard Brook's resignation in *The Guardian* on 13 March 2004, Charles Medawar expressed alarm that they would be put under so much pressure, that it was typical of the UK drug regulatory authorities that they would seek to silence Richard Brook. Calling for a formal parliamentary investigation into the British drugs control regulatory system, Medawar said that a sequence of serious errors has been made by British drug regulatory authorities.

According to Medawar, the current UK SSRI review is akin to the regulators investigating their own mistakes, which is totally unacceptable.

Nevertheless, the basic strategy in the medical profession's fight against suicide is to seek out and find everyone suffering from depression and to put them on antidepressant medication.

Jack's 'breakdown'

I had known Jack and his family for about four years. Married with four children, he always appeared relaxed and cheerful. At the time I was their family GP and he came to my surgery one day, very distressed and extremely anxious. 'Doctor, I think I'm cracking up', he cried. Jack thought he was having a nervous breakdown. Earlier that day, stressed to breaking point, Jack walked out of work without saying a word to anyone. He walked straight to a river and thought about ending it all. Thankfully, his distressed behaviour was noticed by a passer-by who brought him home. In my surgery, Jack was distraught.

Jack thought he was losing his mind. He was keen to see a psychiatrist, so I arranged this for him. Over the next 2 weeks, the psychiatrist adopted one approach and I adopted another. The psychiatrist quickly diagnosed that he was acutely depressed and prescribed antidepressant medication; the psychiatrist did not recommend any other form of therapy. Jack's experience illustrates the differences between a typical psychiatric approach to human distress and an approach which focuses on listening, understanding and working with the person. I asked Jack to write about this experience in his own words:

> Looking back, I can't remember when I started to feel the way I did about myself. But I do know when it began to change for the better. I always thought I was easy-going, on top of things, cool and in control, at work, home and play. I know now that what I was actually doing was filling

up my time with a lot of things to do so I would not have to think about myself or my fears. I always seemed to be worried about what others thought of me. I was preoccupied with doing things to make others happy. It did not seem to matter to me how I felt so long as everyone else was happy.

I went into the career I have today because my father wanted me to have a trade, something he never had himself. I don't blame him. He was trying to give me a better standard of life. But I ended up spending nearly all my life working at something I never wanted to do. This kind of attitude — trying to please others — ran my life for a long time. I couldn't handle saying no. I just took everything on. I was afraid of letting my wife and kids down. I was always scared stiff that if I did not bring home enough money every week to have a good standard of living, I would not be good enough for my wife.

I knew my wife loved me. But to keep this love I felt I had to keep up to a certain standard, or else I was not good enough. I know now that if I had talked to her, I would have found out sooner or later that she loved me for me and not for what we did or did not have in material things. I thought people didn't care about how I felt. I stopped thinking about me and I pushed my own needs deep down inside myself. I hid my feelings away. I felt that I was coping but denying my feelings made me feel bad and was eating me away inside. It all came to a head one day at work when one more small thing needed to be done, and only I could do it. Something just went 'STOP!', a sort of bang inside me.

I felt 'I just cannot do this. I can't keep going. I can't cope any more. I don't want to cope. I want to stop. I want to cry. I can't do this any more. If this is me I would be better off dead'. I just stormed straight out of work without a word to anyone and wandered off. I wandered around *for hours. I am not sure how I felt — full of emotion, full of fear, pain, loss, full of dislike for myself. LOST. I did not know what to do. My emotions were taking me over. I was very afraid. I felt like a lost child. I wanted to hurt myself.*

With encouragement from my wife I went to see my doctor, Terry Lynch. I thought that a little medication would help sort me out, help me relax for a while. Soon I'd get back on top of things like I was before. When I went to my doctor and said 'I can't cope' he really listened to what I was saying. This is when it all came out — a flood of emotions. It was overpowering. I began to see that I was living my life for others. Just talking about it and being listened to, helped me. With my doctor's help I began to learn about myself, who I really was. He helped me to see how low my self-esteem was. He encouraged me to like myself for who I am. He helped me look at my life as if I was on the outside, looking in. This helped me to see the problem areas and also the good areas. He helped me to help myself to relax. He did not prescribe any medication.

During this time, I also went to see a psychiatrist. I initially felt he might be able to help me as well. Though he listened to what I was saying, he did not hear what I had to say. He said 'You're a bit depressed' and prescribed some antidepressant drugs. The next time I went back to the psychiatrist, he was only interested in how the drugs were working. He said 'it's depression, the drugs will work soon'. At my third visit to the psychiatrist, he again was only interested in the drugs. He seemed to get annoyed with me when I said that I wasn't finding the medication very helpful. He then (at my third visit!) decided to talk to me. He began with a lot of questions about my life and my childhood, my social habits, and so forth. From this, he concluded that I was depressed because I did not want to go to work.

He openly wondered if I might just be trying to get off

sick from work for a few weeks. I found that very insulting. He just wasn't getting the message. I had, after all, felt so bad that I had considered taking my own life. He seemed to dismiss that. So I decided I was not going back to him again. Even that decision was an indicator that I was rebuilding my self-esteem! With the help of my own doctor, I began to relax. He encouraged me to like myself, to keep reminding myself that I am a very important and worthy person. He helped me to accept myself as I am. He worked very closely with me over a short period of time. He helped me to build confidence in myself as an individual.

As a result, I became stronger and stronger as a whole person. I never felt better in my life. After four to five weeks I was ready to return to work, where I was soon able to use all I had learned about myself. I was now able to say 'No, I can't handle that at the moment' without feeling the shame of letting people down. I also made a decision to move to a less stressful job. One year later I did just that, but that year proved to me just how strong I had become. All this happened five years ago and I have not looked back. Whatever happens now in my life, I know I can handle it.

I believe that few GPs would have had the courage or the understanding to disagree so strongly with what the psychiatrist was doing. My doctor's stance gave me the courage to stand up to the psychiatrist rather than sit there and accept as gospel every word he said. I know that from hearing people talk about the treatment they and their loved ones receive from the doctors they go to. My philosophy of life now is: 'believe in yourself, like yourself, and encourage yourself'.

I never believed that Jack was 'psychiatrically ill'. His self-esteem was very low, and he greatly relied on approval from others, particularly from his colleagues at work. Jack was extremely self-critical. He constantly put himself under severe pressure to have everything just right, to be the best employee in the company. He wanted to say no when asked to do overtime or when more work was put his way than his fellow workers were being given. But he could not say no because he needed their approval so badly. So he always said 'Sure, I'll do it'.

For years he denied his true feelings, until the bubble burst. He walked out of the job and went to the river in a highly stressed state, eventually ending up in my surgery. Over the next two weeks, while the psychiatrist was diagnosing 'depression' and prescribing antidepressants, I worked with Jack on his self-esteem. I recommended tapes and books on personal growth and inner peace. Because I believed in Jack, I helped him believe in himself. Within two weeks, Jack had attended me five times, each consultation lasting an hour. People in distress sometimes need a lot of time, but in the long run it can be time well spent.

Jack was back at work within four or five weeks. He was calm, relaxed, only this time it wasn't a show. This time round, he really was relaxed and at peace with himself. Jack stopped the antidepressants prescribed by the psychiatrist — who had said he would need them for nine months — within two weeks. He told me that he could not connect with the psychiatrist. They were on different wavelengths — how often I have heard patients say that about doctors.

We doctors are trained to respond as the psychiatrist did; seeking to diagnose and treat rather than to listen, understand and empower our patients. Had Jack attended another doctor, it is likely that he would have been persuaded to take antidepressants for nine months. He probably would not have grown from his experience as he did. Jack had a healing, therapeutic relationship with me. Not so with his psychiatrist, despite seeing him three to four times in two weeks.

Jack's story is typical of many who become diagnosed as

being 'mentally ill'. His story is a classic example of how overwhelmed people can become when they feel unable to say 'no', afraid to be assertive. Jack's experience is one of many examples of a recurring trend I have observed for many years — that a 'breakdown', when properly handled, can be the beginning of a 'breakthrough', a reality which seems to escape many of my medical colleagues.

Geraldine went through an emotional crisis, resulting in her being admitted to a psychiatric hospital for a month. After the admission, Geraldine worked hard to get her life back on track. She decided it would be best for her to return to work a few weeks before Christmas. That way, she would have crossed that bridge before Christmas, and she would be able to relax during the Christmas holidays. Her psychiatrists were totally against this. They felt that Geraldine should stay off work for quite a while longer. She cried for hours after being told that. I could see that going back to work sooner rather that later was very important to Geraldine. Staying off any longer would be counter-productive to her recovery. I felt she could do it. I went against the views of the psychiatrists and certified her fit for work three weeks before Christmas. Since then, Geraldine's recovery had continued steadily, and she has been back at work without any problems for the past six months. Just as they tend to overestimate the value of medication, many doctors underestimate the importance of social reintegration in the healing process. When people are trying to rebuild their sense of self-belief, it greatly helps if they sense that their carers believe in them, and work with them in accordance with the important issues in their lives.

A person or an object?

The American Carl Rogers was a leading therapist of the twentieth century. He pioneered an approach to therapy based upon deep respect for the client, now widely known as client-centred therapy. Irvin Yalom MD, professor emeritus of psychiatry at Stanford University School of Medicine, wrote the introduction to Rogers' book, *A Way of Being*. The following passage from Yalom's introduction demonstrated Rogers' passionate belief that clients must be treated as human beings with great respect and dignity:

> At an academic symposium on Ellen West, a heavily studied patient who committed suicide several decades before, Rogers startled the audience by the depth and intensity of his reaction. Not only did Rogers express his sorrow at her tragically wasted life, but also his anger at her physicians and psychiatrists who, through their impersonality and preoccupation with precise diagnosis, had transformed her into an object. 'How could they have?', Rogers asked. 'If only they had known that treating a person as an object always stands in the way of successful therapy. If only they had related to her as a person, risked themselves, experienced her reality and her world, they might have dissolved her lethal loneliness'.[16]

As mainstream medicine becomes increasingly biological in its approach to human beings, the impersonal approach alluded to by Carl Rogers is becoming increasingly prevalent. When Helen became depressed in her early forties, she sought help from her GP. Without carrying out any tests, her doctor quickly informed her that her depression was caused by a biochemical brain abnormality. That doctor's impersonal clinical approach did little for Helen. She subsequently attended me in my capacity as a GP for a second opinion. I asked her to write about the effect that GP consultation had on her:

> *It is very traumatic to be labelled with the term 'depression' five minutes after walking into the doctor's surgery, especially when you have no idea what is happening to you.*

I believe it is not psychiatric theory or diagnosis that will help a person. Rather, it is knowing and feeling that somebody is there for you at a truly human level; knowing that you can talk to that person and know that you are not being judged or labelled. A depressed person will never open up fully to a person whom they suspect is just waiting to categorize them further like an inanimate object — I wouldn't open up, anyhow.

Depressed people have already received too many negative labels either directly or indirectly throughout their lives. Further negative messages are very detrimental to the image they have of themselves especially when they are given by a psychiatrist or GP who is not prepared to nurture them in a caring relationship. I can only see the medical profession's approach of psychiatric diagnosis and tablet prescribing as adding to the feelings of worthlessness and isolation being experienced by the depressed patient. What people need most is just to be listened to and to know they are being listened to.

Labelling a person with 'clinical depression' and telling them it is caused by a biochemical imbalance or genetic defect is as traumatic as telling a person they have a terminal illness. The medical profession must wake up to this and realise what they are doing. Doctors have the power in their hands to wreck people's lives. People with depression who contemplate suicide do not have a psychiatric disorder. Depression is not a 'disorder'— it is a range of very strong overwhelming feelings. Surely feelings are not disorders or abnormalities. Psychiatrists take people's power away from them with such statements.

The most difficult part of the depression for me is the feeling of loneliness and loss. I know this is a feeling and I know I've got to listen to it and understand it. If the medical profession label that as being mentally ill, well then the whole of humanity is mentally ill, because every human being is a feeling being. Some of us feel more than others. We are made to feel guilty for this and we are labelled for it. Better to write us all off as being the same, all our lives explained away by a magical convenient medical abnormality that we were all unfortunate enough to develop. How tidy!

In my opinion, a person's greatest need is to belong. When you don't feel you belong anywhere, you are lost. When you feel you don't even belong to yourself, you feel a huge loss and despair. When you are lost to yourself, then who can pull you through? Who is left? Of course these feelings cause despair. You will think of any way out, including suicide. That is your protection. It is the one control that you have after so much has been taken away from you — and you won't let go of that. I don't think you are mentally ill because you choose to cling to that one part of you that you still have power over.

Antidepressant drugs cannot combat the pain I feel inside. No tablet will heal what I've seen at home growing up — alcohol, extreme violence, terror, pain, silent resignation. I am stronger in ways because of my life experiences, but very damaged too. It is the internalisation of the painful feelings from these sort of experiences and the burial of these emotions into the most private areas of your being that probably sets the seeds for the loneliness of depression. You knew that loneliness at the time of the painful and terrifying experiences in childhood — but only for a split-second, because that is all the pain you could cope with at the time. I took antidepressants which were prescribed for me. They made me feel far worse — weird and spaced out. I came very close to heading for the river while I was on them.

Helen's description of depression is quite similar to that of psychiatrist Dr Mike Shooter, president of the Royal College of Psychiatrists. The episode that launched him into depression many years previously was seeing a doctor comfort and support a dying man:

> I thought, 'I can't do this, I can't get that close to someone in distress and survive'. The next day a message came down from the same patient that he wanted to talk to me. It terrified me . . . by the time I went to see him, he had died, and I knew I had failed him.[17]

Mike Shooter discussed his experiences of two forms of treatment — psychotherapy and medication. His medical colleagues might take note of his comments. Dr Shooter enthuses about the benefits he experienced from psychotherapy:

> *What I had was good old fashioned face-to-face psychotherapy. The talking therapy was a godsend; it was a luxury to be able to explore those awful feelings with someone who is not going to be overwhelmed by them, who is not going to be made anxious by them, not made angry by them, and who could understand.*

In contrast to his experience of psychotherapy as a 'godsend', he speaks somewhat less glowingly about medication:

> *The pills probably helped biochemically. The pills also helped in that, for me, they represented the fact that this was an illness and it wasn't my fault.*

There is no way of knowing whether the pills helped Mike Shooter biochemically, since there has never been any way of confirming this hypothesis in any patient. The medications used at the time he first experienced being depressed were primarily sedating drugs. The most likely beneficial effect from those drugs is sedation, a calming of his great distress, which seems to resemble Helen's experience above, of 'very strong overwhelming feelings', an experience which is ever-present in people who become diagnosed as being depressed. There are many ways of ensuring that a person believes that their experience of distress is not their fault — one of the benefits Mike Shooter attributed to his medication.

One of psychiatry's current aims is to de-stigmatise psychiatric illness. In my opinion, the stigma of 'mental illness' will continue as long as the experiences of the people diagnosed as 'mentally ill' remain stigmatised. As long as society views depression, severe anxiety, so-called hallucinations and delusions, paranoia, eating distress issues, suicidal tendencies and manic behaviour as bad, wrong, incomprehensible, weird, crazy — the stigma will continue. The tragedy is that society's interpretation of these experiences is misguided.

The judgements the public make about depression and other so-called 'psychiatric illnesses' stem largely from how society sees 'psychiatric illness', which in turn is informed by how psychiatry views these 'illnesses'. To remove the stigma, the public need to receive a different message about 'mental illnesses': that they are a sane and understandable human reaction to major emotional distress. It took Helen months to recover from the stigma she felt when her GP told her that her depression was caused by a biochemical brain defect.

Depression: a withdrawal within

Depression is an understandable withdrawal reaction in a person who has experienced an overwhelming degree of emotional distress. I believe that in the case of every person who develops depression — including people with severe depression for which psychiatry has been unable to find a cause — there is always a reason. The reason can be understood in the following context. In order to defend fundamental human emotional needs — to feel safe and secure, to avoid being hurt, exposed, overwhelmed, out of their depth, intensely anxious, not good enough, rejected — the person reacts by protecting themselves when feeling threatened. Many people who become depressed protect themselves by withdrawing from people and from life. Reaching out, taking risks and interacting with others has become too risky.

The severity of the depression depends on how threatened the person feels and how much they need to withdraw. This can vary greatly. For some people, the depth of the pain of depression is indescribable. Depression can occur when a person finds themselves in a difficult, stressful situation, particularly when all possible solutions seem excruciatingly painful or threatening. As if paralysed by the enormity of their pain and the seeming impossibility of finding an acceptable resolution, the person withdraws and becomes depressed. Depression can sometimes be a protective mechanism to avoid experiencing feelings that terrify the person, such as severe anxiety; fear of emotional annihilation; rage and other feelings for which there seems to be no outlet, no resolution. It is inaccurate to label people who become overwhelmingly distressed — who as a coping mechanism may feel a strong need to protect themselves by withdrawing — as 'mentally ill' and suffering from 'abnormal brain biochemistry'. The following two case stories illustrate the link between depression and the need to withdraw from life. They also demonstrate how important life events can be as a trigger for depression.

Alice's story
Alice was happily married with three children, and had a good relationship with her husband. Soon after I ceased working as a typical GP Alice contacted me because she had a long-standing relationship with me as her GP. A row with the neighbours escalated out of all proportion and ended up in court. Alice had no history of depression or severe emotional

distress, but all that changed coming up to the court case. Unable to face life, Alice began to withdraw, spending most of the day in bed. She lost interest in her work and her family. Alice spend most of her day crying. She felt very depressed and saw no point in living any more. She was distraught when she came to see me. The court case was the following week.

Alice cried and sobbed her way through the consultation. Throughout our meeting, I kept referring back to her uniqueness as a human being, and suggesting that it was possible for her to separate her true value as a unique human being from what was going to happen in the courts. I gave her ample time to express herself, to get it all out. Alice felt a good deal better after our meeting, having released pent-up emotion in a safe and supportive environment. She left, not with a prescription, but with a new-found sense of energy and awareness of her self-worth. I would have been quite happy to prescribe medication for her as a temporary, interim measure to help her cope with the court case.

Our meeting helped Alice put things in perspective, not because I made a diagnosis and put her on drug treatment or because I told her where she was going wrong. That consultation worked well because I did not judge or criticise her. From the outset, I sought to convey to Alice that her feelings made sense. I listened intently to her. Alice did far more talking than I did. She needed a lot of time that day. She spent one and a half hours with me. Extra time is often well spent, allowing the crisis to be thoroughly expressed and reducing the need for future therapy sessions. Had she attended a different doctor I believe, as does she, they would have given her fifteen minutes at most and a prescription either for tranquillisers to calm her down or an antidepressant.

When I met Alice three months later, the court case was over. The dispute with her neighbours was settled. Her depression had disappeared. She was eagerly planning to redecorate her home. She told me that her consultation with me had helped enormously, giving her the encouragement to face the court case.

Hilda's story

Hilda was in her forties when she attended me in my capacity as a GP. She complained of recurring depression and anxiety for over fifteen years. Hilda had attended psychiatrists and a psychologist. She had been diagnosed as having endogenous depression — medical parlance for depression which has no external cause — and had taken several different anti-depressants which had not helped her. For the previous five years, Hilda had been taking three tranquillisers and a sleeping tablet every day. Hilda believed that she was addicted to these drugs and felt angry about this. She could think of no reason why she became depressed and anxious, but these feelings were ever-present in her life for years. She said that neither the psychologist nor the psychiatrists had come up with a reason for her depression.

After her second session with me I felt I understood her depression, to some degree at least. Hilda had been quite anxious and insecure as a teenager. She coped well enough until her late twenties. Then, within ten months, she lost the three people who were closest to her. Her mother died suddenly. Hilda had always been very close to her mother. Then her marriage broke up. A few months later, her only sister also died suddenly. In the space of ten months, the bottom had fallen out of Hilda's world. Her depression began soon after these losses. I believe that Hilda may have subconsciously reacted to these dreadful losses by withdrawing from people and from the world. At least by withdrawing and not reaching out, she would avoid the risk of repeating the awful pain and loneliness which came with feeling abandoned.

She paid a price for this withdrawal — no intimate

relationships in her life. But anything was better than the terrible pain of trusting and reaching out only to lose the people she trusted and reached out to. Five years after her marriage broke up, she entered another relationship. She had two sons with this partner and fifteen years later they are still together. This man has been wonderful for Hilda, but she has never been able to let down the barriers and really trust in this relationship. It is as if, twenty years ago, when her whole life fell apart, she decided she could never again risk experiencing such pain and abandonment.

This explanation for why she has been depressed for twenty years made sense to Hilda. For years it had been safer for her to stay where she was in her life than to take even tentative steps towards connecting with her partner and others. Medication could never be the solution she needed. Yet the psychiatrists she had attended had prescribed several different drugs, none of which helped. Hilda was now ready to deal with her suppressed emotional pain. She is meeting with a counsellor to explore these issues.

I now believe that depression is not a 'psychiatric illness'. Depression is an unhappy place to be, but for the person who suffers with it, depression can be the lesser of two evils. Rather than being an 'illness', depression is often a coping mechanism, a withdrawal within oneself when reaching out to others has become too painful, too risky.

An autumn 1998 study published in the *British Journal of General Practice* suggested that depression is more likely in people exhibiting certain characteristics. The researchers from Leeds University tracked the lives of more than 130 GPs over a fifteen-year period. The researchers found that the GPs who as medical students experienced depression, high self-criticism, sibling rivalry or excessive alcohol intake were more likely to experience a serious depression later in life. The results also suggested that having difficult relationships with the family of origin increased the likelihood of difficult relationships with medical colleagues during their working life. This research does not support the hypothesis that depression is biological in origin.

Doctors believe that depression serves no purpose. Since 1992 there has been a 'Fight Depression' campaign in full swing in Britain, as if depression were an enemy to be exterminated. These campaigns have received great publicity. But they have made little impression, either on depression or on the suicide rate. I believe that even the most severe depressions make sense and are understandable in the context of the life that person has lived and experienced. Unlike many of my medical colleagues, this is the starting point from which I work with people. I work with people as a 'journey-man'; a fellow traveller in this journey called 'life'.

The process of withdrawal frequently begins many years earlier, gradually escalating into the degree of withdrawal which then becomes labelled 'mental illness'. When Jill attended me as a GP in her mid-twenties, with depression, she recalled feeling like an outsider throughout her school days. In school from age five upwards, Jill remembered feeling separate from the rest of her classmates. She was too timid to get involved in the everyday games and play, regularly standing alone by the yard wall, watching the others play. This pattern of withdrawal and timidity gradually escalated, unnoticed by family and teachers alike, eventually reaching the point where she was diagnosed as having depression.

James, also in his twenties, attended me, in my capacity as a GP, having already being diagnosed by a psychiatrist as having 'social phobia'. He became extremely nervous when in company, and as a result avoided social contact as much as possible. As we explored his life story, he recounted having recently seen a video of his first communion, an important milestone occurring around seven years of age within some religions. James told me that as he watched the video, all the other first-time communicants were happily running all over the place with excitement. He noticed that he did not leave his parents' side throughout the day. James recalled feeling scared and intimidated, staying beside his parents in an unsuccessful effort to feel safe and secure. Quiet children, like Jill and James, often slip through the net. Because they don't draw attention to themselves, and they are compliant at school, their anguish can easily go unnoticed, and therefore unresolved.

'But, where does my depression go every Wednesday?'

Joan had experienced severe anxiety for over a year. Her overwhelming anxiety was dominating her life. One evening, she felt so stressed that she visited her doctor about it. The GP was certainly conscientious — he spent almost an hour with her. Most of that hour consisted of a ping-pong match between Joan and the GP about whether or not she should take medication for her anxiety. The GP concluded that Joan's anxiety was a symptom of depression, a common medical reaction amongst doctors, who believe that depression is the underlying cause for many expressions of distress. The doctor spent a great deal of time explaining the prevailing medical view about depression to Joan; that it is caused by a brain imbalance which is corrected by taking antidepressant drugs.

The GP was insistent. He wanted Joan to take antidepressants. Joan wanted help with her anxiety but was not convinced that an antidepressant drug was what she needed. Exasperated, Joan said, 'if my depression is caused by a biochemical brain imbalance, then where does my depression go every Wednesday, Doctor?' The GP stopped in his tracks. 'What do you mean?' he replied. Joan repeated, 'if my depression is due to a biochemical brain imbalance, why am I never depressed on Wednesdays?' The doctor asked Joan if there was something she did on Wednesdays that made her feel better.

Joan knew the answer to her own question. Every Wednesday she attended a counsellor, who was based quite a distance from Joan's home. So on Wednesday, most of Joan's day was spent preparing for the consultation which she eagerly looked forward to every week, travelling to the counsellor, and home again. Joan explained all this to the GP, who was still unable to account for why she did not experience depression on Wednesdays. Joan then outlined to the doctor why she did not feel depressed on the days she visited her counsellor, with whom she had a wonderful relationship. That hour every week was like gold to her. She felt safe, she felt cared for every Wednesday, so she did not feel depressed. The doctor admitted that her version made sense.

Little wonder that the GP was knocked off his stride. In one fell swoop, Joan, a mere 'patient', exploded the medical profession's doggedly-held theory about depression being caused by a biochemical imbalance. How could a biochemical imbalance revert to normal on Wednesdays and suddenly become abnormal again the following day? He had no answer to her common sense. In fairness to the GP, at the end of the consultation he said to Joan that they had both learned something. He was half right. *He* had certainly learned something. Joan was the teacher; the doctor was the pupil.

It is good that Joan feels accepted and understood by her counsellor. This has helped Joan greatly. However, it says something about our society that such understanding and acceptance is not commonly available for people in their lives. A healthy society gives appropriate recognition to each individual's inner reality and experience. In many ways, our society does not give such appropriate recognition. Censorship — of feelings, experiences, life issues and problems — is alive and well in the twenty-first century. Throughout this book, there are many examples of such censorship. For example, there is a subtle but powerful censorship of feelings and their

147

expression. 'Positive' feelings and expression (joy, laughter, humour) are considered valid, while so-called 'negative' feelings (anxiety, fear, sadness, loneliness etc.) are generally less welcome in conversation. The very division of feelings and expression into 'positive' and 'negative' itself illustrates the censorship; something positive is to be welcomed, while something negative is 'not-a-good-thing', and must be eradicated, removed or pushed underground.

Where does this leave a person who experiences 'negative' feelings on a regular basis? They quickly get the message that society doesn't want to hear about their distress. What do they do with, to whom do they go to with, their fear, anxiety, unhappiness, uncertainty, loneliness? If they are lucky, they may have one or two people in their lives in whom they can confide. But because there is such censorship of feelings and expressions in our society, there are few people who will be able help them in their great emotional distress. They feel they have to keep this part of themselves locked away from people, from the world. But since this is a major part of who they are, they then must create a mask, a front, when they meet people. Having to do this greatly increases their sadness, their isolation and marginalisation, their loneliness.

There is a considerable amount of research suggesting that counselling is at least as effective as antidepressant medication. In the late 1980s, the USA National Institute of Mental Health (NIMH) funded a large study comparing the effectiveness of psychotherapy and antidepressant drugs. Twelve prominent psychologists and psychiatrists published their research in the *Archives of General Psychiatry,*[18]. After sixteen weeks of treatment, psychotherapy and antidepressants produced similar results, two thirds of patients responding to either form of treatment.

If antidepressants help some people, and counselling helps some people, it seems reasonable to suggest that the optimum treatment might be a combination of both medication and therapy. In research terms, the jury is still out on this question.[19] Some studies have suggested that a combination of both works better than either on their own, while several others have found that people receiving both modalities of treatment do not fare better. In my work, I have found that medication can be valuable, particularly in the short term. However, I have found that the more medication a person is taking, the less potential there is for psychotherapy to facilitate real growth, change and empowerment, which are important aspects of the recovery process.

Postnatal depression

Depression is relatively common after childbirth. The prevailing view within the medical profession is that postnatal depression is primarily a biological disorder, requiring treatment with antidepressant drugs. Consequently, the personal, social and relationship changes a woman goes through during and after childbirth receive inadequate recognition from the medical profession. Postnatal depression is sometimes attributed to the hormonal changes which accompany childbirth. While there may be a biological element to postnatal depression, this possibility is purely speculative. But the emotional upheaval associated with childbirth is not speculative; it is a fact of life.

Suddenly the woman finds herself responsible for a helpless infant. Her life has changed forever. As if life wasn't busy enough already, this tiny creature will need feeding, clothing and minding for the next twenty years, and the buck stops with her. Her relationships — with herself, her partner, her whole world — have irrevocably changed. Her plans for her own life have to be put on hold. While the joys of new motherhood are well recognised in society, the stresses are not. Some women find themselves with very little support. They have to cope more or less alone.

Caring for her own baby sometimes triggers memories and emotions of her own childhood. If as a child she experienced a great deal of loneliness and sadness, these emotions may come flooding back as she cares for her own child. A woman who has been barely coping with life may find childbirth and motherhood overwhelming. Subconsciously withdrawing into depression may be the only way the woman can avoid being overwhelmed by this new situation in which she finds herself.

A psychologist told me the following case history. A woman became severely depressed after childbirth. She had all the treatments psychiatry could offer, including antidepressants and admission to a psychiatric hospital. Her depression did not improve. As a last resort, the woman was referred to this psychologist. The root of the woman's depression remained elusive. The breakthrough came when the psychologist asked the woman at what times she felt most depressed. She replied 'when I'm brushing my baby's hair'. It emerged that brushing her daughter's hair sparked off memories of her own childhood: memories of sadness, of feeling unloved. Her intense love for her child reminded her of how unloved she felt when she was growing up. These painful memories were at the root of her depression. In the ensuing months, she worked with the psychologist to explore and come to terms with her emotional pain. In the process, she emerged from her depression.

What women with postnatal depression need is social, emotional and psychological support. Postnatal depression is not a 'mental illness'. It is an understandable human response to one of the most challenging human experiences of all — becoming a mother. Why do we need psychiatric reasons when there is a perfectly adequate human explanation?

An exploratory study presented at a meeting of the All-Ireland Institute of Psychiatry in Autumn 2003 evaluated the effectiveness of a ten-session cognitive behavioural therapy group for women suffering from postnatal distress. The study concluded that this was a 'promising' treatment, which could be offered before or after individual treatment or independently. I found it interesting that, while for over half a century women in postnatal distress have been readily treated with medication, the idea that women would benefit from meeting in groups to share their experiences and thus gain support, confidence and self-esteem is at an 'exploratory' stage within psychiatry.

Antidepressants

As is the case with 'antipsychotics', the term 'antidepressants' is a misnomer. It suggests that antidepressant drugs have been proven to act specifically against depression, and that is not true. Bruce Charlton MD[20] recommended that antidepressants should be made available on request. He believes that antidepressants will help people who are not depressed to feel 'better than well'. He is, in effect, saying that life is tough, so why not take antidepressants if they make you feel better, even if you are just frustrated or unhappy? That antidepressants make non-depressed people feel better demonstrates that these drugs are not specifically antidepressant in their action. This supports my belief that these drugs act as non-specific mood-altering drugs.

Initially, I was shocked by the lack of any scientific perspective on the use of antidepressants in Dr Charlton's article. Then I realised that he is merely describing current trends in medical practice. Antidepressants have become so widely prescribed that all a person has to do is to show signs of emotional distress, which is then interpreted by doctors as depression. In his annual report published in 1998, Sir Kenneth Calman, Chief Medical Officer for England, noted the sharp rise in the prescribing of antidepressants. He indicated that in the previous two years, prescriptions for antidepressant drugs had risen by 15 per cent in men and 19 per cent in women. He noted that one in twelve women and one in twenty-eight men were prescribed these drugs. Antidepressant prescribing in

Britain has more than doubled in the past ten years, jumping from 9 million in 1992 to over 22 million prescriptions in 2002. And the prevailing medical view is that many more people should be taking them.

Although the older antidepressants (many of which are still widely used) have been on the market for over forty years, the medical profession has never established how they work. The only thing which can be said with any certainty about the older antidepressants is that they certainly do tend to sedate. If they do make people feel better the sedation may well be the reason. Commenting on the sedating effect of the older antidepressants, psychiatrist Dr Peter Leyburn wrote in *The Lancet,*[21] twelve years after these drugs were first introduced, 'it is difficult to feel depressed when you are unconscious'.

Doctors do not understand how newer antidepressants such as Prozac or Seroxat 'work', though this is not the impression one gets when medical experts speak in the media. In the case of the majority of these newer antidepressant drugs, the profession believes they act by re-balancing the levels of serotonin or other chemicals in the brain. This is guesswork, since no proof exists that depression is caused by an imbalance of either serotonin or any other brain chemical. Nor is there any evidence that antidepressants have a balancing effect on the level of any chemicals in the brain.

In October 2002, I became aware that the Seroxat patient information leaflet contained — for the previous eleven years — wording which I believed seriously misinformed the public and doctors throughout the British Isles and worldwide. The wording in question was:

> This medicine works by bringing the levels of serotonin back to normal. Seroxat is one of the antidepressants that work by returning your serotonin levels to normal.

Knowing that these statements were untrue, I wrote to the Irish Medicines Board expressing my surprise that international regulatory bodies — such as the UK Committee on Safety of Medicines and the Irish Medicines Board — would permit this to occur. The following extract from the letter I wrote in October 2002 to the Irish Medicines Board outlines the true situation:

Patients put on Seroxat *never* have their serotonin levels measured prior to treatment to assess whether their serotonin levels are normal or abnormal to begin with. Patients *never* have their serotonin levels checked while on treatment to see whether their so-called 'abnormal' serotonin levels have returned to normal. It has not been scientifically established what the normal range of serotonin levels actually is; and obviously if we don't know what constitutes 'normal' serotonin levels, our scientific knowledge of 'abnormal' serotonin levels is inevitably seriously deficient.

When treatment with Seroxat (and the other SSRIs) is stopped, no attempt is made by the doctor to assess serotonin levels. If Seroxat was working all along by 'returning your serotonin levels to normal' as the leaflet so emphatically states, what happens to one's serotonin level when Seroxat is stopped? Does it now somehow miraculously remain 'normal' in the absence of treatment? Or does it become 'abnormal' again? The bottom line here is that we doctors haven't a clue what happens to our patients' serotonin levels when the drug is stopped because we have no way of measuring our patient's serotonin levels, and we do not know what constitutes 'normal' or 'abnormal' levels. The bottom line is that we doctors have no idea whether the patients we treat with Seroxat (and other SSRIs) have a normal, low or raised serotonin level at any stage of the entire process of diagnosis and treatment. And we have absolutely no idea how our patients' serotonin

levels are responding to the treatment on an ongoing basis.
In 20 years as a medical doctor, I have never, ever heard of
a patient anywhere having their serotonin levels checked.

In their reply to my letter, the Irish Medicines Board did not
take issue with any of these points:

Dear Dr Lynch,

Thank you for your letter dated 19th October 2002 which
was received by the Irish Medicines Board on 30th October
2002. The Irish Medicines Board has been reviewing this
matter with its experts for some time and is in agreement
that the statement that SSRIs 'work by bringing the levels
of serotonin back to normal' is not consistent with the
scientific literature. The company has been asked to review
the patient information leaflet accordingly.

Thank you for your interest in this matter.

Not satisfied with this response, between November 2002 and
January 2003 I wrote two further letters to the Irish Medicines
Board, seeking answers to many questions, including:

• How it ever could have transpired that the wording that
  Seroxat 'works by bringing the levels of serotonin back
  to normal', wording acknowledged by the Irish Medicines Board as 'not consistent with the scientific literature', was allowed on the patient information leaflet by
  international medication regulatory bodies. Furthermore,
  I sought an explanation as to how this wording remained
  on the leaflet for over eleven years, since the initial licensing of Seroxat.

• How the wording 'Remember, you cannot become addicted to Seroxat' had been allowed by the international
  medication regulatory bodies for over eleven years,
  given that the SSRI antidepressants had never been systematically tested for their addictive potential.

The replies I received from the Irish Medicines Board were, in my opinion, far from comprehensive or satisfactory. Then, in May 2003, I received a letter from the Irish Medicines Board which contained the following remarkable information:

Dear Dr Lynch,

Further to my letter of 10 February 2003, I now wish to confirm that the package leaflet for the Seroxat range has been revised. Regarding mechanism of action, the original phrase *'Seroxat . . . works by bringing serotonin levels back to normal'* has been replaced with the following: *'Seroxat . . . works by altering serotonin function. There is evidence that such function is disturbed in depression'*.

For your information, the company have removed the phrase *'Remember you cannot become addicted to Seroxat'*.

This change of wording also applied to Britain. These two changes are enormously significant. Neither phrase should ever have appeared on the patient information leaflet. The new wording — that 'Seroxat works by altering serotonin function' is also unsatisfactory. There is evidence that Seroxat and SSRI antidepressants do alter serotonin function. However, it is not at all clear whether altering serotonin function is a good or a bad thing, or whether serotonin function needed altering to begin with. We are therefore not in a position to say that the drug 'works' by altering serotonin function. Like its predecessor, this wording conveys an impression of scientific authenticity beyond what is truly known about the drug's effects on the brain. The wording will have the effect desired by the drug's manufacturers; it will persuade people to take the drug. Regarding the decision to remove the words phrase 'Remember you cannot become addicted to Seroxat', in what I believe is a cynical exercise of self-interest, GlaxoSmithKline still insist that Seroxat is not addictive. According to a company spokesperson: 'Nothing has changed, we still maintain that it's not addictive'.[22]

Why would GlaxoSmithKline change the wording so suddenly, so dramatically, whilst insisting that 'nothing has changed'? I believe that self-interest — an attempt to reduce the company's liability to legal actions — prompted this change, rather than genuine concern for the consumers of Seroxat. My hunch is that the company realised that to state 'remember, you cannot become addicted to Seroxat' is untenable, since it is regularly contradicted by the experience of thousands over many years who have become addicted to Seroxat. By June 2003, over four thousand people in the United Kingdom were initiating a class action against the manufacturers of Seroxat. Because of the power of the drug companies, it appears that Seroxat's manufacturers may never be called to publicly account for putting this deceptive, inaccurate wording there in the first place, despite its major repercussions for the public.

While the medical profession and the pharmaceutical industry go to great lengths to convince people that antidepressants are not addictive, the public are reluctant to accept this. A British MORI survey back in 1996[23] revealed that 78 per cent of those interviewed believed that antidepressants are addictive. Only 16 per cent thought that people with depression should be offered antidepressants. But 91 per cent said that counselling should be available to depressed people.

As discussed earlier, most doctors remain convinced that antidepressants are not addictive. With great authority, in public and in consultations with patients, doctors repeat over and over again that there is no risk of addiction with antidepressant drugs. The public are not convinced. I believe the public are right to be concerned, given that many medications prescribed by the medical profession for emotional distress have turned out to be addictive, ineffective, or likely to cause major side-effects, particularly with long-term use.

American Neurologist Dr Fred Baughman Jr, a Fellow of the American Academy of Neurology, has some strong words to say regarding the medical profession's claims regarding biological causes for mental health problems. In a letter to the William Glasser website in 2003, he wrote:

> Whether disease is present or not is not a matter of vote or consensus, but whether or not, one patient at a time, a physical abnormality is demonstrable. All physicians know this. We do not start insulin without proof of an elevated blood sugar. We do not surgically excise without proof of cancer cells. We do not treat the thyroid without proof of subnormal thyroid hormone. What makes organised psychiatry's claims a total, 100 per cent fraud is that they never — I repeat — never, demonstrate, diagnose, prove, the presence of an objective abnormality within the brain or body of a single patient. They can't, they do no physical examinations or testing. Nonetheless, they call you and I, your relatives, neighbours, and friends, brain-'disordered'/ 'diseased'/'chemically imbalanced' and proceed to drug, shock and perform psychosurgery upon us. Believing them, failing to ask for proof of an abnormality, the power we give them over us is totally arbitrary and inconsistent with the ideals this country [USA] is based upon. Dr James Scully, Medical Director of the American Psychiatric Association recently stated that emotional problems are in fact 'brain diseases', and that this fact is as 'incontrovertible as the earth going around the sun'. There being not a single mental/ psychiatric 'disorder'/'disease'/'chemical imbalance' verifiable in a single patient, I publicly charge that such claims are a total fraud against the American public.[24]

Psychiatry's fundamentally unscientific tendency to accept biological hypotheses as facts — and inform the public accordingly — is not new. Regarding this recurring tendency,

Scottish psychiatrist R. D. Laing wrote the following common sense over thirty years ago:

> That the diagnosed patient is suffering from a pathological process is either a fact, a hypothesis, an assumption, or a judgement. To regard it as a fact is unequivocally false. To regard it as a hypothesis is legitimate. It is unnecessary either to make the assumption or to pass the judgement.[25]

Certainly, some people who take these newer antidepressants do feel better. Many people get a buzz, a sense of energy from these drugs. For a person who has had neither a buzz nor a sense of energy for quite some time, this can be a most welcome development. But this does not mean that these drugs work to counteract a specific — and as yet unproven — chemical imbalance in the brain.

Many people feel worse when they take the newer antidepressant drugs. Many people's experience of symptoms such as anxiety, agitation, insomnia, numbness and unreality is heightened. Just as the only statement regarding how the older antidepressants work which can be made with any certainty is that they sedate, the only thing which can be said with confidence about how the newer antidepressants act is that, for many people, they have a largely stimulant action. Adverse effects of Seroxat, Prozac and other SSRI antidepressants which point to its stimulant effect include fever, nausea, diarrhoea, loss of appetite, nervousness, insomnia, anxiety, tremor, dizziness, convulsions, hallucinations, psychosis, hypomania and mania.

For many years — before the newer antidepressants such as Prozac and Seroxat were on the market — psychiatrists claimed that many people with depression were not being adequately treated by GPs because the prescribed dosage was too low. Prozac, launched in the late 1980s, has been widely prescribed for over ten years, as have several other newer antidepressants. Like many of the newer antidepressants,

Prozac was initially marketed as a one-dose strength antidepressant. The vast majority of people taking Prozac are prescribed the recommended dose of one 20-milligram tablet a day. The risk of prescribing an inadequate dose of Prozac and other newer antidepressant drugs had apparently been eliminated. Yet neither Prozac, Seroxat nor other newer antidepressants has ever been shown to be any more effective than the older antidepressants.

In recent years, in my opinion because the initial buzz people feel from Prozac, Seroxat and related antidepressants wears off within a few months, doctors have been increasing the dosage of these drugs. Many people are now being prescribed three-to-four times the dosage of SSRI antidepressants recommended just a few years ago. I believe that there are parallels here with addiction to prescribed drugs such as the benzodiazepine tranquillisers, and in earlier times, to amphetamines and barbiturates. On the *Antidepressant Web*[26] discussion forum, many patients describe their experience of steadily having their dose of Prozac or other antidepressant increased. With each increase, the buzz returns for a short period, then fades. This phenomenon has become known as 'poop-out' among those taking the drugs, and as 'tolerance' within the medical profession. As Charles Medawar, the creator of the Antidepressant Web points out, this need to increase the dose to get that buzz raises the possibility that these people have actually become addicted to the drug.

Also in the *Antidepressant Web*, Charles Medawar outlines how the goalposts regarding what constitutes addiction were changed in the early 1990s. In 1980, the then current edition of the *DSM-III* defined drug dependence as the presence of *either* tolerance (needing more of the drug to get the same effect) *or* withdrawal symptoms. In 1990, according to the American Psychiatric Association, 'The presence of a predictable abstinence syndrome following abrupt discontinuance of benzodiazepines is evidence of the development of physiological dependence'. However, in the updated version of the *DSM-IV* (1994), the American Psychiatric Association changed the definition of drug dependence, making it more difficult to define drugs as addictive. They now define drug dependence as the presence of *both* tolerance *and* withdrawal.

In other words, rather than become more alert to the important issue of dependence to prescribed drugs as one might expect, the American Psychiatric Association has both moved the goalposts and heightened the bar. As Charles Medawar comments in the Antidepressant Web, 'this definition would exclude all but the most exceptional cases of dependence on benzodiazepines'. This definition also results in the gross under-recognition of dependence problems with SSRI antidepressants.

The World Health Organisation's view of drug dependence contrasts with that of the American Psychiatric Association. According to the World Health Organisation, 'when the person needs to take repeated doses of the drug to avoid bad feelings caused by withdrawal reactions, the person is dependent on the drug'.[27] Unfortunately, this common-sense definition of drug dependence is largely ignored by the medical profession.

It seems contradictory that Prozac, Seroxat and related drugs are being used to treat one so-called 'psychiatric illness', yet they can precipitate four states which are themselves considered to be evidence of psychiatric illness — hallucinations, psychosis, hypomania and mania. A fifth serious side-effect of Prozac — convulsions — is itself a medical condition, for which long-term medical treatment is usually recommended. Prozac has also been implicated as a possible cause of suicide and of violent outbursts, including murder. The huge drive from the medical profession towards the wider prescribing of antidepressant drugs is based, not on scientific proof that they work, but on a combination of faith and wishful thinking.

Sometimes the drug companies who manufacture antidepressants are economical with the truth. One explanatory leaflet produced by Dista, the manufacturers of Prozac, states that Prozac and related drugs work by 'restoring the balance of serotonin in the brain'. I believe this is an attempt to create the impression that the medical profession and the pharmaceutical industry know precisely what they are doing when they prescribe these drugs. As discussed earlier regarding the Seroxat patient information leaflet, the reality is that how Prozac or similar drugs 'work' has not been determined.

One of the few established actions of Prozac and similar drugs is that they inhibit the reuptake of serotonin, an important brain chemical, hence the name SSRIs (selective serotonin reuptake inhibitors) for this group of drugs. However, there is no evidence that this action ameliorates depression, or that these levels were abnormal in the first instance. As it is a highly complex organ, the brain may well attempt to compensate for any such interference by becoming less sensitive to serotonin release in the brain. Since serotonin is present throughout most parts of the brain, interfering with the normal functioning of this chemical could have far-reaching consequences.

Any mood-altering drug which stimulates the nervous system, which gives people an energy buzz, has the potential to be addictive. Many people who take the newer anti-depressants find that when they stop taking them, they feel worse. For years, doctors and drug companies have maintained that this occurs because the 'depression' has resurfaced, proof of the appropriateness of the diagnosis and treatment. While this may sometimes be the case, this argument becomes flawed when one considers that many of the symptoms experienced upon stopping SSRI antidepressants are completely new to the person — they were not symptoms previously experienced by the person. Dizziness and electric-shock-like sensations in the head are two such experiences.

In recent years, doctors and drug companies accept that many people who come off the newer antidepressants experience a 'discontinuation syndrome'. However, doctors and drug manufacturers alike go to great lengths to try convince themselves and the public that a 'discontinuation syndrome' is a totally benign event, not at all related to a 'withdrawal syndrome', which by definition points to addiction to the drug. In reality, this is a mere play with words. What is authoritatively described as a 'discontinuation syndrome' is in reality a 'withdrawal syndrome'.

This scenario is not new. In the 1970s and 1980s, the medical profession collectively made a major error of judgement regarding tranquillisers such as Valium, Ativan, and diazepam. Thousands of people reported to their doctors that when they discontinued these tranquillisers their symptoms returned, often with a vengeance. Doctors decided that this occurred because the condition for which these drugs had been prescribed had not yet been cured. They needed a longer period of treatment. The real reason for the recurrence of symptoms was subsequently found to be a withdrawal reaction from an addictive drug. The medical profession's reluctance for decades to admit that these tranquillisers were addictive resulted in the creation of millions of addiction problems. This would not have occurred had the medical profession heeded the warning signs.

There is a very real possibility that, in the case of the newer antidepressant drugs, the medical profession is making precisely the same error of judgement all over again. Meanwhile, the underlying emotional distress — which brought the person to the doctor in the first place — frequently remains unexplored and unresolved.

It seems unrealistic to expect a drug to 'cure' the very powerful emotions which a person with depression experiences. These feelings are of inferiority; isolation; loneliness; a deep desire to reach out and talk to somebody but often being afraid to do so; confusion; reduced concentration; indescribable feelings of grief and loss; panic; self-hatred; feeling useless and totally unworthy of love; immense feelings of inferiority sometimes to the point of feeling sub-human; emptiness, feelings of having already died; beliefs and value systems crushed; illusions of family relationships shattered; constantly questioning the purpose of life and searching for new meaning.

For many years since its introduction in the late 1980s, Prozac was the largest selling antidepressant worldwide. It is still one of the most prescribed antidepressants. The public understandably presumes that this drug was tested and scrutinised thoroughly and with great care before making it publicly available. This is not the case. According to Charles Medawar in the *Antidepressant Web*, the USA Food and Drugs Administration's testing of Prozac was far from thorough and scientific. The FDA licensed Prozac on the evidence of four trials. In three of these trials, patients were allowed take other mood-altering drugs (such as tranquillisers) at the same time as they were taking Prozac. How can the effectiveness of one mood-altering drug be properly and scientifically assessed when many patients in the trial are taking other mood-altering drugs, and this fact is not taken into account in the final results? The fourth trial — the only one where patients taking other mood-altering drugs were excluded from the trial — showed that Prozac was no more effective than a placebo.

According to the manufacturer's own literature — the USA label for Prozac — in 1996, eight years after Prozac was first made available to the public, neither the safety nor the effectiveness of Prozac had been tested for use with in-patient depressive patients, or treatment of more than 6–8 weeks duration:

> The efficacy of Prozac was established in five- and six-week trials with depressed outpatients . . . the

163

antidepressant action of Prozac in hospitalised depressed people has not been adequately studied . . . The effectiveness of Prozac in long-term use, that is, for more than five to six weeks, has not been systematically evaluated in controlled trials.[28]

Yet this drug is widely prescribed for both categories. The standard recommendation for a course of antidepressant drugs is six to nine months. Once the FDA licences a drug, there is no comprehensive procedure in place to scrutinise how safe the drug is in the months and years after it goes on the market.

According to the manufacturer's literature in 1996, eight years after its release, the possibility that Prozac might cause dependence or addiction had not been systematically studied. Two years later, ten years after the launch of Prozac, eight years after the launch of Seroxat, candidly stated that:

One of the most widely accepted tenets of modern psychopharmacology is the value of maintenance [drug] treatment of major depression. And yet this de facto consensus treatment strategy remains largely an article of faith, resting as it does on a tenuous empirical base of a small number of placebo-controlled studies totalling fewer than 600 patients.[29]

The medical management of a depressed person has been largely reduced to deciding what medication, what dosage, and what duration the medication should be prescribed. Rarely do doctors take other factors — such as the life experiences of the person — sufficiently into account. When doctors decide to stop antidepressant treatment, where stands the biochemical abnormality? Is it still there or has it been reversed by the antidepressant? Doctors have no idea. No tests will be done to assess the biochemical status of the person because no such tests exist.

As previously mentioned, antidepressants are increasingly being prescribed for other 'conditions' such as social phobia, eating disorders and pre-menstrual tension. In 2003, they were licensed for 'post-traumatic stress', and what is euphemistically called 'generalised anxiety disorder'. This spreading of the net raises an obvious question, one which seems to have escaped the medical profession. Antidepressants have been marketed as specifically targeting a biochemical abnormality, just as antibiotics target bacteria. However, the extension of use of antidepressants to a wide range of distress situations argues against the notion that antidepressants are refined, specific treatments for a specific biochemical condition. Rather, this suggests that these drugs 'work' through a non-specific, generalised mood-altering action.

When Paula attended me, in my capacity as a GP, for help with her social 'phobia', she had already attended a psychiatrist whose only treatment was to prescribe Prozac for three months. This did not help because it was not what Paula needed. Paula's core issues — such as her need to protect herself from hurt by staying away from people — were ignored by the psychiatrist. Like Paula, many people are caught in an emotional tug-of-war. On the one hand, they desperately want to socialise and have a full life. But on the other hand, deep insecurity, low self-esteem and fear paralyses them into inaction. Making progress entails working with the delicate dance between these two positions.

I mentioned earlier that doctors repeatedly state, in the media and to patients, that the success rate of antidepressant treatment is 70 per cent. What is rarely stated is that the risk of a subsequent episode of major depression following nine months of antidepressant therapy is as high as 50 per cent. Nor is it said that with a second episode of depression, the risk of relapse following nine months of antidepressant treatment is 80 per cent. These figures are hardly consistent with the message being propagated by the medical profession — that antidepressants are a highly successful form of therapy. But this misguided message has got through to the public. For example, an article on depression in the *Irish Independent* of 6 May 2000 stated that '80–90 per cent of depressants, with proper treatment, achieve complete remission and lead successful, happy lives'.

Some doctors do refer patients for counselling and psychotherapy. But the reality is that the vast majority of people who are diagnosed as having a 'mental illness' receive only drug treatment. People often have to wait several months, sometimes up to two years, for counselling appointments. There is something fundamentally wrong with a system which makes one form of treatment available — antidepressants — immediately via the doctor's prescription, while an equally effective alternative — counselling — requires up to two years on a waiting list. Most of those referred for other treatments are also prescribed antidepressants. It is sometimes argued that counselling and psychotherapy is not a cost-effective treatment modality. A thorough appraisal of the cost-effectiveness of antidepressants and of other treatment approaches such as counselling/psychotherapy has not been carried out to date, and is long overdue.

One 2001 study compared generic counselling and antidepressants in the treatment of depression. By generic counselling, the researchers meant 'experienced counsellors, who adopted the counselling approach they believe to be most suitable'. People in the counselling group received six sessions with a counsellor. The researchers found that 'at twelve months follow-up, generic counselling and antidepressants are equally effective in patients with mild to moderate major depression'. The researchers concluded that 'General Practitioners should allow patients to have their preferred treatment'.[30] In terms of cost, the six therapy sessions described in this study over a twelve-month period would certainly compare favourably with twelve months of antidepressant medication.

The British government is becoming increasingly concerned with the escalating cost of antidepressants. National spending for all antidepressants increased 600 per cent during the 1990s. NHS spending on antidepressant medication jumped from £100 million in 1993 to £381 million in 2002, virtually a 400 per cent increase. In less than ten years, antidepressant prescriptions in England rose from 10.8 million in 1993 to 26.6 million in 2002. SSRI antidepressants accounted for the vast majority of this increase. The number of prescriptions written for anxiety, depression and stress in Britain has risen by eight million in the past five years. Roughly two million people in Britain are on antidepressants, at a cost of £380 million annually — and rising — to the National Health Service. According to new guidelines to doctors from the UK National Institute for Clinical Excellence (NICE), antidepressants should not be used as the first treatment option for people with mild depression, who should instead be offered 'simple' interventions such as self-help and exercise.

Questions need to asked regarding why doctors have considered it legitimate to prescribe antidepressants for the 'normal problems of life', a scenario eerily similar to that predicted by an astute author many years ago:

> And it seems to me perfectly on the cards that there will be within the next generation or so a pharmacological method of making people love their servitude, and producing a kind of painless concentration camp for entire societies, so that people will in fact have their liberties taken away from them but will rather enjoy it, because they will be distracted from any desire to rebel by propaganda, brainwashing, or brainwashing enhanced by pharmacological methods.[31]

Similarly in the USA, doctors continue to increase the number of antidepressant prescriptions they write every year. Antidepressants are now the second-largest group of drugs prescribed in the USA. Over 136 million prescriptions for antidepressants were filled between mid-2002 and mid-2003, an increase of 13 per cent over the previous twelve months.

In the USA, the national average for cognitive-behavioural therapy is $100 per session for a standard course of 15–20 sessions, working out at about $1,500–$2000 for a full course of treatment. Branded antidepressants cost about $1,000 per year, plus the bill for the doctor's appointments needed to continue the medication. Given the evidence that counselling may have much better long-term benefits than antidepressants, it is high time that a thorough, independent assessment of the true costs and benefits of antidepressants and counselling was carried out. In spite of the enormous growth in antidepressant prescribing in the 1990s, long-term incapacity due to depression in Britain continued to rise rather than fall throughout the 1990s.[32] The cost of mental illness in England was more that £77 billion in 2002, according to a study from the Sainsbury Centre for Mental Health. This figure is inclusive of full economic and social costs, and is greater than the £60 billion annual cost of crime. Where is the evidence that the British public are getting good value for this enormous expenditure on mental health care?

A research study from the Faculty of Medicine at the University of Iceland, published in February 2004, evaluated the overall public health impact of the escalating sales of antidepressants in Iceland.[33] The researchers used nationwide data from Iceland to study the effect of antidepressant prescribing on suicide, depression-related disability, hospital admissions and out-patient visits for depression. In keeping with international trends, between 1989 and 2000 anti-depressant prescribing increased by a massive 388 per cent, while the total quantity of all medications sold in Iceland during that 11 year period increased by just 48 per cent. The cost of antidepressant prescribing in Iceland between 1989 and 2000 increased by 461 per cent. The authors state that in the decades prior to 1990, antidepressant prescribing remained at a relatively stable level. Since 1990, however, sales of antidepressants 'increased very markedly'. In spite of this dramatic increase in antidepressant usage, the rates of psychiatric out-patient consultations and hospital admissions for depression in Iceland actually increased significantly since 1990; suicide rates and depression-related disability remained largely unchanged since 1990. The researchers note the 'energetic' marketing of newer antidepressants over the past 15 years, awareness campaigns to combat depression and prevent suicide, and clear medical guidelines regarding the treatment of depression. The researchers state that these developments might reasonably have been expected to have a significant impact on disability, suffering and mortality arising from depression. They point out that the cost for society of depression has not been reduced, and the impact of antidepressants on public health has been 'limited'.

The medical profession's preoccupation with antidepressants in the treatment of depression means that few other options are considered. We could do with more imagination, more lateral thinking in medicine. Jemima Nielson outlined her experience of depression in the *Irish Independent*.[34] She had been depressed since childhood. After her grandmother died when she was 16 years old, Jemima became anorexic. When aged twenty, suicidal although on antidepressants, Jemima went swimming with dolphins in Dingle Bay. She swam and frolicked with Fungi, Dingle's most famous tourist attraction. Her connection with Fungi changed her life. She immediately felt an immense calm. Jemima felt an enormous sense of love from Fungi. She started playing with him. All the emotions she had kept bottled up poured out in that magical interaction between human and dolphin. This was the turning point in her life. She soon came off antidepressants, felt less socially isolated and completed her university degree. Thirteen years later, she is happily married with two children.

I have never heard any prominent psychiatrist contemplate the idea that dolphins may be worth researching in the treatment of depression. But perhaps dolphins and other natural life experiences could have significant therapeutic effects on people, as happened with Jemima.

Notes

1. Dr William Glasser (2003) *Warning: Psychiatry Can Be Hazardous to your Mental Health*. New York: HarperCollins.

2. Lucy Johnstone (2000) *Users and Abusers of Psychiatry,* pp. 220–21. Hove: Brunner-Routledge.

3. Detailed in *American Journal of Psychiatry*, February 2002.

4. *Irish Medical News,* 17 November 2003.

5. *Science*, June 2003.

6. Z. Segal et al. (2004) *Archives of General Psychiatry,* January.

7. *Wall Street Journal*, 6 January 2004.

8. Patrick McKeon, *The Irish Times,* 1 September 1997.

9. Dr Tony Bates, *Business and Finance,* Jan 16–29 2003. Tony Bates is a senior clinical psychologist at St James Hospital, Dublin and lecturer in the Department of Psychiatry, Trinity College, Dublin. Tony Bates is the author of *Depression: The Common-sense Approach*.

10. Dr Peter Breggin (1993) *Toxic Psychiatry*. London: Flamingo.

11. Dr Peter Breggin (1994) *Talking Back to Prozac*. NY: St Martin's Press.

12. Seymour Fisher and Roger Greenberg, (1997) *From Placebo to Panacea*. London: John Wiley.

13. *Journal of the American Medical Association*, April 10, 2002.

14. Herman van Praag (2003) A stubborn behaviour: the failure of antidepressants to reduce suicide rates, *World Journal of Biological Psychiatry*, *4*: 184–91.

15. Dr David Healy (2001) The SSRI suicides. In C. Newnes, G. Holmes and C. Dunn, *This is Madness Too*, pp. 59–70. Ross-on-Wye: PCCS Books.

16. Carl R. Rogers (1995) *A Way of Being*. New York: Houghton Mifflin. Introduction by Irving Yalom.

17. *British Medical Journal,* 14 June 2003; *326*:1324.

18. I. Elkin, et al., 1989, 'National Institute of Mental Health Treatment of Depression Collaborative Research Program: General effectiveness of antidepressants', *Archives of General Psychiatry, 46*, 971–82.

19. B. Duncan, S. Miller, J. Sparks, G. Jackson, R. Greenberg and K. Kinchin, (2004) The myth of the magic pill. *The Heroic Client: A revolutionary way to improve effectiveness through client directed, outcome informed therapy,* San Francisco: Jossey Bass.

20. Bruce Charlton (1998) 'Psychopharmacology and the human condition'. *Journal of the Royal Society of Medicine, 91*: 599-601.18. *The Lancet, 25* November 1967.

21. *The Lancet,* 14 November 2002.

22. *Irish Times,* 10 May 2003.

23. Professor Robert Priest et al. (1996) *British Medical Journal, 313*: 858–9 (5 October) Lay people's attitudes to treatment of depression: results of opinion poll for Defeat Depression Campaign just before its launch.

24. Dr Fred A. Baughman Jr., Neurologist, Fellow, American Academy of Neurology, from e-mail on the William Glasser website http://www.wglasser.com/whatsnew.htm)

25. R. D. Laing (1970) *Sanity, Madness and the Family.* London: Penguin.

26. Charles Medawar, *The Antidepressant Web,* http://www.socialaudit.org.uk

27. World Health Organisation (1998), Selective serotonin re-uptake inhibitors and withdrawal reactions, *WHO Drug Information, 12*, 3:136–8.

28. Prozac (fluoxetine) product information, in Anon, *Physicians' Desk Reference*, 50th edition, Montvale, NJ: Medical Economics Co, 1996, 919–23.

29. *Journal of the American Medical Association* (1998) *280*: 1671–8.

30. C. Chilvers, et al. (2001) Antidepressant drugs and generic counselling for treatment of major depression in primary care: randomised trial with patient preference arms. *British Medical Journal, 322*: 772.

31. Aldous Huxley (1959) *Brave New World.* London: Chatto and Windus.

32. J. Moncrieff and J. Pommerleau (2000) Trends in sickness benefits in Great Britain and the contribution of mental disorders. *Journal Public Health Medicine, 22*: 59–67.

33. T. Helgason et al. (2004) Antidepressants and public health in Iceland. *British Journal of Psychiatry, 184,* 157–62.

34. *Irish Independent*, 22 April 2000.

4

Other 'mental illnesses'

Deciding that a symptom or a human behaviour is evidence of 'mental illness' is an arbitrary decision, a form of moral judgement. A hundred years ago, masturbation was widely believed to trigger many mental health problems. Thirty years ago, homosexuality was considered to be a 'mental illness'. But now, within the diversity of modern society, people are demanding more freedom to express themselves sexually. Consequently, homosexuality is no longer believed to be a 'mental illness'. Similarly, 'mental illnesses' are diagnosed when a person exhibits characteristics which are judged by society to be abnormal, or unacceptable. Society has decided that it is not normal or permissible to hear voices; to become seriously depressed; to become 'high'; to want to end one's life. Rather than pigeon-hole the 'abnormality' (and consequently the person) into the appropriate diagnostic box, perhaps we should be asking ourselves if the boxes themselves need to be re-examined.

Schizophrenia

It is said that approximately one per cent of the population receives a diagnosis of schizophrenia, amounting to over 500,000 people in Britain. Schizophrenia accounts for 15 per cent of suicides. Almost half of those people diagnosed with schizophrenia attempt suicide. One in ten succeed in ending their own life. Most psychiatrists and GPs believe that schizophrenia is a chronic brain disease. The medical consensus is that the hallucinations, delusions and other symptoms of schizophrenia are so bizarre that they must be caused by a brain abnormality of some kind. When speaking in public about schizophrenia, medical experts usually present an upbeat message. They outline how the medical profession now knows that schizophrenia is a brain disease, a 'mental illness', which can be 'managed' or 'controlled' with medication.

In developed countries, many people diagnosed as having 'schizophrenia' seem to make little progress over many years. As Harding maintains, this does not mean that the problem lies within the person's brain structure:

> The possible causes of chronicity [of mental health problems] may be viewed as having less to do with the disorder and more to do with a myriad of environmental and other social factors interacting with the person and the illness.[1]

When describing schizophrenia as a chronic, life-long condition, psychiatrists frequently compare it to diabetes or other medical life-long conditions. But to compare diabetes with schizophrenia is misleading for several reasons. It has long been established that diabetes is due to an insulin deficiency. In contrast, no biochemical or other physical defect has been identified in schizophrenia. No doctor would dream of diagnosing diabetes without appropriate blood tests. However, as is the case with all 'mental illnesses', no biochemical or other tests are ever carried out to confirm a diagnosis of schizophrenia, because no such tests exist.

Treatment for diabetes involves daily replacement therapy of insulin, the exact compound which is lacking in diabetes. In contrast, schizophrenia is treated with drugs for which no precise brain biochemical action has been established. These drugs are blunt instruments; their main mode of action is to sedate, to quieten the person. Insulin in correct dosage can be used for a lifetime without risk of serious adverse effects, unlike the medications used to treat schizophrenia, which can cause serious adverse effects that can be irreversible even when the drugs are stopped.

Once a person is diagnosed as having diabetes, they have the condition for life; they will never again become free of their condition. In contrast, one-third of people diagnosed as having schizophrenia make a full recovery from their 'condition'. As discussed later in this chapter, the recovery rate is higher in developing countries, where up to 66 per cent reach full remission.

In reality, there is a great deal of uncertainty and confusion about schizophrenia within psychiatry:

> Of all the major psychiatric syndromes, schizophrenia is much the most difficult to define and describe. The main reason for this difficulty is that over the past 100 years, many widely divergent concepts of schizophrenia have been held in different countries and by different psychiatrists. Radical differences of opinion persist to the present day.[2]

This textbook states that a diagnosis of schizophrenia in one country might well be diagnosed as depression in another:

> In New York, the concept [of schizophrenia] included cases that were diagnosed as depressive illness, mania, or personality disorder in the United Kingdom.

Mary Boyle is a clinical psychologist, a professor at the University of East London. In her book *Schizophrenia: A Scientific Delusion?*,[3] Boyle questions the scientific basis for diagnosing schizophrenia. In *This is Madness*[4], Mary Boyle explores the diagnostic process as it exists within psychiatry. She makes the point that, while within psychiatry there may be debates and disagreements regarding what diagnostic category a person 'belongs' to, there is never any debate or questioning of the validity of the actual diagnostic system, and the process by which people become diagnosed.

I believe that the process by which doctors diagnose 'mental illness' is fundamentally flawed. In the process of diagnosis, doctors actively seek out certain characteristics or 'symptoms' which are considered by doctors to be highly significant. In contrast, other characteristics that present within the person are deemed unimportant. They are not sought out; rather, they are virtually ignored. Regarding what is called 'schizophrenia', doctors actively seek to establish whether or not the person is experiencing hallucinations; delusions; paranoia, several withdrawal and thought patterns (described in more detail below in the case of Alison) considered to be evidence of a thought disorder. Once satisfied that some or all of these characteristics are present in the person, a psychiatric diagnosis of schizophrenia is likely to follow.

There are several fundamental flaws in this diagnostic process. For starters, other characteristics present in the person are, as a result of collective medical 'wisdom', deemed unimportant and ignored. I discuss some of these characteristics later in this chapter, such as low or absent self-esteem; ever-present anxiety and terror; an ever-present feeling of being powerless to shape one's own destiny, powerless to make oneself safe in one's world.

A second fundamental flaw, discussed in more detail later, is the way in which experiences are interpreted by the medical profession. Doctors tend to presume that symptoms such as hallucinations, delusions and paranoia have no meaning, and therefore are proof of *illness*. However, when one takes the time to connect with the person's story, it becomes obvious that these experiences have deep meaning for the person, mirroring their *distress*. A third flaw is the medical profession's presumption that the person's experiences are evidence of brain disease. This issue is discussed throughout this book.

The late Scottish psychiatrist R. D. Laing expressed reservations regarding the medical approach to schizophrenia in his book *Sanity, Madness and the Family*.[5] Laing wrote that, in more than eighty per cent of patients, even two psychiatrists trained in the same medical college cannot — independently of each other — agree on a diagnosis of schizophrenia. According to Laing, there is no condition over which there is more dispute in the whole field of medicine. Afro-Caribbeans living in Britain and having repeatedly to deal with discrimination, poverty and low-class status are up to 16 times more likely to develop schizophrenia than their counterparts who continue to live in their Afro-Caribbean country of origin. Unless this group of people have undergone a rather sudden genetic change since coming to live in Britain, this points to the importance of social and environmental pressures as potential triggers of major mental health problems rather than a genetic predisposition.

Psychiatrist Dr Peter Breggin does not believe that schizophrenia is a mental illness. In *Toxic Psychiatry*,[6] Dr Breggin outlines in detail his view that people so diagnosed are in reality going through a psycho-spiritual crisis, often revolving around basic, fundamental human issues such as identity, shame and overwhelm. He outlines how they communicate in metaphors which have meaning and which often hint at the heart of their problem.

The consensus view within psychiatry is that schizophrenia is a physical brain disease, although this presumption is not backed up by solid medical research. The early warning signs of schizophrenia strongly point not to a physical problem; they clearly suggest that the central issue in schizophrenia is a major emotional crisis characterised by intense fear and emotional distress rather than a physical brain disease:

Early warning signs include social withdrawal, isolation, reclusiveness, suspiciousness of others, deterioration and abandonment of personal hygiene, flat emotions, inability to express joy, inability to cry or excessive crying, inappropriate laughter, excessive fatigue and sleepiness or an inability to sleep.[7]

Schizophrenia typically develops in the late teens and early twenties. Most psychiatrists presume that, whatever may be causing this condition, it isn't pressures within the person's life. Yet some studies have shown a striking excess of major, stressful life events in the months prior to the onset of schizophrenia.

While it is not fashionable within medicine to seriously consider possible psycho-social triggers for schizophrenia, there is evidence that emotional and psychological distress and social issues may precede the overwhelming distress which becomes diagnosed as 'schizophrenia'. A 2001 study looked at possible childhood risk characteristics in children who later go on to develop schizophrenia-type problems later in life. The researchers found a significantly increased frequency of the following, in people who later in life were diagnosed as having schizophrenia:

Social maladjustment in school; a strong preference for solitary play; self-reported social anxiety at age 13; teacher-reported anxiety at age 15; passivity; social withdrawal; social anxiety; hypersensitiveness to criticism; disciplinary problems; antisocial behaviour; peculiarity; odd behaviour; flat affect, e.g. seldom laugh or smile, no reaction when praised or encouraged.

Very significantly in my opinion, the researchers found that:
The more anxious children were, the more likely they were to develop schizophrenia.[8]

The above findings are consistent with my own observations. Over the years, I have met and worked with many people who have been diagnosed as having schizophrenia. Without exception, every one has exhibited most if not all of these features as children, many years before their diagnosis. Such findings have major implications regarding the cause of schizophrenia, implications which collectively the medical profession have largely decided to ignore.

In *Sanity, Madness and the Family*, Psychiatrist R. D. Laing described how he and his co-workers spent a great deal of time (20–40 hours in each case) with eleven patients diagnosed as having schizophrenia, and their families. They concluded that the symptoms which psychiatrists had labelled as bizarre and abnormal were understandable given the nature of the relationships within those eleven families.

Internationally renowned psychologist and author Dorothy Rowe describes so-called 'psychiatric symptoms' as defence mechanisms:

> When we value and accept ourselves we need only a few modest defences, but when we lose confidence in ourselves, when we turn against ourselves, we have to resort to the most desperate of defences, those behaviours which psychiatrists call mental disorders.[9]

I believe that the behaviours exhibited by people diagnosed as having schizophrenia are the consequence of deep insecurity and severe emotional turmoil. The person withdraws because life has become too terrifying for them. Hallucinations and delusions occur as a frantic attempt to create meaning in life and to protect from further humiliation. Feeling totally unimportant, a young man attempts to convince himself and others that he is extremely important — Jesus, or a famous rock star, for example. Typically, the persona adopted will be one which has deep meaning for the person, or has major significance within the person's culture. For example, within a strongly Catholic culture, such people are far more likely to state that they are Jesus than Buddha, or Allah.

Feeling invisible or terrified, a young woman believes that everyone is looking at her. Feeling so unimportant and invisible that no one would be bothered talking to him, a person believes that they are being talked about on TV. Feeling too hurt and scared to interact with people, they withdraw into isolation. The hallucinations and delusions create a fantasy world where the person is important and safe, to some degree at least. These so-called hallucinations and delusions, typically dismissed as meaningless by doctors, can have immense meaning for the sufferer. They typically revolve around issues of importance to all humans, which become profoundly important for people struggling for their emotional survival: issues such as identity, belonging, the meaning of life and one's life purpose. Who am I? Am I a really good, important person (Jesus Christ, Buddha, a popstar or sportsperson) or an I evil or bad (the devil, smelly, a piece of dung). Do I matter? Am I invisible? Exploring these symptoms with the person can be very productive.

Having gradually dismantled the tunnel vision of my medical training, I now see that there are certain characteristics which are virtually always present in people diagnosed as having schizophrenia. Although rarely picked up by doctors, it has become evident to me that these characteristics are central to the experience of people so labelled.

Terror is one such characteristic. I have rarely encountered a person diagnosed with schizophrenia in whom terror was not a virtually ever-present feature. One young man so diagnosed recently described how he felt 'under threat' every time he left his home. Another young man, diagnosed as having schizophrenia for three years, appeared very frightened during his third meeting with me. I asked him what he was feeling and thinking and he replied, 'I'm wondering how I can get out of here alive'.

Powerlessness is another characteristic which is virtually ever-present. I have yet to meet a person diagnosed as having schizophrenia who felt they had a sense of power to shape their own destiny. Feeling totally powerless, at the mercy of everything and everyone, is it really surprising that people become withdrawn, paranoid and believe that people can read their mind?

Feeling totally unsafe is another common feature, a feature which makes people withdraw and cut themselves off from people. Feeling totally unsafe, is it really surprising that people become paranoid, when one constantly feels in danger? Other ever-present features include very low self-esteem and self-confidence.

Most psychiatrists believe that the 'thought disorder' experienced by people diagnosed as having schizophrenia is evidence of a breakdown in the brain's normal biochemical functioning. However, there is no scientific evidence to confirm this view. The prevailing medical view of 'schizophrenia' can reasonably be described in the following manner: 'these features are so unusual that they must be caused by a physical defect in the brain. How could there possibly be any other explanation for such bizarre behaviour?'

Searching for symptoms such as paranoia, hallucinations and delusions, it does not strike doctors that these symptoms are understandable in the context of how that person is in their life. Doctors instantly presume that such symptoms are always irrational, that they could not possibly have any value or meaning. The vast majority of doctors have never experienced anything like the depths of powerlessness, overwhelm, terror, lack of safety, absent self-esteem and identity issues experienced by people who become diagnosed as having schizophrenia; medical training does not teach doctors that these characteristics have any importance when assessing a person's mental and emotional distress. Hence, most doctors do not spot these characteristics in their patients, and certainly would never contemplate the very real possibility that so-called psychiatric symptoms — such as delusions, hallucinations, paranoia, thought disorder and becoming withdrawn — may be the result of the type of characteristics and experiences I have just described.

One young man, diagnosed as having schizophrenia, told me that he likes his 'delusions' and 'voices'. They give him a sense of security; they occupy his mind, and distract him from the realities and anxieties of his life. He told me that he is afraid that without the voices he would be panicky. Another young man similarly diagnosed described how the bullying and intimidation he experienced early in life at school 'would make you want to crawl into a shell'. Having no belief that he can defend himself in this world, that he has any power to stand up for himself, he has indeed crawled into a shell of detachment and withdrawal. Another man diagnosed as having schizophrenia told me that for years he has watched how people turn their head. If they turn their head to the right, this means that something bad will happen to him. If they turn their head to the left, this means that something neutral will happen to him. At first hearing, this might sound illogical, weird, psychotic. How on earth could the way a stranger turns their head affect what will happen to a person?

But if you take a broader view, and see it from the person's perspective, it makes sense. This young man has all the characteristics just discussed. He constantly feels unsafe, threatened, powerless. He totally doubts his ability to cope with and survive around people. Feeling so unsafe, he is always on guard to see where the next attack, hurt or invasion might come from. At least if he is on guard, he may not be taken by surprise. Watching people to see which way they are turning their head became a way for him to anticipate where the next threat might come from; gave him some sense of predictability

181

in a world which seems beyond his control. Interestingly, the way people move their heads doesn't ever suggest to him that something good will happen; the best he hopes for is a neutral situation, where nothing bad happens to him. This reflects his sense of threat, of foreboding that he feels almost constantly.

Within the past few months, two people diagnosed as having schizophrenia told me how anxious they became while on holiday. When one realises how ever-present fear and terror is in people so diagnosed, this comes as no surprise. Being on holiday takes people out their familiar routine, brings them in contact with new experiences, which can be very scary for a person who sees themselves as powerless, at the mercy of others, and who has no faith in their own ability to cope with change and challenge.

A young woman began attending me recently, after having read the Irish edition of this book. She attended me in my capacity as a GP with a special interest in mental health. Four years ago she was diagnosed as having schizophrenia. Since then, she has been on four drugs simultaneously – two major tranquillisers, a drug to attempt to counter adverse effects of these drugs, and an antidepressant. Her main experience upon which the diagnosis of schizophrenia is based is that she hears 'voices'. Despite being on four drugs, her 'voices' continue unabated. She hears them virtually all day, every day. I asked her to tell me about the voices. She replied that there is an almost constant struggle going on in her head between two 'voices' each with their own name; a male voice, which is aggressive and very critical of her, and a female voice which argues with the male voice, defending her, stands up for her in the face of the male voice's aggression and criticism. To date, we have met three times. We have just begun to explore the 'voices'. While it may be a coincidence, I was stuck by the fact that in her life, this woman has been in a series of difficult relationships with men. Her father had in general been very critical of her. She is currently has a loving, supportive partner. However, in her previous two long-term relationships, she was subjected to repeated criticism, emotional and physical abuse. My immediate reaction was that the male, abusive voice may represent her repeated experience of trauma and abuse from important males in her life, and that the supportive, defending female voice may represent herself. It was as if unresolved traumas from the past were playing themselves out in a drama, projected outside of herself onto an external screen — the 'voices'. Rather than being psychotic, meaningless, the very presence of these 'voices' may well point to where her conflict, her unfinished emotional and psychological business, lies. The fact that these voices began at a time when she felt overwhelmed in her life and the abuse was particularly intense may be no coincidence. As she was with me one day, she said that the voices were outside the window. The female voice said to the male voice, 'serves you f***ing right'. I asked her what she felt this meant. She quickly responded that it was about her being with me, that the female voice was telling the male voice that he was in trouble now that she was seeking help. She immediately knew the meaning of the words of each voice. She told me that this was the first time that any doctor had explored her 'voices' with her, although she had been attending the psychiatric services for four years. Once her psychiatrists became aware that she was hearing 'voices' four years ago, further exploration ceased. Schizophrenia was diagnosed, and medication commenced. Drugs were seen as the only appropriate ongoing treatment modality for her. Since then she has lived in a twilight zone; too sedated to function fully, sleeping until after noon each day, lethargic, with four stone weight gain in those four years. All of these problems are attributable to her medication. She is embarrassed about her weight gain, which her psychiatrists dismiss as an insignificant issue. It may be irrelevant to them, but not to her.

Three years ago, I worked with a young woman who taught me a great deal about so-called 'thought disorders', widely considered within medicine as pointing to brain abnormalities, as evidence of schizophrenia. When, as a GP, I first met Alison she was diagnosed as having schizophrenia. She had been attending a psychiatrist for six months. Heavily sedated by the major tranquillisers prescribed by the psychiatrist, Alison appeared out of touch with what was going on around her.

Alison did not trust her psychiatrist. She felt that all he did was prescribe medication without listening to her. Alison did not believe that drugs over a long-term basis would help sort out what she believed were psychological problems. I sensed that to make progress with Alison, I first had to create a trusting and respectful relationship with her. I set no goals for her. I concentrated on creating a relationship where Alison felt safe and not judged. Consequently, Alison opened up to me far more then to her psychiatrist. People will only open up when they feel safe enough to do so.

The psychiatrist repeatedly set targets for Alison. He insisted that she get up and go to bed at 'normal' hours. Each week he would set different goals, which he expected Alison to achieve. Alison felt there was no way she could achieve these targets. Anyway, these goals did not seem that important to her at the time. Trying to understand what was going on within her seemed more important to her than what time she got up in the morning. The psychiatrist became frustrated with her failure to comply with his recovery plan. Consequently, Alison learned to lie to the psychiatrist. She learned to tell the psychiatrist what he wanted to hear. By insisting that Alison follow his instructions, the psychiatrist inadvertently created a barrier between them. This gulf grew wider with each consultation.

Within weeks, I felt that Alison would make little progress while taking such powerful drugs. Her thinking and speech were fuzzy from the medication. Fortunately, after six months of medication and getting nowhere, her psychiatrist acceded to Alison's request to reduce her medication. Three weeks later, tension was running high. Alison was spending hours — sometimes twenty-four hours — without moving, as if in a trance. Her parents, who clearly loved her deeply, were very worried. Admission to a psychiatric hospital became a real possibility. By this time, Alison had finished with her psychiatrist. The psychiatrist's final recommendation to Alison was that she should now take Prozac. Alison and I wondered why, after six months taking major tranquillisers, the psychiatrist saw fit to recommend Prozac, a supposedly entirely different category of drug for a separate 'psychiatric illness'. She declined the offer of Prozac.

Alison was locked into her thought pattern and could find no way out. Her parents were prepared to do anything to improve her condition, including hospitalisation if that would help. But I felt that the local psychiatric hospital would have little to offer except more medication. Alison, her parents and I came to an agreement. Alison would attend me twice a week for a fortnight. We would then arrange hospital admission if Alison's condition remained unchanged.

The turning point came that week. Alison had repeatedly expressed a craving that someone would understand her current way of thinking. She had desperately wanted to discuss this with the psychiatrist, but she felt the psychiatrist did not want to know. Most psychiatrists view 'thought disorders' as crazy, purposeless thinking, confirming the diagnosis of schizophrenia. They do not see any point in exploring the person's thinking patterns. Satisfied that the person's thinking processes are different from 'normal' thinking, clear evidence of 'illness', they switch to a consideration of what drug treatment would be appropriate. I believe that this is a gross miscalculation.

That week, Alison and I devoted two hours to an exploration of her thought processes. When a thought came into her head, she felt a need to explore that thought to the nth degree. She would hold on to a thought in her mind until satisfied that she now understood every possible aspect of it. When other thoughts inevitably crept into her mind, as they naturally would, she tried to put them on hold until she had completed her work on the first thought. She then came back to the next new thought and repeated the whole process. She could stay locked in this thinking process for hours on end, dealing with each thought queued up in designation order, thinking each thought through.

Her explanation made sense to me. Alison's 'thought disorder' mirrored her current state of deep emotional insecurity and fear. She had dissociated herself from life. The emotional turmoil she had experienced in recent years had shaken the foundations of her existence. She had nothing to hold on to, no anchor in the storm. Holding on to a thought for hours on end gave her a sense of control and safety which was missing in almost every other aspect of her life. She was hanging on to her thoughts literally for dear life. For hours she would not talk to her family. To talk would risk losing her train of thought. Alison felt that by losing her train of thought, she might literally be lost. She feared that she might then never be able to think straight again — a terrifying possibility to be avoided at all costs.

Alison felt that the medication really contributed to her dilemma, closing down her mind and her thought processes, increasing the fog, preventing her from connecting with happy memories, which Alison felt might give her something to hold on to, numbing the spark and inspiration she sought to guide her through this time. She had experienced insecurity in the years preceding this crisis and this insecurity suddenly escalated. She held the worry inside her, precipitating its growth and eventual climax. The medication — one the newer so-called 'antipsychotics', which are regularly touted as not causing the major sedation caused by older drugs — blurred everything, reducing her ability to clear her head and to find inner peace. Alison felt that the major tranquillising drugs disabled her brain and her thinking processes.

Alison was thrilled that her thinking patterns made sense to me. I had connected with her way of thinking. This had a profound effect on her, and was a major turning point. Alison had found someone with whom she could discuss and explore her thinking processes. We discussed ways of letting go of this way of thinking. I did not pressurise Alison to change her way of thinking. I reassured her that her need to hold on to her thoughts would diminish as her sense of inner safety and security increased. Her parents reported a major improvement during subsequent weeks. The crisis now over, the possibility of hospital admission no longer arose.

In the ensuing months, Alison began to find her feet again. Step by step, at her own pace — not mine, or the psychiatrist's — she has reintegrated with her family and with life. Alison stopped coming to me over two years ago, when she felt ready to move on. Through annual Christmas cards, her parents have kept me up to date regarding Alison's progress. She is back in full-time work, living a fulfilling life. It probably helped that Alison had not been attending the psychiatric services long enough to have become institutionalised within the services, something which occurs much more frequently that most doctors realise.

My medical training taught me that so-called 'thought disorders', 'delusions', 'hallucinations', 'paranoia', 'highs' and other experiences had no meaning. I was taught to look for them only in the context of making a diagnosis; that there was no point in exploring them with people. I realised many years ago that my medical training got this wrong — that exploring what matters most to the client is extremely important. With Alison, the key to her recovery was being able to talk in great detail about her so-called 'thought disorder'. With others, people have had similar 'breakthroughs' by exploring their so-called 'psychotic' symptoms in detail with me.

I know of very few doctors who work in this way. I was therefore not surprised at the findings of a research paper published in the *British Medical Journal*.[10] The researchers looked at how willing doctors are to engage with people's so-called 'psychotic' symptoms. They analysed 32 consultations between psychiatrists and patients in London, diagnosed as having schizophrenia or schizo-affective disorder. They found that doctors have trouble talking to patients about psychotic symptoms. As was the case with Alison, the researchers found that patients actively attempted to talk about the content of their psychotic symptoms, such as hallucinations and delusions, and the distress associated with these symptoms. However, the study found that doctors tend to hesitate and avoid answering the patients' questions, indicating a reluctance to engage with these concerns. The researchers concluded that

proactively addressing patients' distress about their psychotic symptoms may lead to a more satisfactory outcome of the consultation itself and improve engagement of such patients with health care services.

The researchers comment that

no research has been published on how doctors engage with these patients with psychotic illness in consultations.

Thousands of research papers are published in medical journals every year. It is therefore truly remarkable that something as vital to the doctor–patient interaction as the way doctors engage with patients with psychotic symptoms, has been the subject of no research. How could this be? Could it be that, as is often the case in life for us all, doctors will only ask a question if they feel the question has value, and if they are ready to hear the answer?

Typically, when a new, interesting finding emerges from medical research — such as the finding in the above study that patients may benefit from fully exploring their psychotic symptoms with their psychiatrist — other researchers take up on the thread, and explore this findings further. Over the years, I have noticed one exception to this pattern. Research which runs counter to current medical beliefs tends not to be explored and developed to the same degree as research findings which are compatible with current medical beliefs. If the medical profession is not comfortable with the answer, it won't ask the question. Research likely to be embarrassing to the medical profession, or fundamentally challenging to the beliefs and practices of the medical profession, is less likely to be carried out or find its way into prestigious medical journals. And the findings of the above research are potentially embarrassing for doctors. If it were established that 'merely' listening to people in this manner could improve outcomes of schizophrenia, this begs the question — why has it taken the medical profession so long to realise this?

While the tide within psychiatry flows firmly with the view that psychotic symptoms have no meaning, some psychiatrists in other countries hold a different view. There are a few psychiatrists in Britain whose concerns regarding mental health care are similar to mine. Some of these psychiatrists are part of the Critical Psychiatry Network. Dr Duncan Double, one such psychiatrist, has expressed his concerns in a paper entitled 'The Limitations of Psychiatry':

> Much of the expansion of psychiatry in the past few decades has been based on a biological model that encourages drug treatment to be seen as a panacea for multiple problems. Psychiatrist Dr Duncan Double is sceptical of this approach

and suggests that psychiatry should temper and complement a biological view with psychological and social understanding, thus recognising the uncertainties of clinical practice.[11]

Pat Bracken and Phil Thomas are both psychiatrists. Working in Bradford, both have been actively involved in the Critical Psychiatry Network. In 2001, they published a paper entitled 'Post-psychiatry: a new direction in mental health'.[12] They envisage a new era in mental health care, where the 'voices of service users and survivors should now be centre stage'. The use of the term 'survivor' [of the mental health system] by these two psychiatrists is interesting. As a general rule, the term 'survivor' refers to a person who has survived something dangerous, something threatening to their being, perhaps to their existence. Many mental health service users who have emerged from their distress refer to themselves as 'survivors', and many service user groups similar use the term 'survivor' in this context. While in part this term may be used to convey having survived the deep distress previously experienced, it is also frequently used in the context of having survived the mental health system itself. That many service users have experienced the mental health system as something to be survived is alarming.

On occasion, people under the care of other areas within the health services may refer to having 'survived' the services, referring to the difficult aspects of their experiences such as certain tests, procedures and treatment. However, the term 'survivor' is used far more by users of the mental health services than within any other area of health care. Rarely do ex-patients refer to them self as survivors of the cardiac, surgical, or respiratory health care services, for example. In contrast, regarding the mental health services, the term is frequently used with a vehemence and passion which illustrates the degree to which many service users have experienced mental health services as something to have 'survived'. Many people attending the services on an ongoing basis experience it as quite a challenge to survive within the services.

I fully agree with the two psychiatrists mentioned above, that the voices, views and experiences of service users and survivors should now become centre stage. They can offer a unique, valuable perspective, one largely ignored to date — insights and perspectives based on their own personal and collective experience of their distress and of the services, which are designed predominantly by non-service users.

Peter Chadwick was once himself diagnosed as having schizophrenia. He now lectures in psychology at Birkbeck College, the Open University and the City Literary Institute. In common with many service users and survivors, he has many interesting views and insights:

> A profession which focuses so heavily on the dysfunctions and limitations of schizoid, schizotypal, and schizophrenic people can hardly be producing research findings which give an accurate and adequate description of the various client groups and this is a serious impediment to interaction with service users at an individual level. Deficit-obsessed research can only produce theories and attitudes which are disrespectful of clients and are also likely to induce behaviour in clinicians such that service users are not properly listened to, not believed, not fairly assessed, are likely treated as inadequate and are also *expected* not to be able to become independent and competent individuals in managing life's tasks (p. xii–xiii, preface).

> It is time to reassess our attitudes to psychosis-prone people and to start seeing them as total human beings with dignity and with capacities of choice and discernment rather than as malfunctioning organic entities to be plied with pills and bus passes.[13]

Dr Douglas Turkington is a British psychiatrist. In an interview with *Openmind*, he expressed views very similar to my own:

The medical model said that patients' experiences had no meaning, but I thought they were full of meaning. I had to rip up my old training. I have realised that even the most 'insane' patient can make a recovery.[14]

The interviewer comments that Douglas Turkington believes that:

past experiences, not biology, lie behind many of his patients' distress; he is pushing for a seismic shift in how psychiatrists interact with their patients. And with an emphasis on the psychological rather than the physiological, Turkington is urging for an appraisal of medication; 'medication does not make a person's beliefs go away. It just submerges them'.

Dr Douglas Turkington's comment that 'I had to rip up my old training' illustrates the enormous challenge doctors face when, as I did, they come to realise the enormous deficiencies in our medical training regarding mental health. Doctors are human. Doctors are prone to the same insecurities, vulnerabilities, self-interest, biases, limited vision, external influences, defence mechanisms and wishful thinking which can occur in any person, in any area of life. This point came forcefully home to me five years ago. I had been asked to give a three-hour talk with recently qualified doctors. During this talk, I expressed my concerns about mental health care, and about what I saw as major inadequacies in the training these young doctors had experienced. At the end of the talk, most of these young doctors were visibly unsettled. Never before had their absolute faith in the medical system been questioned in such a manner. After the meeting, one doctor wryly commented 'Great! Now we don't know who we are!'

This apparently casual comment helped me to see the role played by the human aspects of doctors in maintaining the status quo within mental health. Their unquestioning, absolute belief in the medical approach to mental health problems had been questioned, and this was a deeply disturbing experience for them. A brief review of history illustrates how tenaciously we human beings tend to hold on to our belief systems — religious, political, social, and other belief systems — and how we frequently seek not only to defend our belief systems, but to impose them on others. Psychiatrists, and to a lesser extent GPs, have an enormous investment in the current medical approach to mental health care; an investment which affects doctors' identity, status, their way of working, their financial and professional status and their belief systems. In reality, the biology of mental health problems is a belief system. It is a belief system because doctors have such faith in it, even though their patients never, ever have their supposed brain abnormality confirmed by biochemical or other tests.

Three characteristics of belief systems include:
• An investment in the continuation of the belief system by those who run and believe in the system
• A resistance from within the belief system to question the fundamentals of their belief system and to resist such questioning from others
• A resistance to the exploration and development of other beliefs, beliefs which might challenge or reduce the power and influence of the said belief system.

Any person can potentially feel paranoid from time to time. The more vulnerable we feel, or the more we need to protect ourselves, the greater our paranoia. Some people become extremely paranoid, describing elaborate scenarios of being watched or followed. Because this paranoia appears groundless to the onlooker, doctors state that the person's experience is inappropriate, makes no sense, has neither meaning nor purpose. It does not occur to them that, for the person having these experiences, the paranoia may indeed be appropriate, and have both meaning and purpose.

A client of mine recently related the following story of her uncle's experience. The mother of the fifty-five-year-old man had just died. Desperately lonely, he visited his GP every week with a wide variety of symptoms. The GP concluded that he was schizophrenic and put him on antipsychotic medication. The man quickly became very depressed, barely getting out of bed. This went on for months. Encouraged by his family, he consulted another doctor, who stopped his medication. The man soon returned to his old self. The medication sedated and depressed him so much that he could not function. What the man needed all along was human contact, to help him express and come to terms with the enormous grief he experienced when his mother died. Instead, his grief was medicalised, pathologised, and drugged, an all-too-common scenario.

The human thinking process is very dynamic. We frequently experience more than a hundred thoughts a minute. Medical science does not know how thoughts are created. The biochemical activity which underpins the human thinking process has not yet been identified. No scientific basis exists which justifies the presumption that thought patterns such as Alison's are caused by abnormal brain biochemistry. Yet modern psychiatry presumes that this is the case.

Bertram Karon PhD and Anmarie Widener of the Psychology Research department at Michigan State University wrote on schizophrenia in the *Ethical Human Sciences and Services* journal.[15] They discuss the key role emotions play in the creation of schizophrenic symptoms:

> Eugen Bleuler (who first coined the term 'schizophrenia' in 1911) assumed wrongly that schizophrenics have no feelings. In fact, schizophrenic persons feel very intensely,

although they may mask or even deny their feelings. The most basic affect is fear, actually terror. Human beings are not easily able to tolerate chronic terror. All of the symptoms of schizophrenia may be understood as manifestations of chronic terror and of defences against terror. Thus, withdrawal from people diminishes one's fear.

The severity of the thought disorder varies with the severity of the terror. Chronic terror tends to mask other feelings. Nonetheless, the schizophrenic experiences — continuously or intermittently — anger, hopelessness, loneliness and humiliation. 'Inappropriate' affect [mood, expression] is usually *socially* inappropriate, not inappropriate to the patient's inner experiences. We do not want to know about schizophrenia because we do not want to feel such intense terror. Given enough stress, any one of us may experience schizophrenic symptoms.

I recently met an old friend whom I had not seen for many years. As we reminisced, he spoke of Jim, a boy who grew up with us. My friend mentioned that Jim had been diagnosed as having schizophrenia in his twenties, and wondered about it as he pointed out that Jim had grown up in a happy home. But sometimes we do not know what is really going on in people's lives, within the four walls of home. I had spent more time in Jim's home than my friend, but I never felt comfortable there. The atmosphere in Jim's home was usually tense, and the tension escalated greatly whenever his father was at home. When Jim was about eight years old, I recall seeing his mother on several occasions physically shoving food down his throat, roaring at him to eat his food. This terrified me, though at least I was secure in that it wasn't my throat which was being attacked. As a child of ten, Jim was anxious and very insecure; he had several behavioural problems, including daily bedwetting and soiling, for which he was again shouted at.

His parents were pillars of the local community. Looking back now, I see that his parents were themselves highly stressed. They were doing their best, but they needed help and support which was not available to them. In his teenage years, Jim became very distressed, and was diagnosed as having schizophrenia. I do not think it was a coincidence that this boy who as a child was extremely insecure went on to be diagnosed as having schizophrenia. It is a pattern that I have seen, over and over again.

In January 2001, I attended a conference in Cork which marked the foundation of Cork Advocacy Network, a group seeking to give support and a voice to people diagnosed with 'mental illness'. One speaker, Paddy McGowan from Omagh, County Tyrone, spoke of how, after three years of contact with psychiatry and the mental health services, he told a psychiatric nurse about the voices he had been hearing for years, which to Paddy were as normal and familiar as the sun in the sky. The nurse sat up immediately, suddenly paying attention to his every word. The next day, his diagnosis was changed from post-traumatic stress (an appropriate 'diagnosis', precipitated by his experiences of working as a fireman during the Troubles in Northern Ireland, having to deal with the aftermath of shootings and bombings) to schizophrenia. His whole life changed as a consequence. That happened in 1984, when he was twenty-three years old. It did not matter to the psychiatrists that he had heard voices for the previous fourteen years, and that to him they seemed entirely normal. Had the doctors explored the voices with him, they would have discovered that the voices began two weeks after the death a much-loved relative, his grandmother. This surely pointed to a stress or grief reaction rather than evidence of a 'mental illness'.

Paddy was immediately put on major tranquillisers. He remained on medication for ten years. Eventually, he decided that he was getting nowhere on this medication. With the help of friends who were themselves familiar with the process of weaning oneself off medication, he gradually came off the drugs. His final prescription would have knocked out a horse: Largactil, a major tranquilliser, 1,600 mgs daily (300 mg is the highest recommended daily dose); Depixol, another major tranquilliser, injection of 80 mgs weekly; Prothiaden, an antidepressant with sedative side-effects, 150 mgs twice daily (twice the highest recommended daily dose of 150 mgs). Ironically, the only things not tranquillised by this concoction of medication were the voices for which he was put on this medication in the first place.

Coming off the drugs in 1994 was a major struggle for Paddy, but with help and support he got through it. He hasn't looked back since. Apart from the group of people who helped him to come off the medication, Paddy did not tell anyone he was coming off the drugs. Over the years, he had learnt that if he did tell people (including the psychiatrists) they would insist that he continue with his medication. For three years, Paddy found himself in a bizarre situation: he was off all medication, but everyone around him thought he was continuing on the drugs as usual. Paddy's family and friends soon noticed big changes in him. They would often say that Paddy was 'himself' again. They marvelled at the wonders of modern medicine and in particular Paddy's medication, which was obviously now working effectively. Everyone was talking about the miraculous improvement in Paddy's condition. Paddy described this as an 'internal prison'; he wanted to tell everyone he was off medication and doing very well without drugs. But he felt that he could not tell anyone, for fear of being persuaded (or forced) to go back on his medication.

Paddy McGowan is writing his own book about his life and experiences. A central figure within the Irish Advocacy Network, Paddy McGowan has spoken at many conferences about his experiences. He is currently involved in seeking reform of mental health services in Britain and Ireland.

In November 2003, I spoke at a conference organised by Phil Barker. A Scotsman, a professor of psychiatric nursing, Phil Barker is in my opinion a man of vision, common sense, compassion and courage. He is the creator of the Tidal Model, a new vision for psychiatric nursing. At this conference, I had another opportunity to hear Paddy MacGowan speak. Among other things, Paddy spoke of the smoke-room in the psychiatric hospital. This stuck a chord with me, because many patients have described the hospital smoke-room as the place of greatest learning within the psychiatric hospital. Paddy told of how, in the smoke-room, he learned how to be a 'good' psychiatric patient, how to survive within the system that is psychiatry. From people more experienced at being 'patients' than he, Paddy learned what the doctors wanted to hear.

Based on what he learned, Paddy created his own plan — to tell the doctors what they wanted to hear, to behave in ways which the doctors would interpret as signs of improvement. In the smoke-room Paddy learned that, as far as the staff are concerned, the right answer to the question 'are you hearing voices?' is 'no, I haven't heard voices for days now'. As a way of demonstrating to the staff that he was 'improving', every morning Paddy would fill a large jug with water and water the plants on the ward. The staff was most impressed, seeing this as a major step forward. Soon, the psychiatrists decided that Paddy was clearly on the road to recovery, and discharged him. By behaving in the way which he felt would be interpreted positively by the staff, Paddy achieved his own goal — discharge from the hospital. During his talk in November 2003, Paddy commented that perhaps it was just as well that the staff didn't realise what he had realised the first day he watered the plants — that the plants were artificial.

A man called Peter began attending me recently, having read the Irish edition of this book. He felt that my approach to mental health might offer him a different perspective from the one he had repeatedly experienced from doctors. Twenty-five years ago, he was diagnosed as having schizophrenia. At the time, he faced difficult examinations and couldn't cope with the strain. He has extensive experience of the psychiatric system. He had been on medication for the past twenty-five years. He told me he had learned to play the game, to be a 'good' patient, by doing what he was asked to do. He describes his experience of how psychiatrists and nurses he encountered in hospitals kept their distance from the patients, handing out medication as if 'at the end of a forty-foot pole'. He told me that the psychiatric system 'closes you down, giving no springboard towards recovery and reintegration into society'. That was his experience of the psychiatric system.

A common belief among psychiatrists is that schizophrenia is a genetically inherited disorder. Psychiatrists Dr Conall Larkin and Abbie Lane expressed this belief:

> The most solid fact in terms of the cause of schizophrenia
> is that genetic factors play a role.[16]

Having stated this 'solid fact', the authors seem to contradict this assertion in their very next sentence:

> However, no clear pattern of (genetic) transmission has
> been identified.

A similar view was expressed in the *Lancet* medical journal in 2003:

> Schizophrenia is highly heritable, but the genes remain
> elusive.[17]

Given that the genes remain elusive, and no clear pattern of inheritance has been identified, common sense might suggest that it is premature to conclude that schizophrenia is 'highly heritable'.

In spite of decades of research, there is as yet no reliable evidence linking schizophrenia to genetic abnormalities. Whether such evidence emerges in the future remains to be seen. There is an increased incidence of schizophrenia within families of those who have been diagnosed as having schizophrenia, but the increased incidence is not nearly as significant as it is for the majority on known, genetic problems. Only eleven per cent of people diagnosed as having schizophrenia have a parent with a similar diagnosis. This may be due to genetic factors, environmental factors or a combination of both. Prematurely, psychiatry largely presumes that genetic factors are the key, overriding issue within families.

Psychiatrists frequently point to twin and adoption studies as evidence of the validity of genetic claims for schizophrenia. These studies look at issues such as whether twins have an increased incidence of schizophrenia, and whether children or a twin, from families where members have been diagnosed as having schizophrenia, who are adopted and grow up apart from their family of origin, have an increased incidence of schizophrenia compared to the general population. American psychiatrist Dr Peter Breggin has examined twin and adoption studies in detail. In *Toxic Psychiatry* he outlines that, rather than finding a genetic link to schizophrenia, twin studies actually point to environmental causes:

> There is simply no evidence in the most highly touted studies for a genetic factor in schizophrenia. It discredits psychiatry that these studies have been used to prove the opposite of what they really show and that the public has been consciously propagandised with misleading information.[18]

In his book *The Gene Illusion*, US clinical psychologist Jay Joseph questions medical presumptions of genetic transmission of so-called 'psychiatric illnesses'. Joseph presents a detailed analysis of the genetic claims regarding schizophrenia, including adoption and twin studies. He maintains that adoption studies are unreliable due to many factors including selection bias, unsound research methodology and bias:

> In conclusion, the results from family, twin and adoption studies do not support the position that genes influence the appearance of a set of behaviours given the name 'schizophrenia'.[19]

As is the case with hypothesised biological causes, there is a bottom line regarding the much-claimed genetic link to schizophrenia. Unlike known genetic conditions such as cystic fibrosis, Down's syndrome, haemophilia and other conditions where genes have been precisely identified and are routinely tested for in the diagnostic process regarding these conditions, no gene has been identified as causing — or playing a role in causing — schizophrenia, or any other so-called 'psychiatric illness'. This is the current reality. Therefore, presuming — and claiming with authority and certainty — that 'psychiatric illnesses' are known to be genetic in origin is a highly unscientific practice. It is also misinforming the public. No one knows what will emerge from future research; it behoves us all to keep an open mind.

The natural history of mental health problems differs from known genetic illnesses in one important respect. Genetic illnesses do not tend to resolve, to get better. The medical management of genetic illnesses revolves around maintenance rather than cure. People do not become cured of genetic conditions such as Down's syndrome, cystic fibrosis, haemophilia and Huntington's chorea. Where treatments have been developed, they help to manage the condition, sometimes quite effectively. But the condition itself rarely if ever resolves. To date, cure is not an option.

In contrast, one-third of people diagnosed as having

schizophrenia (and up to two-thirds in underdeveloped countries) make a full recovery. Contrary to the prevailing view, many people do fully recover from manic depression. Up to fifty per cent of people diagnosed as having depression will recover on a placebo, and counselling has in many studies been found to be as effective as antidepressants. To even suggest that a genetically known illness — or a known biochemical illness such as diabetes, with which mental health problems are frequently compared by doctors — might be cured with either a placebo or counselling, would be laughable. These realities raise further doubts regarding the current medical belief that mental health problems have a strong genetic component.

While some people who are diagnosed as having schizophrenia do have children, the pattern of severe withdrawal and social avoidance results in a high proportion of people so diagnosed not entering relationships and not having children. Therefore, if schizophrenia were a genetic condition, one might reasonably expect that the incidence of schizophrenia would for decades have been steadily decreasing, since as a group, having children is now nearly as common as in the general population. No such steady decline has been occurring.

Drugs have been the medical profession's treatment of choice for schizophrenia since the 1950s. Yet according to the scientific literature, the recovery rates from schizophrenia remain as they were prior to the introduction of medication. In recent years, much has been made of the effectiveness and safety of newer drugs for schizophrenia. The media have picked up on the medical profession's enthusiasm for the newer antipsychotic drugs. For example, a report in *The Times* on 6 September 2001 described the newer medications used in the treatment of schizophrenia as targeting the underlying problem with far greater precision and causing far fewer problematic adverse effects. This report described how these drugs were generally believed to be a major advance on previous treatments.

However, such conclusions may be premature. According to a major analysis of 52 research trials, involving over 12,500 patients, published in the *British Medical Journal:*

> There is no clear evidence that new antipsychotic drugs are any more effective or better tolerated than conventional drugs for patients with schizophrenia.[20]

Doctors still do not understand the mechanism of action of so-called antipsychotic drugs. Most medical researchers believe that schizophrenia drugs work by changing the brain's chemistry in a beneficial way. The human brain is perhaps the most complex structure on this planet. There are billions of brain cells with an infinite number of possible interactions between them. Doctors do not understand the brain and how it functions. Yet most psychiatrists routinely prescribe these powerful drugs to their fellow human beings, not uncommonly for a lifetime.

The recovery rate from schizophrenia, one third in the western world, up to double that in underdeveloped countries where medication is used a great deal less, does not support the idea of medication balancing a lifelong chemical imbalance. In his book, Richard Godsen PhD asks valid questions regarding the presumed biological causation of schizophrenia:

> The most influential biological theories assume that schizophrenic symptoms are caused by an imbalance of brain chemistry. Remarkably, at least to some non-medical observers, the dominance of this theory is not the result of some laboratory work directly linking schizophrenic symptoms with a chemical imbalance. Rather it is derived from observations that drug treatment appears to blunt some of the outward display of the symptoms. As a result, it has been deduced that the cause of the symptoms is a shortage

of the chemicals contained in the medication. This reasoning is, to say the least, not very sound. It could just as easily be argued that a person who counters shyness by drinking alcohol apparently has a shortage of alcohol in the brain.[21]

The drugs most commonly prescribed for schizophrenia are the major tranquillisers, also known as antipsychotic drugs. Increasingly, psychiatrists favour the term 'antipsychotic' in preference to 'major tranquillisers'. The reasons for this shift are worth looking at. These drugs certainly are major tranquillisers. They have a far stronger sedative effect than the better known 'minor tranquillisers' such as Valium. But 'antipsychotic' conveys the impression that these drugs have a specific antipsychotic action, just as the word 'antidepressants' incorrectly suggests a specific antidepressant action. Describing these drugs as 'antipsychotic' conveys a false impression of precision in their mode of action. This portrays modern psychiatric practice as a scientific speciality. But these major tranquillisers are not antipsychotics. They are blunt instruments which induce sedation in most people, whether or not they have been diagnosed as schizophrenic. Indeed, they are used in all sorts of situations to induce sedation, such as in nursing homes, prisons, and some institutions charged with the care of children. This fact alone raises serious questions regarding the supposed specificity of 'antipsychotic' medication for 'mental illness'. Bertram Karon PhD and Anmarie Widener refer to this issue in their aforementioned article:

> It was a public relations coup to relabel major tranquillisers as 'antipsychotic medication', implying that they are as specific and as effective for psychosis as vitamin C is for scurvy. Unfortunately, there is no specific 'antipsychotic' medication in that sense.

According to psychiatrists, antipsychotic drugs are much better at suppressing symptoms such as agitation and restlessness than at surmounting the so-called 'negative' symptoms of schizophrenia: withdrawal or passivity, for example. But is this not disconcerting? Does this not suggest that these drugs act as major tranquillisers, tranquillising the more active symptoms whilst having little or no effect on the 'negative' symptoms? There is evidence that these drugs do not actually reduce the symptoms — such as delusions, hallucinations, paranoia — for which they are prescribed; that in many cases, the now sedated person becomes indifferent to the symptoms.

Many of the people I have worked with over the years were taking major tranquillisers when they began working with me in therapy. I would regularly notice certain patterns in people taking these drugs; sedation, sleepiness, forgetfulness, sometimes speech slightly slurred and slowed, decreased ability to think and feel, for example. In my experience, this occurs with the newer as well as the older drugs. On many occasions, as I reflected on the person sitting in front of me, it has struck me that these features are not unlike the features one would observe in a person who has had a few drinks. If this is the effect of these drugs on people when they are with me, is it not possible that these effects are interfering on a daily basis with the person's ability to function, to think, to recover? I can see the logic of short-term use of these drugs. The logic of the current widespread long-term use is another matter altogether.

In 1999, psychiatrist Dr Tom McMonagle wrote an article on the treatment of schizophrenia. He candidly expressed his concern about the effectiveness of medical interventions in schizophrenia. The medical approach to schizophrenia is similar in all developed countries, so his concerns apply to all modern, developed countries:

Between 1950 and 1998, over 2,000 randomised controlled trials have taken place of interventions for schizophrenia.

These were surveyed by Adams at the Cochrane Schizophrenia Group in 1998 and his results must cause us to have reservations about the quality of data available for supporting clinical decisions. Nor is it correct to assume that the higher quality trials are necessarily the more recent ones. The combination of low numbers, massive drop-out rates, unrepresentative patients and short duration — the studies lasted an average of six weeks — make most of the trials irrelevant to everyday clinical practice.[22]

It is worrying that drug treatments prescribed continuously for many years to millions of people worldwide have been tested in clinical trials only lasting an average of six weeks. Common sense suggests that six weeks is nowhere near long enough to assess the effectiveness and side-effect profile of powerful mood-altering drugs. Perhaps common sense is less common in medicine than it ought to be. A 1978 study in *International Psychiatry* found that patients treated with placebo in hospital and no major tranquillisers on follow-up showed greater clinical improvement and less pathology at follow-up, fewer hospitalisations and less overall functional disturbance in the community. Only 8 per cent of those on no medication were re-admitted, while between 43 and 73 per cent of those who received major tranquillisers were re-hospitalised.

Dr Trevor Turner is a consultant psychiatrist at Homerton Hospital, London. He is a strong advocate of the use of antipsychotic drugs in schizophrenia. But in the Summer 1998 edition of *Community Mental Health* he conceded that these drugs work principally by sedating the patient:

Sedation, rather than any genuine antipsychotic effect, is often the main role of standard antipsychotics.

An eighteen-year-old told me of his experience of taking a newer major tranquilliser, olanzepine (Zyprexa), for his 'schizophrenia'. He was repeatedly falling asleep in school and was unable to focus on schoolwork. He could not concentrate and his speech was slurred. He was totally unable to retain information, having to read schoolwork over and over, and then taking in only a fraction of what he was reading. Last year a woman who had been on a major tranquilliser several years previously, recounted how 'out of it' she was while on this drug. On one occasion, she looked at her watch. She knew it looked familiar, but she could not figure out what it was, or what it was for.

Whatever the truth about creating a physical dependency to major tranquillisers, doctors fail to appreciate the very real possibility of creating a psychological dependence on major tranquillisers by prescribing them over long periods of time. We all know that it is not a good idea for people to take alcohol and benzodiazepine tranquillisers in this way over long periods of time. Common sense would suggest that repeatedly giving major tranquillisers which create sedation and indifference to people who experience a great deal of anxiety and fear may not be such a good idea. The person may become psychologically dependent on the substance for relief of their symptoms. Over time, this does little to build up the person's sense of confidence, self-reliance, self-determination, empowerment, self-belief and their sense that they can survive in this world and shape their own destiny.

In 1998 Schizophrenia Ireland, a national schizophrenia association, produced a leaflet which was widely distributed. The leaflet states that this support group 'seeks to provide accurate, factual information about schizophrenia'. But since the medical profession has little accurate, factual information about the nature of schizophrenia, in reality the leaflet reflects current medical opinion rather than established facts. The leaflet emphatically states that 'schizophrenia is *not* caused by pressures within the family'. No evidence exists to prove this.

Psychiatry is not even close to establishing what causes schizophrenia. Yet most psychiatrists presume that whatever may be causing this condition, it is not pressures within the family.

There is a large body of evidence that factors within the family may play a part in creating and maintaining schizophrenia. British psychologist Lucy Johnstone summarised this research:

certain themes in family relationships have consistently emerged over several decades from a variety of therapeutic orientations. These are:

- extreme difficulty in separating and achieving independence
- blurred boundaries in relationships
- fundamental confusions about identity
- confused and contradictory family communications
- emotional and physical/sexual intrusiveness
- difficulty in dealing with anger and sexuality
- severe marital disharmony
- social isolation.[23]

I repeatedly see these themes in the many people I have worked with who have been diagnosed as having schizophrenia.

It is sometimes implied that, if family stresses and pressures do in part contribute to the distress that becomes diagnosed as schizophrenia, then parents are to blame. I do not concur with this view. I believe that the vast majority of parents do their level best for their children. However, many parents are themselves struggling with major emotional, psychological, social and relationship issues, many of which can greatly interfere with a person's parenting capacity. The blame, and the ensuing guilt and shame, is a major reason why parents who might otherwise be very open to such ideas, are fearful of coming forward and seeking help with such issues.

No brain malfunctions or genetic causes have been demonstrated in schizophrenia. Prematurely, psychiatrists and GPs concluded that schizophrenia is caused by some as-yet-undiscovered brain abnormality. Doctors treat people, on the presumption that they are right, with potent drugs which can have major side-effects. Doctors have long since concluded that it is not worth researching other possible causes of schizophrenia, such as relationship conflicts, emotional, psychological, social and relationship issues. My experience in dealing with people who have been labelled as schizophrenic is that family pressures and disharmony can sometimes play a part in triggering or exacerbating schizophrenia.

In a research paper, Al Siebert PhD concluded that the brain disease hypothesis for schizophrenia is actually refuted by all the evidence. He points out that most people with schizophrenia do not progressively deteriorate. They tend to improve over time, which would not occur if brain chemical abnormality were present. He also points out that:

> Psychotherapy, without medications, has led even the most severely disturbed individuals with schizophrenia to full recovery and beyond.[24]

Psychotherapy and counselling are frequently dismissed, from within and outside the medical profession, as just 'talk therapy'. It is often stated that talk therapy is just that — talk — and how could mere 'talking' solve 'mental illnesses'? My view is that psychotherapy involves talk, yes, but a great deal more. I see myself as a 'journeyman' who becomes part of the person's life, for as long as the person deems appropriate. Sometimes therapy focuses on building the person's self-esteem, hearing their story, empathy, believing in the person when they can't believe in themselves, releasing pent-up emotions, among many other things. Sometimes, therapy will involve practical, down-to-earth collaboration with the person, assisting them to deal with the issues in their lives. Exploring the benefits of therapy in his book *Prozac Backlash,* US psychiatrist Dr Joseph Glenmullen refers to the importance of

> hands-on, pragmatic help . . . a willingness to get into the nitty-gritty details with patients is an important part of collaborative therapy.[25]

Many of the features which people commonly believe to be due to chronic mental illness are in fact caused by the treatment these people receive from the medical profession. Take tardive dyskinesia for example. This devastating complication of psychiatric drug treatment causes repetitive involuntary movements which are slow and writhing in a snakelike fashion. The face is most commonly involved, with repetitive sucking or chewing movements, lip movements, tongue movements in and out of the mouth, grimacing and other facial movements. Fidgeting hands, tapping feet and other bizarre involuntary body movements may also occur.

This condition can be extremely distressing to the sufferer, who knows these movements are occurring but cannot stop them. For the person who develops tardive dyskinesia there is no escape, no respite. Any person who is prescribed a major tranquilliser for more than four to six months may end up with this dreadful condition. Typically, once these drugs are prescribed for a person diagnosed as having 'schizophrenia', they are prescribed for many years, often for life.

Using figures made available from psychiatry and the drug industry, Dr Peter Breggin estimated that by 1980, between fifteen and thirty million people worldwide had developed tardive dyskinesia as a result of their medication. It is reasonable to assume that there are a great many more cases now than in 1980, because millions more have been put on these drugs during the intervening years. Research suggests that the risk of developing tardive dyskinesia is 5 per cent after one year of treatment, rising to over 40 per cent after five years. In my experience, patients prescribed these drugs are rarely informed that they are at risk of developing a serious, irreversible, drug-induced neurological disorder.

These figures clearly represent a worldwide epidemic of a devastating and an irreversible health problem. The medical profession is usually quick to inform the public at length and in great detail about health problems that reach epidemic proportions. Perhaps psychiatry's reluctance to publicise the tardive dyskinesia epidemic is because psychiatry itself created it.

Psychiatrists are quick to point out that adverse effects such as tardive dyskinesia occur mainly with the older group of drugs, that this problem is much less likely with newer medications. I am not convinced. The tendency to underestimate the adverse effect potential of new drugs is a well-established pattern in medicine. A legal case in the USA should serve as a warning for doctors and the public alike. In May 2000, a Philadelphia court awarded $6.7 million to a patient who had developed tardive dyskinesia caused by Risperdal, a new antipsychotic drug. Could this be just the tip of the iceberg?

A year ago, I was contacted by a man in his thirties. He told me that he had tardive dyskinesia, and he wanted a second opinion. He had severe, disabling tardive dyskinesia. He entered my surgery holding the back of his head with one hand, his neck with the other. He had to hold his head like this all the time, to prevent his head from rolling around and jerking violently and uncontrollably. He had never been prescribed the older antipsychotic drugs. Risperdal, a newer antipsychotic drug, was the only drug this man had been prescribed. His symptoms began within 6–8 months of commencing the drug, and continued when it was stopped, as is usually the case with tardive dyskinesia. Since then, I have become aware of several other instances of this condition attributed to newer, major tranquilliser drugs. There is no cure for this condition.

Thioridazine (trade name Melleril, Melzine, Thiozine) is a major tranquilliser which has been widely prescribed internationally for well over thirty years. Recently, this drug was associated with a rare but potentially serious heart complications. In January 2001, doctors were notified that the prescribing of thioridazine was to be restricted to schizophrenia only, and only then as a second-line treatment under the supervision of a consultant psychiatrist. In future, patients for whom this drug is prescribed are required to have regular heart checks and blood tests. Why did it take over thirty years to discover this serious adverse effect? Since coming on the market, thioridazine has been widely used in the treatment of schizophrenia, agitation, and anxiety. How many people suffered this serious adverse effect over the years? How many people may have died as a result? We will never know.

Dutch psychiatrist Jan Foudraine gradually moved away from the idea that the so-called 'psychotic' person was suffering from a 'disease'. In his book *Not Made of Wood* he outlines the tendency amongst psychiatrists to believe that their theories are proven facts, and to treat people on this basis:

> I discovered that this idea — that psychotic people are suffering from a 'disease' — was a delusion entertained by a lot of psychiatrists and very much harder to tackle than the 'fantasies' of people I met in the psychiatric institutions.[26]

Admission to a safe haven has its place. Sometimes people feel so overwhelmed that they need a safe, temporary retreat from the world. Such safe havens were created in the 18th century by Phillipe Pinel and other practitioners of 'moral treatment'. Moral treatment involved treating patients with respect and dignity, without cruelty or humiliation. Work and social relationships were encouraged and fostered. Practitioners of moral treatment endeavoured to understand the patient as an individual, unique human being. Admission to a psychiatric hospital does not necessarily provide a safe haven. Many patients describe admission to a psychiatric hospital as the most terrifying experience of their lives. Psychiatric inpatient treatment is often cold and impersonal.

In recent years, there have been a few centres internationally which provided a safe haven based on principles akin to that of 'moral treatment'. Soteria House in California was one such centre, run by psychiatrist Loren Mosher. Results from Soteria House were impressive. Several carefully constructed research studies found that, for people who were going through their first schizophrenic breakdown, admission to Soteria House produced better outcomes compared to admission to a mental hospital. In one study, just eight per cent of patients during their stay at Soteria House received medication, whereas all of those admitted to hospital with similar experiences were treated with major tranquilliser medication. A two-year follow-up study found that people who were initially admitted to Soteria House received significantly less medications, needed to attend outpatient clinics less frequently, were more successful at living independently and maintaining employment than those admitted to psychiatric units. A separate group of Soteria patients, admitted with schizophrenia-type symptoms, were given no medications during the first six weeks. Just ten per cent of this group received medication at any stage, whereas all of the matched, similar group admitted to psychiatric units received medication. Recovery in these Soteria patients was significantly better than a matched, similar group of patients admitted to psychiatric units.

Soteria House was a success story run at a fraction of the cost of a psychiatric unit. The 'recovery-on-the-minimum-of-medication' philosophy ran contrary to the prevailing psychiatric reliance on medication, which sees medication as an essential, central pillar of treatment. Mainstream psychiatry did not want to know about this method of helping people in emotional turmoil. Funding Soteria House became a problem. The Californian Department of Mental Health refused to finance it. As Dr Breggin wrote in *Toxic Psychiatry* regarding Soteria House: 'we have a blueprint for easy-to-develop, effective programmes, if only they could get funded'.

Several cross-cultural studies carried out by the World Health Organisation over several decades have found that the outcome for people diagnosed as having schizophrenia is significantly better in developing countries that in the developed world. These studies went to great lengths to ensure that like was being compared to like. Outcomes for people with schizophrenia-type symptoms and experiences are approximately twice as good in underdeveloped countries compared to developed ones. This is a remarkable fact. One might reasonably expect that — in keeping with trends across a wide spectrum of medical conditions and specialties — the evidence would point in the opposite direction; that recovery rates from treated schizophrenia would be significantly greater in the developed world than in underdeveloped countries. Developing countries were found to have greater social support for patients and to put less emphasis on psychiatric treatment.

Dr Richard Warner is the Medical Director of the Mental Health Centre of Boulder University, Colorado. In his comprehensive book *Recovery from Schizophrenia*, he discusses the World Health Organisation schizophrenia studies in detail. According to Dr Warner:

> The general conclusion is unavoidable: schizophrenia in the Third World has a course and prognosis quite unlike the condition as we recognize it in the West. The progressive deterioration which Kraepelin considered central to his

definition of the disease is a rare event in non-industrial societies, except perhaps under the dehumanizing restrictions of a traditional asylum. The majority of Third World schizophrenic people achieve a favourable outcome. The more urbanized and industrialized the setting, the more malignant becomes the illness. Why should this be so?[27]

According to American medical journalist Robert Whitaker:
The World Health Organisation studies had demonstrated that the American belief that schizophrenics necessarily suffered from a biological brain disorder, and thus needed to be on drugs for life, wasn't true.[28]

Courtenay Harding, then a psychologist at the University of Colorado, reported in 1987 on long-term outcomes of people diagnosed as having chronic schizophrenia who were discharged from Vermont State Hospital in the late 1950s. Harding found that one-third had completely recovered. She also found that those who recovered all had one thing in common: they all had successfully weaned themselves off their medication. Harding concluded that the idea that people diagnosed as having schizophrenia needed life-long medication was a 'myth'.[29]

Regarding patients diagnosed with chronic, unremitting schizophrenia, researchers in Finland found that by actively involving the person and their family in every stage of treatment planning (termed the 'Open Dialogue' method), by providing support within the community, by putting less emphasis on medication, patients improved significantly. Within the Open Dialogue approach, all relevant issues are openly discussed from the beginning. Significant others in the person's life including the family, GP and when relevant, employers, are all involved in a collaborative approach to the problems being experienced by the person. What a contrast to the isolation, stigma, shame and hopelessness typically experienced by people diagnosed as having 'schizophrenia' and their families. In a study carried out between 1992 and 1997,[30] clients receiving this Open Dialogue method were hospitalised less frequently and used less medication; 35 per cent required medication compared to 100 per cent of the comparison group who received traditional psychiatric treatment. At the second year follow-up point of this study, 82 per cent had no, or only mild, psychotic symptoms, compared to 50 per cent in the comparison group. The Open Dialogue group had better employment status; only 23 per cent were receiving disability allowance compared to 57 per cent in the comparison group. The Open Dialogue group also had a far smaller relapse rate of 24 per cent, while the comparison group had a relapse rate of 71 per cent. Recent studies suggest that the Open Dialogue model has improved the outlook for people suffering from their first episode of psychosis, significantly reducing the rate of hospitalization, the rate or relapse, and the use of medication.[31]

Clearly, the time has come for a thorough independent review of how the major human distress experience we call 'schizophrenia' is seen and dealt with within modern, developed countries.

Major tranquilliser drugs can sometimes be helpful in a crisis situation. By sedating the person, they may give them some breathing space, a break from the intense emotional experience they are going through. They may calm a person to the point where carers may be able to get through to them. However, if these major tranquillisers continue to be prescribed for months or years after the crisis, as well as exposing people to their adverse effects, the resulting sedation may reduce the person's ability to work through the issues relating to their crisis. And contrary to the prevailing medical view, taking these drugs long-term increases the risk of people becoming psychologically dependent on the medication. Many people have told me of their experience of becoming addicted (their word) meaning that they came to believe they could not live without major tranquillisers.

Bipolar disorder (manic depression)

When considering possible causes of manic depression, the prevailing medical view again favours physical causes such as a brain biochemical imbalance or a genetic defect, despite the fact that no biochemical or genetic abnormality has been identified regarding what is called 'manic depression' or 'bipolar disorder'. Doctors base this judgement on the premise that there could not be any other explanation for the major swings of mood experienced by people who have been diagnosed as having manic depression. Given the apparent extremes of depression and elation sometimes experienced by those so diagnosed, the medical — and consequently the public — interpretation is that the mood swings could not possibly be caused by emotional or psychological issues. Yet research suggests that the onset of manic symptoms is preceded by stressful life events in more than two-thirds of cases.

The medical stance fails to take into account that there is at least one condition where people experience extremes of behaviour triggered by underlying emotional distress. People who suffer from eating disorders may swing between an abhorrence of food so strong they eat little or nothing (anorexia), and protracted periods of food bingeing where they consume huge amounts of food (bulimia), frequently followed by vomiting up the consumed food. In my opinion, emotional, psychological and relationship issues are the underlying cause of eating disorders. Sufferers always have desperately low self-esteem.

Just as the swings between anorexia and bulimia relate to underlying emotional issues, the theory that the mood swings in manic depression may originate from emotional and psychological issues is a plausible one. But the medical profession does not seem interested in this possibility. This theory does not fit into the medical view of how things should be, so it is discarded without proper evaluation. The prevailing medical view regarding manic depression could reasonably be described in similar terms to that outlined earlier in this chapter regarding schizophrenia:

> These features are so unusual that they must be caused by a physical defect in the brain. How could there possibly be any other explanation for such bizarre behaviour?

And as with schizophrenia, the medical profession erroneously presumes that the highs and lows of manic depression have no inherent meaning or appropriateness. This certainly does not concur with my experience of working with many people so diagnosed. A letter published by an American medical researcher in the *British Medical Journal* in 2003 illustrates the profound meaning within the writer's personal experience of a so-called 'psychotic', 'manic' episode. He wrote in response to Dr Mike Shooter's account of his depression (see Ch 3, p. 139)

> EDITOR—Mike Shooter's narrative is remarkable for the fact that as a patient he developed his own form of treatment. Implicit in his account is a recognition of the shortcomings of the medical model of mental illness.
>
> Advocates for mentally ill people seek the removal of stigma. They emphasise the role of biology in generating the experiences of madness. They hope that seeing mental conditions as brain disorders and not as reflections on the sufferer's personal make up will alleviate shame and societal disapproval. As one advocate put it, 'depression is something you have, not something you are'. But Shooter finds benefit in saying 'I have to challenge the assumptions I make.' This implies a third way of thinking about

depression and manic depression, not as something we are, not as something we have, but as something we do. This outlook deserves exploration. 'I have written elsewhere about being picked up by police late at night wandering the beach in my underwear thinking I was Elijah the prophet, looking for the coming of the Messiah. My sense of this incident, now nine years past, was that it was the most profound and meaningful healing experience imaginable; I had never felt more sane and purposeful.'

Sometimes mania has an importance that cannot be captured by medical paradigms that focus on brain disorders. Biological models remove self knowledge and moral agency from the picture. Let us enlarge our frames of reference for manic depression, so we can remove stigma not just from the diagnosis of mania but from the experiences themselves.[32]

So-called 'mania' is like a polar opposite to depression, hence the term 'bipolar'. 'Mania' can be an escape from enormous inner pain and depression into a fantasy world of elation. It can be a reaction to stress. But beneath the elation there often lies a deep sense of worthlessness, hurt and humiliation. While the term implies elation, many people who experience so-called 'mania' are aware at the time that they are very distressed, that all is not well though they may not admit this to themselves or others at the time.

Fred had been diagnosed as having manic depression years before our first meeting. In the early years of our doctor–patient relationship, I experienced him as quite difficult to be with. In subsequent years, we developed a deep trust and mutual respect. Fred's difficult, nit-picking persona masked a deeply vulnerable man. His bouts of mania and depression had more to do with deep-seated emotional distress than a 'mental illness'. A brief history of Fred's life story told by his son demonstrates how loneliness, emotional, psychological and relationship conflicts were key issues in Fred's manic depression:

As a small child I remember very vividly his bad moods and the silences that seemed to go on for days. It seemed as if our house was always filled with tension and I felt relieved when my father was away from home. It was as if I had two fathers — one of them was a kind, caring, loving father, the other man scared me when he woke me at night shouting at my mother. He sulked over the most trivial things, and many aspects of our family life revolved around keeping him in 'good humour' at all costs.

He was a strict disciplinarian and ruled our home with an iron hand. We all knew who was the boss in no uncertain terms! He made the decisions, no one else was consulted. It was as if he had an enormous need within himself to be in command. No one in my family dared to question him or go against his wishes. He could not handle any threats to his authority. He was ALWAYS right! It makes sense to me now that his chosen career was one where he was very much 'in charge'. In my adult life I can recall a few episodes when I questioned his authority. Although he always apologised to me afterwards, his response each time illustrates his determination to be the 'boss'.

Once he barred me from the family home, putting a chain on the door. Another time he struck me and on two occasions he demanded immediate payment of a long-term loan he had previously given me. With the possibility of such a response I didn't have the courage to challenge him too often! He was admitted to hospital on several occasions to be treated for depression. For the last twenty years of his life he was always on antidepressant medication in one form or another. While he did not like taking any medication, he particularly resented taking lithium. He believed that this drug masked his real self in

220

some way. As for us, as a family, we wanted him to take it because anything that would keep him calm and subdued was better than enduring his mood swings.

Looking back now I feel both angry and sad that the doctors who treated my father simply plied him with medication and never tried to understand why he was depressed. If the underlying cause of his depression had been explored with him, perhaps he could have emerged from its dark shadows. I recall on one occasion how he was discharged from the psychiatric hospital extremely 'doped' due to a combination of sedatives and antidepressants. He literally did not know what day of the week it was. Alarmed, I phoned his doctor who told me that my father was now senile and I would have to accept this. I assumed the doctor was right and that he knew what he was talking about. However, my father lived for five years after that incident and he never became senile up to the day he died. His confusion was entirely due to the drugs prescribed by the 'expert' doctor.

My father's family background was not a happy one. His parents did not communicate very well and his father sought consolation in alcohol. At night his mother and father sat in separate rooms. His mother entertained visitors in one room while his father was ignored and left sitting in another room. In a similar fashion, in his later years my father often confined himself to one room in the house; cut off from family life for hours on end with only television for company. His mother was obsessed with religion and spent most of her day praying in the church. She was rarely at home so a housekeeper assumed the mother's role. As he was considered to be a 'difficult child' my father was sent to school at a very young age. Being a small child, he may well have felt this as a form of rejection.

My father liked to travel and went to many exotic places,

always on his own. While he was away he was the life and soul of the tour-group. He was the centre of attention and everyone thought he was great fun. We dreaded his return as he invariably came back from these trips as high as the proverbial kite and had to readjust to mundane home life. I can see now that he had a great need within himself to be liked and accepted. These foreign holidays fulfilled this need, for a while at least. Sometimes he would wear flamboyant clothes. These made him stand out from the crowd, which was what he wanted, but they were a great source of embarrassment to me. He would often take to the bed for a few days and summon us by means of a bell to wait on him. This was another strategy to get attention.

When he was depressed he often said that he felt worthless and a burden to my mother and the family. He would often be full of remorse for his behaviour. At times he would dress in a shabby and unkempt manner, giving a visual message to the world as to how he felt about himself. My father was an unhappy man. He provided well for his wife and family, often having to make a little go a very long way. He tried to be the best father he could, given his own family background and the life experiences he had. Though he caused unhappiness to me, I realise now that he never set out to be a bad parent and I bear him no ill-will. My relationship with him has healed. My one regret is that during his lifetime he never had the opportunity to heal himself.

In her book *An Unquiet Mind*, psychiatrist Kay Redfield Jamison writes of her own experience of manic depression.[33] While lithium kept her on an even keel, reducing the extremes of depression and mania, she believes that psychotherapy heals. However, psychotherapy is rarely offered to people diagnosed as having bipolar disorder, either as an alternative treatment or in conjunction with medication. As in Fred's case, the vast majority of manic depression sufferers receive drug treatment only. Contrary to repeated medical pronouncements that lithium and other 'mood stabilisers' act by returning brain biochemistry to normal, the *Monthly Index of Medical Specialties (MIMS)*, the reference book Irish doctors refer to when they prescribe medication, 'the mechanism of action of lithium is not known', as mentioned earlier.

Doctors sometimes say that lithium is a naturally occurring substance, a salt, as a way of encouraging the acceptability of taking lithium. That lithium is a naturally occurring substance conveys little regarding its safety or appropriateness for human consumption. Many naturally occurring substances — lead, for example — are toxic to the body. Lithium is a naturally occurring substance in our world, but not within our bodies. Unlike minerals such as zinc, iron etc., lithium does not naturally occur within the human body. Unlike minerals and vitamins, the human body not does need a regular supply of lithium.

Publicly, most doctors convey the message that the effectiveness of lithium and other 'mood stabilising' substances is established beyond all doubt. Within medical journals however, some psychiatrists have some concerns about the effectiveness of these drugs. In 2003, a psychiatrist referred to earlier comments by British researchers that 'the real-world effectiveness of lithium treatment is therefore unclear'.[34] In a review of lithium effectiveness in 1997, British psychiatrist Joanna Moncrieff concluded the following regarding the use of lithium in the prevention of manic-depressive episodes:

> Over the past 25 years, the most uncontroversial indication for lithium has been in the prophylaxis (prevention) of bipolar disorder. Follow-up studies suggest that the natural history of bipolar disorder has not improved since the introduction of lithium, and patients who are taking lithium

appear to be little better than those who are not. Some authors have suggested that noncompliance and under-prescribing might explain these disappointing findings, but another explanation could be the ineffectiveness of the drug itself. Overall there appears to be little evidence that lithium is effective for three of its commonly recommended uses: treatment of acute mania, prophylaxis (prevention) of bipolar disorder and augmentation of treatment in resistant depression. In addition, naturalistic follow-up studies fail to reveal any beneficial effect of lithium on the course of bipolar disorder. It is known to be associated with various forms of harm. Its place in psychiatry needs discussion and re-evaluation.[35]

Two problems regarding lithium treatment which have apparently been underestimated by the medical profession for decades are (i) serious methological problems in many of the studies which in the early days of lithium treatment found the drug to be effective, and (ii) the development of symptoms of mania on cessation of the drug. As many as 50 per cent of patients who are abruptly withdrawn from lithium begin to experience symptoms of mania within four weeks. For decades, most doctors have interpreted this in a similar way to the apparent 'deterioration' which many people experience when stopping antidepressants; that this occurrence indicates a recurrence of the illness on stopping the drug, 'proving' both the presence of the illness in the first place and the effectiveness of the drug. However, some psychiatrists believe that such a high rate of acute mania within weeks of stopping lithium abruptly may have more to do with the inherent properties of lithium itself, just as some doctors are belatedly realising that many of the problems experienced by people who stop taking antidepressants relate to the drug rather than to the perceived 'illness'.

Reflecting on the people I have known who were diagnosed as having manic depression, I noticed that manic episodes typically followed a stressful period or event in their lives. Yet these people were not offered counselling or any other help by their doctors to cope with the stresses in their lives. Many psychiatrists dismiss the value of psychotherapy and counselling in the treatment of manic depression and in the treatment of 'mental illness' in general. A woman recently contacted me about her husband who had been treated with medication for manic depression for ten years by the local psychiatrist. She felt that her husband was getting nowhere, and that it might help him to talk to someone about his life and stresses. I agreed, and suggested that she seek out a good therapist in their area. However, when she mentioned to her psychiatrist that they wanted counselling for her husband, the psychiatrist would not hear of it. He was totally against this idea, and threatened to refuse to see him again if he went for counselling.

Virtually all of the people I have met who have been diagnosed as having manic depression share most of the following; low self-esteem; deep loneliness; major unhappiness and despair in their lives. I have repeatedly noticed that many people diagnosed as having manic depression exhibit patterns in their lives which contribute significantly to their so-called 'mental illness'. In my experience, becoming aware of their patterns and working towards balancing them can be a valuable addition to a person's treatment plan. The so-called 'high' can be triggered by feeling overwhelmed. Patterns in a person's life can contribute to becoming overwhelmed. One pattern I have frequently noticed in people diagnosed as bipolar is the inability to say 'no' to others, due mainly to their low self-esteem, their fear of what people might think if they assert themselves. Another recurring tendency is an inability — more accurately an intense fear of — expressing what they are really feeling, and asking for help and support in their lives. Such

225

people risk becoming very stressed and overwhelmed through repeated, excessive commitments they make to others. Consequently, there is little time in their life to take care of themselves, or to ensure that their own needs are being met, even the most basic needs of rest and relaxation. The feelings of stress and overwhelm can escalate into the state we call a 'high'. Such patterns tend to be deeply ingrained, and do not change easily. But I know through working with many people that such patterns can be changed, with patience, affirmation and support. In twenty years as a medical doctor, I have heard very few psychiatrists comment on the relevance of such patterns to people's so-called 'manic depression'.

A thirty-year old woman began attending me recently. To date we have met on six occasions. Four years ago, she was diagnosed as having 'bipolar disorder'. Since then, she has attended the psychiatric service regularly, having been admitted to hospital on three occasions. Medication has been the only treatment modality offered to her. The fact that her mental health problems began shortly after her father's death went unexplored by her psychiatrists. Regarding people diagnosed as having 'bipolar disorder', I frequently observe that in subtle ways, their lives are way out of balance. In this woman's case, she gives far more than she allows herself to receive. She takes care of others far more than she takes care of herself or lets others care for her. When 'well', she feels there is not enough time in the day to get everything done. She puts herself under great pressure to get a mountain of things done, ending up exhausted and becoming depressed. She is an extremely good listener to other people, but rarely tunes into her own needs or expresses her own needs to others. To date we have met six times over four months. One area I have focused on with her is the importance of taking care of herself, of not over-extending herself, of becoming more aware of her own needs, that she doesn't have to give two hundred per cent of herself to everything she does. Conservation of one's energy is important for us all, but particularly so with people who have the tendency to swing between 'highs' and 'lows'. It is early days in our work, so it is far too soon to come to any conclusions, though she feels that the past four months have been the most balanced she has had since being diagnosed as having 'bipolar disorder'.

Observing and tuning on to one's patterns can be helpful to people diagnosed as having manic depression in one further way. I have repeatedly observed a 'slippery slope' phenomenon in people so diagnosed. They begin to become overwhelmed — this is the start of the slippery slope — and they become increasingly anxious. Their sleep becomes disturbed; their eating suffers. As a reaction to reduce their sense of overwhelm, in a frantic attempt to climb back up the slippery slope, the speed of their thinking and actions increases.

Over the ensuing days or weeks, they continue to slip down the slippery slope. One thing feeds into another. Sleep remains disturbed, sometimes to the point where the person will sleep only a few hours at night, sometimes not at all. Like a train careering out of control, the human 'brakes' systems do not kick in. Inevitably, the sense of overwhelm grows larger and the person spirals more and more out of control. Something has to give. Either the person hits a 'wall', or the person — or those around the person acting on the person's behalf — call for medical help to stop the train careering further down the slippery slope. The 'brake' which doctors exert is typically major tranquillising medication, and possibly admission to hospital. Such situations are a good example of the benefit of medication, and the benefit of hospitalisation.

Once the careering human train is brought to a stop, what strategies does psychiatry employ to prevent further episodes in the future? The only preventative strategy offered is medication, so-called 'mood stabilisers' and major tranquillisers. These drugs do somewhat reduce the chances of a recurrence, and they have their place. But in my experience, working with a person's patterns is a valuable addition to medication treatment. This approach also offers a person increased hope of understanding their 'condition', and of ultimately mastering it, something which medication can never achieve.

One person currently attending me is on two medications following a hospital admission, an admission which was necessary as she had become quite agitated, distressed and 'high' in the face of stress in her life. Now out of hospital for six months, she is on a mood stabiliser and a major tranquilliser. As a consequence of these drugs, she is sleeping for twelve hours a day, barely able to get out of bed before one o'clock in the afternoon. She has gained three stone in weight. She is keen to get her life back on track, but the sedating effect of her medication is now slowing her progress. Her psychiatrists do not seem to see this as the major issue it is for her. They see her for five minutes every two months, check her mood, and leave her medication unchanged. This woman's case is one which illustrates the importance of seeing recovery in far broader terms than just the suppression of symptoms, which can have the unwanted — and often unrecognised — effect of suppressing the person also. Of course, medication should not be stopped suddenly or prematurely. But I believe it behoves us doctors to consider gradually reducing medication while working in collaboration with the person, identifying issues which the person needs to deal with, and working with the person as they strive to get their life back on track.

While bipolar disorder is portrayed as a life-long condition to be managed rather than recovered from, people can and do make a full recovery. As discussed elsewhere regarding other mental 'illnesses', doctors should be paying a great deal more attention to the people who do recover fully. These people may offer a rich, fertile ground of information regarding recovery which can be harvested, collected and used to formulate realistic recovery plans for others. Unfortunately, the medical profession displays little interest in such an approach.

I have been in contact with Gayle for over three years. Now in her late forties, for over twenty years Gayle has been diagnosed as having manic depression. In recent years, she set about creating her own recovery path. Gayle did not attend me as a client. She described the Irish edition of my book published in 2001 as a great support as she sculpted her recovery journey.

Having been on antidepressants and lithium for virtually twenty years, over four years ago Gayle gradually weaned herself off her medication over a two-year period. Her main support during this time came through her husband, with whom she has a loving, supportive relationship. Gayle has not felt depressed for over four years, and has now been off all medication for over two years. In Autumn 2003, Gayle attended her psychiatrist, whom she had not attended for many years. Gayle visited the psychiatrist to make the point to the doctor that she was now very well mentally without medication, better than she had been for twenty years.

When greeted with such a story of recovery, hope and personal achievement, one might expect that the psychiatrist would be very pleased to see his 'ex-patient' doing so well. Certainly, this might be how less 'educated' people might respond on hearing Gayle's story. Not so. The doctor expressed no sense of pleasure at Gayle's mental well-being, and did not even explore it with her. Gayle told the psychiatrist that my book had been a major help in her journey of recovery. The psychiatrist dismissed this, replying that she knew of me and had no time for anything I said or believed in. The psychiatrist cautioned Gayle that one can never know what is around the corner. Gayle then asked the psychiatrist if he knew what was around the corner for himself. When he replied that he didn't, Gayle suggested to him that perhaps he should be more circumspect about giving people a message without hope, such as the one he had just given her, the message he had always given her. Gayle now believes in herself; the psychiatrist's abject pessimism did not throw her. She went to that meeting knowing that the psychiatrist was probably more comfortable with the notion of lifelong 'illness' and maintenance with drugs than of recovery and living a full life off medication. As far as Gayle's recovery was concerned, her psychiatrist did not want to know.

I personally know a man who had a similar experience with his psychiatrist, who found it very hard to contemplate that he had made a good recovery from manic depression. Off medication for several years, this man is living a full life. He has a full pilot's driving licence, having passed every requirement, including psychological testing. He attributes his recovery largely to working with a good psychotherapist.

As discussed later in this chapter, there is much more to recovery than the issue of medication. I always encourage clients not to feel pressured by anyone to come off their drugs. I say to clients that there may be times when they need to increase medication, and that's okay. There may be times when a person who is off medication for some time may need to take it again for a while, and that is okay too. There is no point in making the issue of whether one is on or off medication so big that the person feels pressured, or a failure if they need to restart medication or increase the dose for a while. Such an approach can be counterproductive.

A therapist friend related the following story to me. A client of hers, a man in his fifties, had been treated for bipolar disorder for over twenty years. He had just commenced coming to her. In all his years attending psychiatrists, no doctor had ever suggested to him that counselling might help in any way. Within the first few meetings, his enormous emotional and mental distress was patently obvious to her, yet had never been deemed worthy of attention other than medication. Knowing how his psychiatrist was likely to react, this man referred himself for counselling without telling his psychiatrist.

During their third meeting, this man outlined to the therapist what had transpired three days previously with his psychiatrist. He arrived at the psychiatrist's office at the appointed time. His psychiatrist eventually saw him two hours after the time of the agreed appointment. The appointment lasted the usual 5–10 minutes, without an apology for keeping him waiting or any mention of this from the psychiatrist. The patient had been calm on his arrival at the office. But having been kept waiting for two hours, and especially because the psychiatrist did not refer to this delay at all, in the consultation the man was furious, agitated. Seeing his agitation, the psychiatrist quickly concluded that he was going high, increased his medication, and arranged a further meeting the following week.

During his consultation with the therapist, this man expressed his fury at being treated with such disrespect by the psychiatrist. Unfortunately, such examples of disrespect are experienced by some mental health service users, disrespect which would be not be tolerated in most areas of life. Due to his very low self-esteem and fear of expressing himself — features which are virtually always present in people diagnosed as 'mentally ill' but regularly missed by service providers — he did not tell the psychiatrist why he was agitated, nor did the psychiatrist ask him why. The therapist, a warm, empathic woman, helped him to express himself, his anger and hurt. She gently suggested to him that he had every right to say all this to his psychiatrist at their next meeting. He did precisely that. The psychiatrist apologised and immediately reduced his medication back to its previous level. This one session with his therapist helped him take a step in a direction vital to his recovery — to express his true feelings, especially to a person in authority such as the psychiatrist.

The point is, if not for the encouragement this man received

231

from his therapist, this man may never have plucked up the courage to express himself to the psychiatrist. Most likely, the psychiatrist's error of judgement would never have come to light. Rather, his psychiatric notes would state that he was going high, requiring further 'stabilisation' of his 'condition'. How many other such misinterpretations of peoples' behaviour are occurring in psychiatric hospitals and clinics? How frequently are doctors interpreting people's behaviour in various situations as evidence of 'illness' rather than understandable human reactions?

Another therapist friend told me about the experience of a client, diagnosed as having 'manic depression', 'bipolar disorder'. A man in his mid-twenties, he made his own decision to stop medication and instead to work through his problems in conjunction with his therapist. He told his psychiatrist that he had been off all medication for over six months and wanted to continue attending the mental health services as he continued on his recovery journey. His psychiatrist refused this request, telling him that if he was not on medication, he had no business attending the clinic. A client of mine told me a similar story. She had become overwhelmed in her life, and I admitted her to hospital as a temporary measure, for her own safety since at the time she was quite suicidal. While in hospital she was not keen on taking medication, and her psychiatrist did not push her to take medication. After a few days the psychiatrist said to her that since she wasn't on medication, how could he justify her continued hospital stay? In other words, if you are not taking medication, then your distress is not really legitimate, not a 'real' problem' for which you might need 'real' help.

Paul, in his mid-twenties, has been on medication for manic depression for five years. Apart from medication, no other intervention has been recommended by his doctors, so he decided to come to me, in my capacity as a GP with a special interest in mental health. As in my experience is usually the case with people diagnosed as having 'manic depression/

bipolar disorder, a whole world of distress opened up as we chatted, a world previously unexplored. Paul came from a loving home, but his father died when he was just six years old. Throughout his life, he greatly missed the support and safety of having his father around. For as long as he could remember, Paul was extremely shy, quiet and unsure of himself. As a yardstick of his sensitivity and lack of confidence, I vividly recall him telling me that he hated having the TV remote control when there were other people in the room, in case he picked programmes they did not like. Any minor comment about the TV programmes seemed like a major criticism to Paul. Because he felt totally unable to stand up for himself, he was frequently bullied in his life. All his life but especially from the teenage years onwards, high anxiety was a virtually ever-present experience for him. In his own words, he just did not know how to survive in this cut-throat world of business, demands and expectations. Having so little confidence, he easily became overwhelmed and agitated, which was interpreted medically as a 'high', even though he describes this experience in terms of feeling overwhelmed and distressed.

Paul and I have embarked on a gentle, patient recovery journey, where Paul knows that we work as a team. I see the gradual development of Paul's self-confidence and assertiveness as essential elements of his recovery process. This will inevitably take time. Paul knows that. He is already making some progress and, for the first time in five years, has a slight glimpse of hope that he may actually be able to move on with his life. My approach to Paul's recovery journey is along the lines discussed later in this chapter, on recovery.

I received the following important learning from one client. She had been diagnosed as having manic depression for several years. Soon after we started working together, she was going through a very stressful time in her life. She became agitated, 'high'. She needed to go into hospital, and following her

233

discharge we continued working together. I asked her if there was any gain for her when she was 'high'. She immediately responded that she felt extremely powerful in that state, something she never felt at other times in her life. I was struck by the polar opposites she was outlining to me; swinging from never feeling powerful to feeling very powerful. When she was 'high' in my office one day, she gave out to me that the paper towels in the toilet were not soft enough, telling me that this wasn't good enough. As she said herself, the 'high' gave her a sense of power and control of her life that she craved at other times in her life. Usually feeling unimportant and unable to express her views, when 'high' she made damn sure that her views were heard by those around her, that nobody took her for granted. It makes sense to me that one of this woman's challenges in life is to take more control and be more assertive in her everyday life. By doing so, she may not need to swing from one extreme to the other. It is most unfortunate that such issues are deemed irrelevant and unimportant by doctors when they are often central to the person's life and distress.

In February 2004, the aforementioned Derry mental health group STEER published *A Journey of Hope*, a booklet containing eight personal stories of mental 'illness' in the words of the people themselves. Two personal narratives were by people who had been diagnosed as having manic depression. Similarly to my client's experience, both mentioned that when they were 'high' they felt all powerful, that anything was possible', a great contrast to their more familiar feelings of despair, powerlessness and hopelessness.

Some people doubt whether a person's experiences could really cause such distress, especially when there seems to be no obvious major trigger. Because not everyone who goes through a particular type of experience reacts in the same way, people sometimes doubt whether life experiences could cause such distress. It is sometimes said that, since all members of a family have the same upbringing, how could some emerge deeply distressed and others remain apparently unaffected? Surely if life experiences were that relevant, all family members would be similarly affected?

These reasonable questions do not take certain realities of life into account. Even regarding relatively uncomplicated scenarios, not all human beings are similarly affected. For example, cigarette smoking does not affect all people equally. Some smokers develop lung cancer; others develop heart disease, or circulatory problems. Others develop chronic bronchitis or emphysema. The degree to which people's health is affected by cigarette smoking varies considerably, even amongst people with similar smoking habits. Indeed, some smokers seem to emerge unscathed from decades of smoking, living to a healthy old age.

The same applies to many things in life. Take exposure to asbestos for example, which is well known to cause major health problems including cancer. Not everyone exposed — even amongst people who share the same degree of exposure to asbestos — will be effected in the same way. Some will develop major health problems soon after exposure. Others may develop the same or different health problems, to varying degrees of severity, and at varying times after exposure. Some people will never develop any health problems in spite of their exposure to asbestos. Precisely the same scenario occurs following, for example, the exposure of a community to radiation. Given such diversity in the human response to a relatively uncomplicated scenario such as the exposure to an external toxin, it should not surprise us that the individual human response to the complex, intricate stresses, strains and demands of life may vary considerably.

Because children are raised in the same family does not mean that they share precisely the same upbringing. Rather, each child's world is unique. Dynamics within the family often change through the years. A second child can never experience precisely the same childhood as a first child, or a third or fourth child for that matter. The second child comes into a family of two parents and one sibling, whereas the fifth child comes into a family of two parents and four siblings. Parental attitudes, expectations and fears regarding the first child are most unlikely to be precisely the same as with the third or fourth child. Life is dynamic, ever-changing. The relationship between parents may have changed from the time of the first child to that of later siblings. Family and individual circumstances will inevitably have changed as the years progress. Given the myriad other interactions which young people have in their lives, each unique to the individual, it is clear that no two children can ever experience precisely the same childhood. Add to this the unique, personal way in which each individual is continuously reviewing their sense of themselves in their world, and their own unique personality which prompts responses to people which may be quite different to responses evoked from people by their siblings, and it is clear that every person's experience of their life is unique to them.

Before they rush into diagnosing human beings as being 'mentally ill', doctors should explore whether the person's problem can be explained in human terms, in the context of how their life has unfolded for them. By jumping to the 'mental illness' explanation, I believe the medical profession is doing the public a great disservice. In my experience, if you build a trusting relationship with people, giving them time to let them tell you how their life is, and has been for them, there is rarely a need to resort to 'mental illness' explanations.

Anorexia and bulimia

In his book *Making the Prozac Decision*, psychiatrist Eliot Kaplan speaks of psychiatry's view of the role of Prozac in the treatment of anorexia:

236

What Prozac and other antidepressants can do is to address
the underlying biological problem that may be causing the
eating disorder.[36]

People reading this are likely to conclude that the cause of
anorexia is some 'underlying biological problem'. The truth is
that no underlying biological problem as a cause of anorexia
has been established. What is presented here as scientific
thinking here turns out to be little more that wishful thinking.

In 1998, the *Sunday Independent* carried an article about
eating disorders.[37] Reporting on the Edinburgh International
Science Festival of that year, journalist Sarah Caden referred
to Dr Chris Freeman, a prominent researcher who presented a
paper at that conference. In the article, Sarah Caden described
how Dr Freeman compared anorexia to schizophrenia. Dr
Freeman outlined how, just 15 years ago, it was believed that
schizophrenia was caused by behaviours within the person's
family. However, according to Dr Freeman, it has now been
established that schizophrenia is a genetically inherited
condition. He predicted that in another 15 years, anorexia will
also be proven to be caused by a genetically inherited condition.

Because there were several inaccuracies in this article, I
wrote to the newspaper to set the record straight. My letter
was published in the *Sunday Independent* the following week:

I cannot allow this statement to go unchallenged. It is most
certainly *not* proven that schizophrenia is a genetic disorder.
The way this paragraph is structured conveys the clear
impression to the reader that the medical profession now
know for certain that the cause of schizophrenia is genetic.
The truth is that the medical profession has not yet
established the cause of schizophrenia.[38]

Medical doctors and researchers frequently convey to us the
impression that medical science is making great strides in its fight

237

against illness. This message comes across clearly in this article. Quoting Dr Freeman, the journalist wrote that just 15 years ago, it was believed that schizophrenia was caused by behaviours within the person's family, that it has now been established that schizophrenia is a genetically inherited condition.

In my opinion, this sentence could be interpreted as follows: 'Fifteen years ago, as far as understanding schizophrenia is concerned, we were in the dark ages. We hadn't a clue. Now though, we really do understand schizophrenia. Now, thanks to medical research we really do know what it is all about. We have made huge progress in the past 15 years.'

The reality is that modern medicine's understanding of schizophrenia has not changed significantly during the past 15 years. There have been no major breakthroughs, no wonderful discoveries which have revolutionised the medical understanding of schizophrenia. Psychiatry certainly has moved away from the possibility that schizophrenia may be caused by, as Dr Freeman puts it, the behaviour of a patient's family. With little proof to substantiate their stance, psychiatry has formed a strong consensus view that the cause of virtually all so called 'psychiatric illness' is physical — either genetic, or biochemical, or a mixture of the two.

Referring in my letter to Dr Freeman's predictions about anorexia, I wrote:

> I am fascinated by the sentence 'In another 15 years, Dr Freeman predicted, it will be proven that anorexia is also the result of a genetic disorder'. As I have not yet perfected the art of reading the future, I am personally very wary of making such a dramatic prediction. I doubt that many psychologists would agree that the cause of anorexia is genetic. At this point in time there is no convincing evidence that anorexia is a genetic illness. Whether there will be in the future remains to be seen.

That Dr Freeman's paper was presented at a scientific meeting did little to allay my concern.

Most of the medical experts who speak so eloquently about anorexia have never suffered from the condition. They have never experienced what a person with anorexia goes through. When those who know most about anorexia — those who have it — describe their experience of this condition, it becomes obvious that severe emotional distress is a key factor.

Claire Beeken had anorexia nervosa for 13 years. Following her recovery, she set up the charity 'Caraline'[39] in England. She named the charity after a friend and fellow sufferer who did not survive the condition. Claire wrote a book describing her life and her anorexia — *My Body, My Enemy, My Thirteen Year Battle with Anorexia Nervosa.*[40] It becomes quite clear from reading this book that Claire's anorexia had little to do with either a biochemical abnormality or a genetic disorder. Claire's loneliness and emotional suffering screams out at the reader throughout the book.

By the time she wrote the book, Claire had recovered and had been working for a number of years with her own self-help group. Her words are based on a great deal of personal experience, and the experiences of other people with eating disorders. In her book, she describes anorexia as 'a symptom of stress or other profound emotional damage or psychological problems'.

Throughout her book, Claire Beekin outlines her own emotional and psychological issues, issues which feature again and again in the lives of people with eating disorders. She describes how in her case the underlying trigger for her eating disorder was sexual abuse, by her grandfather. Her desperately low self-esteem, deep self-rejection and self-hatred are evident throughout her story, as is her intense loneliness and isolation. She speaks of not belonging anywhere, of wanting to disappear, of preferring animals to people because animals 'don't hurt you'.

Claire never opened up to her doctors. She did not trust them or feel safe with them. She spent all her time with the doctors concealing her problems from the psychiatrists and most of the other health care workers. Faced with the prospect of yet another admission to the psychiatric ward, she speaks of her dread that her life will be 'in enemy hands', where even her family will have no say in what happens to her.

Claire identifies a central reason why preoccupation with food becomes such a life-dominating issue for people with eating disorders. Speaking about a friend who later died from anorexia, she described how her friend began controlling her eating, because it was the one thing in her life which she could have some control over. The rest of her life was overwhelmingly difficult for her, and seemed beyond her control. At a time when so many aspects of everyday living seem overwhelming, impossible to cope with, becoming preoccupied with food can seem a relatively safe activity. Claire describes how, on the rare occasions she felt safe and loved, her eating disorder did not surface.

Psychiatrists frequently hold case conferences about patients, particularly those who are not responding to treatment. Claire's description of her case conference demonstrates how intimidating and degrading the experience can be for the hapless patient, and how far out of touch psychiatrists can be with their patients:

'Come in' says Dr Pinto [her psychiatrist] as I tap on the door. I am expecting to see just Dr Pinto, but I open the door and at least half a dozen pairs of eyes swivel in my direction. In the middle of the seated circle sits Dr Pinto. 'Hello, Claire. Come and sit down' he says, gesturing to the empty chair next to him. This, apparently, is a case conference. 'How do you feel?' 'Do you feel in control when you don't eat?' 'Do you this?' 'Do you that?' There are no introductions, no niceties — these doctors, psychiatrists, nurses, social workers, or whatever they are, launch in with questions from every angle. As I struggle to find an answer to one question, a different mouth chimes in with another query. They are relentless and I am reduced to tears. I feel like a slimy little specimen under a microscope. I pray hard that night. 'Dear Lord Jesus Christ, please let this whole thing be just a nightmare. Please let me wake up at home'. Trouble is, it's very, very real.[41]

The immense intimidation felt by patients during case conferences was echoed in *Out of Me, The Story of a Post-Natal Breakdown* by Fiona Shaw:

The nursing staff seemed as intimidated by the prospect as the patients. I felt on trial there: at first I used to assume that I'd been found guilty and I took what I saw as my punishment quietly. I had Dr A. [her psychiatrist] acting judge. She always seemed to me less interested in finding out what I thought or felt than in having confirmed some assessment she had already made. And in that environment, organised around her own style of communications, all her statements were self-confirming.[42]

When approached holistically, the symptoms people present with can, by their symbolism, reveal what the person's real need is. Writing about an episode of binge eating, Claire Beekin recognises that she is really trying to satisfy a hunger not for food, but for love and understanding.

The psychiatrists and their methods played little or no part in Claire's recovery. The first steps on her recovery began when she joined a self-help group for people with eating disorders. That was when Claire met Lorna, the person running the self-group. Lorna related extremely well to Claire, and this relationship was a major factor in Claire's first tentative steps towards recovery.

Psychiatrists believe that people with anorexia deliberately resist the doctor's efforts to help them recover. Indeed, throughout Claire Beeken's book there are many examples of how Claire resisted and thwarted the psychiatrists. This happened because she felt so threatened by the psychiatrists and so misunderstood that she felt she had no choice but to resist. Her survival depended on it. In contrast, when confronted by Lorna — someone who understood Claire — she welcomed being challenged. Claire wrote how Lorna worked at raising her self-esteem, highlighting her good points. Working with people with eating distress issues can be complicated; progress can be very slow. But if the person does not feel safe, heard and cared for within their relationships with their carers, then the likelihood of a favourable outcome may be further jeopardised.

Shortly before she died from anorexia, Claire's friend Caraline spoke to Claire. Caraline had also been through the medical and psychiatric mill, and was none too impressed:

Doctors need to learn from people like you — someone who knows what it feels like and who understands. They need to know that brutal treatment doesn't work. The professionals never listened to me; perhaps they'll listen to you.

Like Claire Beekin, Rosemary Shelly has recovered from anorexia. Editor of the book *Anorexics on Anorexia,* she alludes to patients' lack of emotional support from the medical profession and to doctors' preoccupation with patients' food intake:

Too many hospitalised sufferers are being treated in ways that have proved to be detrimental to their long-term physical and mental health. This is particularly the case when anorexics are fed vast amounts of food to produce rapid weight gain that they are unable to cope with mentally and subsequently lose on discharge from hospital. The patient's mental condition is often overlooked. That should not be the case.[43]

Shelly outlines one anorexia sufferer's experience with the medical profession:

What really surprised and shocked me was the fact that the focus was on feeding me up to produce a change in my body, but never once did they take my mind into consideration. The way I was feeling did not seem important to them. I received very little in the way of counselling.[44]

Eating disorders represent a major challenge to the medical profession. Anorexia does not fit comfortably into traditional medical disease models. Medical training concentrates on understanding the human body. Understanding human feelings and the psyche barely feature in the training of doctors. Consequently, many doctors find themselves out of their depth when faced with people whose deep emotional turmoil is presented in a complex manner, as occurs in anorexia. Not understanding the condition, doctors are often suspicious of eating disorder sufferers. Patients sense this suspicion. The bemusement and suspicion exhibited by doctors towards eating disorders is, I believe, exemplified in an article in the *Irish Medical News* of 2 November 1998 by Dr Andrew Rynne. An experienced Irish GP and medical journalist, Dr Rynne is seen a modern-thinking and compassionate GP amongst his peers. Dr Rynne was expressing his views while reviewing *Hope: Understanding Eating Disorders*, views which in my opinion make it very difficult to create the open, trusting relationship which is critically important for recovery:

At the very least, anorexia and its accompanying conduct do not fit comfortably into any traditional disease models as I understand them. The cure for all this suffering is in the hands, or at least tantalisingly close to being in the hands, of the sufferers themselves. If the cases described in this book are typical, then so-called eating disorders, anorexia, bulimia and so on, have to be the single most self-centred and self-obsessed type of behaviour on this planet. These people are suffering all right, but they are control freaks. At one level they are 'patients' yet at another level they are power freaks and self-indulgent manipulators and, as such, are extremely powerful attention-seekers.[45]

If, as Dr Rynne says, a condition does not fit comfortably into traditional medical disease models, is it not possible that the problem lies with the disease models rather than the person? In *Anorexics on Anorexia*, editor Rosemary Shelley outlined the experiences of many contributors to the book as they sought help from their GP for their anorexia:

Contributors speak of being sent away by their GPs, after initially presenting them with their food problems, and being told to 'Go home and eat' or 'Go for a walk around the garden'. If only it were that simple. To admit to having an eating problem, having the courage to seek medical help, but then being sent away with nothing is humiliating and even fatal.[46]

In my professional experience of people with eating disorders, emotional issues are always the core of the problem. Many of the emotional, psychological, social and relationship issues discussed elsewhere throughout this book are experienced to a high degree by people with eating distress. Seventeen-year-old Angela was brought to me, in my capacity as the family's GP, by her distraught mother. Angela had been bulimic — repeatedly inducing herself to vomit her food — for the previous three months. It quickly emerged that Angela had very low self-esteem. She described her relationship with her father as 'difficult'. Angela felt under great pressure to perform well in school examinations.

During that first consultation, I explored various aspects of their family relationships with Angela and her mother. I arranged to see Angela and both parents the following day. In a non-judgemental fashion, I attempted to improve the communication within the family. Angela needed to know she was loved and valued. She was, but she did not realise it. I encouraged both parents to explicitly express their love for Angela to her. Her father explained to Angela that his preoccupation with her exam results stemmed from his love for her. He desperately wanted her to have a much easier life than his. Her father's excessive interest in her school performance was, for him, the way he expressed his love for her.

By the end of the second consultation, Angela's whole demeanour had changed dramatically. Initially withdrawn, she was now radiant. During our consultations one thing became very clear to Angela. Her parents loved her dearly, though they had been expressing their love in roundabout, indirect ways. Three months later I met Angela's mother. Angela's bulimic behaviour had not returned. Relationships within the family had improved significantly. The fact that Angela's problem came to light at an early stage helped to bring the situation to a satisfactory conclusion. Many cases can be much more complicated than that of Angela. Nevertheless, if the right approach were adopted from the client's first contact with the health services, perhaps recovery would be more frequent and more speedy.

A GP colleague to whom I recounted this case history was intrigued by my approach to Angela's bulimia. Recognising his own limited understanding of emotional distress and family relationships — and reflecting the medical profession's limited understanding — he replied uncomfortably: 'And I probably would have just put her on Prozac'.

Alcohol and drug abuse

According to the prevailing medical view, drug and alcohol abuse account for 15 per cent of suicides. I do not believe that these are 'psychiatric conditions'. They are caused by a combination of factors including low self-esteem; troubled family relationships; feeling alone and unsafe; lacking emotional closeness to others; social isolation and social problems; peer pressure; painful losses; deep insecurity; avoiding dealing with one's life problems, issues and unfinished emotional baggage. These issues, combined with the addictiveness of alcohol and illicit drugs, are the real issues behind drug and alcohol abuse. For many people, drugs and alcohol are powerful anaesthetics, temporarily numbing their emotional distress.

In my experience with people who drink excessively, a combination of the following are frequently present; low self-esteem; social awkwardness; insecurity; being easily hurt; fear of facing and dealing with problems; shyness; relationship difficulties; loneliness; a lack of a sense of safety, predictability and openness within the family when growing up; financial pressures; feeling easily threatened; work stress; inability to say 'no'; great difficulty expressing feelings and emotional needs; bottling up feelings and fears; anxiety; hopelessness; being easily stressed; past experience of many painful losses.

A study carried out in 1998 by doctors at the National Drug Treatment Centre in Dublin revealed that 44 per cent of drug addicts had suffered either physical or sexual abuse when they were young. Some 21 per cent of addicts had been the victims of sexual abuse and a further 23 per cent had been subjected to physical abuse. The researchers found that addicts who had been sexually or physically abused began their drug-taking at an earlier age and were more difficult to get off drugs. According to the study's co-author Dr Roy Browne, psychiatrist at Cork University Hospital, the link with sexual and physical abuse is a very relevant finding. He said that if the underlying psychological causes of drug abuse are not addressed, many people will be drawn back to heroin. But in my experience, the underlying psychological causes are rarely addressed. This study focused on the link between drug usage and physical and sexual abuse. Had the study included emotional, psychological and social abuse, it is likely that the final figure would have greatly exceeded 44 per cent.

Taking mood-altering drugs such as hash/marijuana can cause many 'psychiatric' symptoms. They can cause people to become depressed, paranoid and/or psychotic. When people present to doctors with such symptoms, it is important to check whether the person has been taking illicit, mood-altering drugs.

As with alcohol abuse, drug addiction is not a 'psychiatric condition' and should not be labelled as such. Rather than label these people as 'mentally ill' and treat their 'illness', the medical profession should approach drug addiction in the wider context of the person's life, relationships and experiences. I believe that overcoming substance abuse is far more likely when the issues which prompted and maintain the abuse are addressed.

There is evidence to suggest that in many developed countries, alcohol intake amongst young people has increased significantly in recent years. Many young people have more money at their disposal than their predecessors of past generations. Many young people who drink excessively do so for the 'kick' alcohol gives them. Not everyone who drinks excessively does so to quell shyness and insecurity. Being under the influence of alcohol is no excuse for violent, abusive behaviour. However, as a society we need to be more mindful of the reasons why people drink excessively.

Recovery

This entire book is infused with the perspective that recovery from so-called 'mental illness' is a realistic possibility. One of

247

the most promising developments within mental health in recent decades has, ironically, come from outside the traditional mental care services providers. Service users are becoming increasingly vocal. Supported internationally by a small number of psychiatrists, psychologists and other service providers and support groups, service users are increasingly insisting that their voices be heard. One important result of this has been the growth of the concept of recovery. Many of the pioneers of this development are people who themselves have recovered from major mental health problems, such as diagnoses of schizophrenia and manic depression. Based on numerous personal testimonies of recovery, many service users and user groups are challenging psychiatry to shift its focus from lifetime symptom maintenance towards a philosophy and vision of recovery. This position was outlined in the *Derry Journal* by John L. James of STEER, the mental health group based in Derry City. John James has himself been a mental health service user:

> One of the most enduring myths within society is about mental illness and the idea that a person never recovers from it . . . However, despite the tremendous challenge that people with mental health difficulties experience, recovery is an achievable outcome. The concept of recovery is a challenge to the existing psychiatric profession. Up until very recently, they considered people, who had to be admitted to institutions and hospitals with serious mental illness, as having 'chronic' conditions that would entail a lifetime of care and treatment. This perception created a 'self-fulfilling prophesy', in that they did not structure the treatment and care towards recovery because they simply could not accept that it was possible, let alone probable. This led people with these conditions to simply accept their fate, have low expectations, and surrender any hope of a 'normal life' and little or no effort was made to challenge

this negative assumption. It is the hangover from this ethos that still haunts long-term institutions and hospitals, which hinders the development of more positive and progressive attitudes, and obstructs the rehabilitation and recovery of many people with mental health difficulties.

Despite its late arrival to these shores, the concept of recovery is not a new one. It first originated out of the American civil rights movement in the 1960s and the 1970s. At this time, social consciousness was raised and the rights of people who had previously been marginalized by society were beginning to be raised by the marginalized people themselves. The mental health service user movement has been very slow to emerge, the difficulties experienced by people with mental health difficulties have seemed overwhelming: the condition itself, the edifice of the psychiatric establishment and the stigma have meant that the movement had many barriers to overcome . . .

What is needed for a person to be regarded to be in the process of recovery? Several factors have been identified; acceptance of the illness; an established social network; taking responsibility for one's actions; making decisions for oneself; independent management of self; owning the condition instead of the condition owning us; the presence of hope and empowerment. A large part of the Recovery Model is about giving respect to people with mental health difficulties. Instead of taking charge of their lives and doing things for them, it is about working with and alongside them to allow them to take control of their own lives and treatment. It is about giving people the tools they need to manage their mental health on a day-to-day basis.[47]

Increasingly, psychiatrists — and consequently GPs, other mental health care workers and service users — speak of mental problems as long-term (typically life-long) illnesses to be managed for life rather than overcome. If the service providers, to whom people in distress look to for hope, do not see people as capable of recovery, service users pick this up. Herein lies the main source of the message of hopelessness service users frequently speak of.

This misguided approach ignores an important reality: people can and do recover from even the most overwhelming mental health problems. In developed countries, approximately one in three of people diagnosed as having schizophrenia recover. As discussed earlier, the recovery rate in underdeveloped countries is closer to sixty per cent recovery rate. While it is not easy to obtain figures, many people who have been diagnosed as having manic depression do recover. Up to fifty per cent of people diagnosed as having depression recover on placebo. People can and do recover from anorexia, and from severe anxiety.

Why has the concept of recovery from 'mental illness' not been championed by psychiatry? Why have service users had to provide the lead? There are many possible reasons for this. Doctors many argue with some justification that focusing on recovery rather than maintenance may not be realistic for many patients; that recovery is too high a goal to set. However, it is possible to hold a vision of recovery for people without pressuring them with expectations of recovery. The role and influence of the pharmaceutical industry in shaping medical beliefs is greatly underestimated. Drug companies will make a great deal more money through a health system which promotes maintenance (on drugs for years, often for life) rather than recovery. Recovery is challenging to the medical belief system, which repackages distress and overwhelm as 'illness'. The concept of long-term maintenance of an 'illness' with medication sits easily with the medical profession and the general public, since it exists within all specialties of medicine. However, the idea that people can recover through a broadly based recovery process in which non-medical interventions play a key role (peer support, empowerment, self-esteem and confidence building, social supports and networks, rehabilitation and training, employment training, counselling and psychotherapy, for example), in which medication is seen as having a role but not the be-all and end-all of the person's possible recovery tools, dilutes the perceived importance of the medical profession's most prized treatment, medication. As a consequence, the role of the medical profession is itself diluted somewhat in the process of recovery, something which may be difficult for many doctors to contemplate.

The process of recovery has a further potential; by helping individuals to recover themselves, the recovery process may help society to reclaim aspects of itself which are currently censored. By legitimising experiences currently deemed within society as unacceptable and undesirable — the experiences explored throughout this book — the widespread acceptance of the recovery process may help introduce a new language and understanding into our society, based on acceptance and respect for human vulnerability and sensitivity.

Common sense would suggest that a great deal of research should be devoted to gathering information regarding the factors which have helped people recover. This information might then become a pivotal part of the approach and philosophy of the mental health services. Serious questions need to be asked regarding why such research is not enthusiastically embraced and developed by those with greatest power and influence within the mental health services.

In 2002, a survey of mental health service users was carried out by Schizophrenia Ireland, a national support group. The survey was targeted at people with enduring mental illness, who had considerable experience of mental health services. 471 people responded. John Farrelly of Schizophrenia Ireland outlined their reasons for undertaking this survey:

The lack of availability of non-medical interventions is a source of ongoing debate in mental health care. A possible reason for ambivalence towards non-medical interventions is that there is no broad consensus as to their efficacy. It would seem logical that the best way to establish efficacy is to ask the people who experience a particular treatment.

Among other things, survey participants were asked of their view and experiences of interventions other than drugs. The most commonly experienced interventions included employment training, counselling/psychotherapy, peer group support and art/music/creative therapy. In each of these areas, an average of over 75 per cent found the interventions either 'very helpful' or 'helpful':

The vast majority of respondents found these non-medical therapies to be either very helpful or helpful. In a system, which is delivered primarily by the medical model of intervention, there is a significant lack of emphasis on a holistic and integrated approach to promoting recovery from mental illness.

Relevant accessible therapies should be available as a matter of course for people experiencing mental distress. The issue of medication and its prescription warrants serious consideration. The constituent health boards, prescribing psychiatrists and general practitioners, must address these issues.[48]

A survey by the self-help group Recovery Inc. found that participants reported fewer symptoms and fewer hospitalisations after joining their group. In another study of 115 former mental patients, those who continued to attend self-help meetings at least once a month over a period of ten months were more likely to improve both psychologically and interpersonally. In 2003, I spoke at a conference held by the

Scottish Association of Mental Health (SAMH) in Glasgow. At that conference, two service users spoke candidly and openly of their experiences within the British mental health services. Both had in the past been diagnosed as having schizophrenia. Both had fully recovered and were off all medication for several years. Both stated that they had recovered in spite of — rather than because of — psychiatry. They attributed their recovery to human values such as support, understanding, patience, and connecting with people who normalised rather than pathologised their experiences (their 'symptoms'), such as the Hearing Voices Network. They had quite an impact on the audience, mainly managers within the SAMH services. The managers were most impressed and enthused, and determined to place greater emphasis on the concept of recovery within their services.

Daniel Fisher is an American psychiatrist who has fully recovered from a diagnosis of schizophrenia. Having been diagnosed as having schizophrenia as a young man, Dan Fisher recovered, went on to qualify as a psychiatrist, and has been off medication for 25 years. He, along with Patricia Deegan and others, is a leading figure in the National Empowerment Centre in America, which has formulated an Empowerment Model of Recovery from Mental Illness, which can be accessed at www.power2u. I find it interesting that the important concept of empowerment, which is central to the recovery process, does not figure in everyday psychiatric language. In Britain, there are many ex- and current service users speaking out, calling for a greater focus on recovery. Ron Coleman, one of those who spoke at the above SAMH conference, has for years been outlining the need for a recovery-focused mental health service. In America, David Oaks and his colleagues at MindFreedom and Support Coalition International http://www.MindFreedom.org have for years been campaigning for mental health services which respect the human rights and dignity of service users, an essential prerequisite to recovery.

William Anthony of the Boston University Centre for Psychiatric Rehabilitation outlines his views on recovery:

> Recovery is a process; a vision; a belief which infuses a system . . . which providers can hold for service users . . . grounded on the idea that people can recover from 'mental illness', and that the service delivery system must be constructed based on this knowledge . . . The consumer literature suggests that recovery is a deeply personal, unique process of changing one's attitudes, values, feelings, goals, skills, or roles. It is a way of living a satisfying, hopeful, and contributing life. Recovery involves the development of new meaning and purpose in one's life as one grows beyond the catastrophic effects of psychiatric disability.[49]

It is possible for service providers to hold a vision of recovery for a person for whom the idea of recovery is currently way beyond them. Recovery is a gradual process. As I see it, it is important for service providers to have a realistic sense of where the person currently is, while also having a sense of where they might, in time, get to. I focus on where the person is, and what small steps the person might be capable of taking. In time, small steps add up.

All of the people involved in a person's care need to know that the idea of recovery can be terrifying for the person, particularly in the early stages. This is why small, gradual, patient steps are usually more productive than attempting too much too quickly. Two years ago, a young English woman attended me. She was on holiday in Ireland for two weeks, and her relatives suggested she talk to me. Her eating distress was immediately obvious; she was very underweight. The woman herself had no expectations at all from her visit to me; she attended purely because her family wanted her to. Always extremely fearful of seeking help, I was the first health professional she attended. In our hour-long first meeting, she was very frightened, reluctant to speak. Rather than pressurise her with a barrage of questions when she was not ready to speak to me, I spent much of that session gently outlining my understanding of eating distress. Without expecting replies from her, I articulated what I felt were the underlying, never-spoken fears, distress, and overwhelm in people who develop eating distress problems such as anorexia, rather than focusing greatly on her weight and eating habits. As our meeting progressed, she became visibly more relaxed and talkative. She seemed pleasantly surprised at how our meeting went. We arranged to meet a week later, just before she returned home to Britain.

At our second meeting, she outlined what had transpired since we first met. Having left our meeting feeling understood, she spoke more freely to her family. She spoke to them of having more hope now. Her family, having watched her in great distress for several years, were understandably overjoyed to see her being a little more positive. Suddenly, the whole family began to talk enthusiastically of her recovering. But the very idea of recovery terrified her. It conjured up thoughts of having to engage with people and situations which seemed light years away from what she felt capable of doing, given her very low self-confidence and self-esteem. So, the very slight sense of hope she felt after her first session with me quickly evaporated. I spent a considerable amount of that second session gently explaining all this to her family, who understandably did not realise that their enthusiasm for her recovery actually increased her stress levels. She seemed relieved by this, and agreed to seek help on her return to Britain.

In recent years, service users are increasingly being involved in decision-making within the mental health services. Rogan Wolf is a User Support Worker for the Westminster Consultation Project in Britain. In a 7 January 2001 opinion article on the website of the Sainsbury Centre for Mental Health, Rogan Wolf wrote that service user involvement must be real and meaningful, warning against tokenism:

> The true strength of the user perspective comes from their direct experience and this has its own crucial and creative authority. But it is a difficult position to speak from, requiring the right conditions for it to be spoken freely. Service providers and users must work carefully together to create conditions by which it is as easy as possible (a) for users to speak freely, with authority and from the heart and (b) for professionals to listen fully, sensitively and accurately.

Robert Bernstein, executive director of the Bazelon Centre for Mental Health Law, acknowledges the challenges to mental health service providers inherent in the philosophy of recovery:

> The consumer movement has rattled what we were taught. The new model is that consumers will define for us how we can be helpful, not the other way around.[50]

Many people I have worked with over the years are a testament to the real possibility of recovery, given sufficient support, affirmation and encouragement. John began attending me eighteen months ago when he was seventeen years old. His mother had heard me speak on the radio regarding my concerns about the mental health services. She brought her son to see me in my capacity as a GP with a special interest in mental health. He was attending school, had been diagnosed as having schizophrenia, and was taking 20 mgs daily of Zyprexa, a major tranquilliser. We meet for an hour every 2–3 weeks. Gently and gradually, at his own pace, he has begun to internalise and believe in the positive messages I had been giving him about himself. With John's permission, I spoke with his parents, and gave them a perspective on 'schizophrenia' which was entirely new to them, though he had been attending the psychiatric services for the previous two years. I explained how fear, terror, absent self-confidence, no sense of being able to protect himself in this world and other related issues, were central to his considerable distress which had been interpreted as 'schizophrenia' by his psychiatrist.

This explanation helped John's loving parents to support him more effectively. When he first attended me, he constantly spoke of other people being able to read his mind, of how being constantly terrified of people made it enormously difficult for him to attend school every day. Rather than see his belief that others could read his mind and thoughts as abnormal, crazy or psychotic, I could see that this view was consistent with his belief that he was powerless in his everyday world. While unable to offer much constructive help on his recovery path, thankfully and in my experience unusually, his psychiatrist was prepared to countenance John attending me, and was prepared to reduce the medication gradually. Now, John is on just 2.5 mgs of Zyprexa a day. He is now going to college, and dealing with the pressures and stresses of college better than he or his parents ever thought possible. He is interacting better with people than at any time in his life. John no longer sees himself as powerless. Together, we created strategies for John to repeatedly reconnect with his sense of power and assertiveness. His parents excitedly tell me that he is doing remarkably well, that they can't believe the change in him. Both with me and with his parents, John's former preoccupation that people could read his mind has greatly diminished. It still happens sometimes when he feels vulnerable, but now he has strategies to deal with this positively. He attributes this to the work we have done together.

As I just mentioned, John's psychiatrist had little to offer in terms of creating a workable, realistic recovery journey with John. This and many other relevant points were made by British mental health services user Linda Hart in 'An Open Letter to Mental Health Professionals'. In my opinion, this letter is a good example of the contribution service users can make to the improvement of mental health services:

> I believe most of you don't actually know what to do. We are all used to the characters on our street corners and housing estates who pass a wrap containing a gram of cocaine, heroin or a few Es in exchange for less money than it costs to buy a packet of fags. We know, too, that these drug pushers will get a hefty prison sentence if they are caught.
>
> But do we recognise the suited men and women, carrying important-looking briefcases and driving expensive cars, who haunt our hospitals, GP surgeries and your conference and training days? They bribe you with mugs and pens, the promise of funding yet more conferences and – if you're a scientist – a lab in which to do research. They won't get caught and given a prison sentence. These are the drug pushers of highly toxic psychiatric drugs. They aren't allowed to talk to patients, so you will know what goes on better than me.
>
> But what I can tell you about is not only what these drugs do to us in their attempt to cure our supposed illnesses, but also what they do to us when we try to come off them. I've seen time and again people coming for help because they're lonely, bereaved, having relationship difficulties and suffering other distressing but natural life-events. I've also seen these people being given antipsychotic medication. Why? What can be the justification if it's not to shut them up or stop you from feeling helpless?
>
> Those suffering from 'real' psychosis are told they have to take these drugs for the rest of their lives. And when they stop, as they invariably do, they get withdrawal effects

which you put down to 'relapse' or to their symptoms returning. It would seem that you psychiatrists have totally lost the plot – and taken nurses, service users and the general public with you. Why do those of you who are not in the least bit control-freaks or agents of the government, as some of us in our enforced helplessness would believe, go hand-in-hand with the drug industry to give us chemical lobotomies?

As clients, we beg you to put an end to our pain, and I think that faced with the human misery and torment that you can't bear, you reach for a quick and easy solution. But you are complicit in a fraud that gives no one a real chance. Maybe you should look into yourself and discover things about helplessness and why in the first place you trained to be psychiatrists or, as it should be, 'healers of the soul'.

There are many situations which actively hinder recovery. Some people talk glibly about moving on – out into the community. Most sufferers from mental distress don't have a community to go out to, especially when we've been marginalized for years, not only by the general public but also by the very services that purport to help us. Patients in long-stay hospitals have only £15.50 a week to live on. Many are ready to move on, but with no community teams in the county to deal with serious and enduring mental health difficulties, they are stuck in a regime that denies them the hope necessary for 'recovery'. We need freedom from this debilitating type of poverty and time to build up our relationships and our lives. We need people who are willing to follow our agenda and to stop doing things to us or for us.

To suffer from a severe mental health problem is like being a prisoner serving a sentence for a miscarriage of justice. Freedom from that prison can be just as

259

overwhelming, and we need people who can understand that. So as a first step we need places where service users can go when they are withdrawing from antipsychotic drugs; places that are adequately funded, and incorporate both medical and peer support. You do spend, quite rightly, hundreds of thousands of pounds on places where people can go to come off alcohol and narcotics. Yet you spend nothing on psychiatric recovery.

If you think I'm too radical then just think about this. To label someone 'radical' is yet another way of not listening to them, and to be fully radical is to make hope possible rather than despair convincing.[51]

Eugene attends me every three weeks or so, has done for eighteen months. In his late twenties, he attended me having been diagnosed years previously as having obsessive compulsive disorder. Prior to me, John had attended five psychiatrists. Each psychiatrist recommended medication as the treatment. John's brother came across the Irish edition of this book and gave it to John. John read it and decided that he would come to meet me. Prior to attending me, no doctor had attempted to explore John's symptoms in detail with him. One of his main distress symptoms was what he called 'intrusive thoughts'; thoughts he did not invite, which unnerved and deeply upset him, which seemed alien to him, being so apparently out of character. These thoughts revolved around sudden impulses of violence towards other people. This upset him greatly, since he was a quiet, passive, gentle person who wouldn't harm a fly. Within our first few meetings, it seemed to me that these 'intrusive thoughts' might more appropriate to Eugene than perhaps he realised. Having lost confidence over the years, Eugene regularly felt 'walked on' by others, and had for years felt unable to protect himself from such intrusion. Through fear and deep self-doubt, Eugene for years

260

had no outlet for his anger. I felt that these 'intrusive thoughts' might make sense, as an outlet for his pent-up anger and frustration. Together, we worked to increase his confidence, assertiveness and self-expression. As his self-confidence has grown, his 'intrusive thoughts' have diminished. They rarely occur now, only when he feels overwhelmed. And like John above, Eugene now has strategies to employ when they occur. Hence they rarely occur, and tend to be short-lived when he does experience them. Eugene feels that my understanding of these 'intrusive thoughts' makes sense, and empowers him to deal constructively with them, as he has done.

It is said that prevention is better than cure. Most specialities within medicine have developed preventative strategies for various conditions. Ask a cardiologist or GP how a person might reduce their chances of having a heart attack, and you will get some good preventative tips — avoid smoking, take regular exercise, watch your weight and your stress levels, reduce dietary fat intake, check your cholesterol, for example. This is an example of primary prevention, which involves taking steps to prevent the onset of the condition. Psychiatry has not managed to develop cohesive primary preventative strategies. Ask a GP or psychiatrist how one might reduce their chances of having a 'nervous breakdown'; of developing 'schizophrenia', 'manic depression' or other so-called 'mental illnesses', and the doctor will quickly run out of ideas. Psychiatrists may argue, with some justification, that this is because few primary preventative strategies have been found to be effective. In the everyday practice of psychiatry, the preventative strategies that do exist predictably revolve around medication. These are secondary preventative strategies, that is, strategies which attempt to reduce recurrence of the problem once it has already occurred. For example, psychiatrists advise that on-going 'maintenance' treatment of bipolar disorder prevents recurrences of the 'condition'. Psychiatrists say that antipsychotic drugs prevent relapses in schizophrenia, and that long-term antidepressants prevent relapse in the treatment of recurring depression. As discussed throughout this book, many of these strategies are not as effective as doctors sometimes claim them to be.

Yet, issues central to the emerging focus on recovery may have considerable preventative potential. Helping people reclaim their self-confidence, self-esteem, assertiveness, self-expression, and helping them reintegrate into society in a phased manner helps people cope with and overcome enduring 'mental illness'. Common sense might suggest that psychosocial issues such as these may offer possibilities in the prevention of mental health problems also. While many GPs and psychiatrists say and believe they are providing a broadly based, holistic biopsychosocial model of mental health care, in reality it is the 'bio' bit of this three-pronged approach which dominates current understanding and treatments within mental health services. In our efforts to improve mental health services, we must examine current services, the reasons why they have developed as they have, and possible resistances to change. Psychiatry has for decades linked its identity both to the pharmaceutical industry and to hypothesised biological concepts of mental health problems and their treatment. Consequently, psychiatry may find it difficult to accept increased focus on psychosocial issues which may have the effect of reducing the perceived central role of medication and the doctors who prescribe it. It does not take a rocket scientist to see potential conflicts of interest, to see where resistances may surface.

In common with the vast majority of my medical colleagues, I received little training in the area of nutrition. Regarding mental health problems, doctors see little role for nutritional approaches. Some mental health service providers, including Patrick Holford[52] believe that nutrition has much to offer in mental health care. It is chastening to admit that I do not know enough about nutrition in mental health to comment one way or another. If natural, nutritional products can help people feel better, I would welcome that. His website contains many testimonials from people who say their mental health has benefited from taking his advice. The one person I know personally who has tried his methods reports a significant improvement in her mental well-being as a result.

Notes

1. C. M. Harding, J. Zubin and Strauss (1987) Chronicity in schizophrenia: fact, partial fact, or artifact? *Hospital and Community Psychiatry, 38,* 477–86.

2. *Oxford Textbook of Psychiatry,* third edition, (1996) Oxford: Oxford University Press.

3. Mary Boyle (1993) *Schizophrenia: A scientific delusion?* London: Routledge.

4. Mary Boyle (1999) Diagnosis. In C. Newnes, G. Holmes and C. Dunn (Eds.) *This is Madness*, pp. 75–90. Ross-on-Wye: PCCS Books.

5. R. D. Laing (1970) *Sanity, Madness and the Family*. London: Penguin.

6. Dr Peter Breggin (1993) *Toxic Psychiatry.* London: Flamingo.

7. *Schizophrenia Ireland* (1998) Information leaflet.

8. M. Morris, R. MacPherson (2001) Childhood 'risk characteristics' and the schizophrenia spectrum prodrome, *Irish Journal of Psychological Medicine, 18*(2), 72–4.

9. Dorothy Rowe (2002) *Beyond Fear*, p. xiv. Harper Collins.

10. R. McCabe, et al. (2002) *British Medical Journal, 325*, 1148–51.

11. *British Medical Journal* (2001) *324*, 900–4.

12. *British Medical Journal,* (2001) *322*, 724–7.

13. Peter K. Chadwick (1997) *Schizophrenia: The positive perspective. In search of dignity for schizophrenic people*, p. 7. London: Routledge.

14. 'Interview with Dr Douglas Turkington' by Adam James, *Openmind,118*, (Nov/Dec 2002) Reprinted with permission © Mind (National Association for Mental Health).

15. Bertram Karon PhD and Anmarie Widener (1999) *Ethical Human Sciences and Services,* Fall/Winter. Authors are from the Psychology Research department at Michigan State University

16. Conall Larkin and Abbie Lane (1998) *Irish Medical Times*, January.

17. Paul J. Harrison, Michael J. Owen (2003) *Lancet, 361*, 417–18. Authors are from the University of Oxford Department of Psychiatry

18. Peter Breggin (1993) *Toxic Psychiatry.* London: Flamingo.

19. Jay Joseph (2003) *The Gene Illusion*, p. 231. Ross-on-Wye: PCCS Books.

20. *British Medical Journal (*2000) *321*, 137–6

21. Richard Godsen PhD (2001) *Punishing the Patient: How psychiatrists misunderstand and mistreat schizophrenia.* Melbourne: Scribe Publications.

22. Tom McMonagle (1999) 'Advances in Psychiatry' supplement to the *Irish Medical Times,* September.

23. Lucy Johnstone (1999) Do families cause 'schizophrenia? Revisiting a taboo subject. In C. Newnes, G. Holmes and C. Dunn (Eds.) *This is Madness,* pp. 119–134. Ross-on-Wye: PCCS Books.

24. Al Siebert (1999) *Ethical Human Sciences and Services,* Summer.

25. Dr Joseph Glenmullen (2001) *Prozac Backlash.* New York: Touchstone.

26. Jan Foudraine (1974) *Not Made of Wood.* Quartet Books.

27. Dr Richard Warner (1994) *Recovery from Schizophrenia: Psychiatry and political economy.* London: Routledge. He is the Medical Director of the Mental Health Centre of Boulder University, Colorado.

28. Robert Whitaker (2002) *Mad in America.* Cambridge, MA: Perseus Publishing.

29. Courtenay Harding (1987) Chronicity in schizophrenia: Fact, partial fact, or artifact? *Hospital and Community Psychiatry, 38.* Also (1994) Empirical correction of seven myths about schizophrenia with implications for treatment'. *Acta Psychiatrica Scandinavica, 384.*

30. The Integrated Treatment of Acute Psychosis Project, Western Lapland.

31. Seikkula, Alakare and Aaltonen (2001) Open Dialogue in Psychosis 1: An introduction and case illustration, *Journal of Constructivist Psychology, 14*, 247–65.

32. Edward Whitney (2003) *British Medical Journal, 327*, 682, September. He is a medical researcher, Colorado Division of Workers' Compensation, Denver, USA.

33. Kay Redfield Jamieson (1997) *An Unquiet Mind.* NY: Picador.

34. Gunnell and Frankel (1994) referred to by M. Arshad M in *Irish Psychiatrist, 4* (6) Dec 03/Jan 04.

35. Joanna Moncrieff (1997) Lithium: evidence reconsidered, *British Journal of Psychiatry, 171*, 113–19.

36. Carol Ann Turkington and Eliot Kaplan (1995) *Making the Prozac Decision.* McGraw Hill.

37. The *Sunday Independent* (1998) 12 March.

38. The *Sunday Independent* (1998) 19 April.

39. Claire Beeken had anorexia nervosa for 13 years. Following her recovery, she set up the charity 'Caraline' in England. She named the charity after a friend and fellow sufferer who did not survive the condition. Contact 'Caraline' on www.caraline.com

40. Claire Beekin and Rosanna Street (1997) *My Body, My Enemy, My Thirteen Year Battle with Anorexia Nervosa.* Harper Collins.

41. Ibid. p. 42.

42. Fiona Shaw (2003) *Out of Me*: *The story of a postnatal breakdown,* pp. 75–6. London: Trafalgar Square.

43. Rosemary Shelly ed. (1997) *Anorexics on Anorexia,* pp. 2–3. London: Jessica Kingsley. Rosemary Shelly has recovered from anorexia.

44. Ibid. p. 3

45. Dr Andrew Rynne (1998) *Irish Medical News*, 2 November 1998. An experienced Irish GP and medical journalist, Dr Rynne is seen a modern-thinking and compassionate GP amongst his peers. Dr Rynne was expressing his views while reviewing Marie Campion (1998) *Hope: Understanding eating disorders*, p. vi. Dublin: O'Brien Press.

46. Shelly, op cit. p. 4.

47. *Derry Journal* (2003) 19 December.

48. John Farrelly (2002) 'Schizophrenia: Choice is paramount' *Irish Medical Times,* 26 July. He is from Schizophrenia Ireland.

49. William Anthony (2000) *Psychiatric Rehabilitation Journal,* Fall.

50. Robert Bernstein (2002) *US News and World Report,* 6 March.

51. Linda Hart (2003) An open letter to Mental Health Professionals. *OpenMind, 124,* Nov/Dec. Permission granted © Mind (National Association for Mental Health).

52. Patrick Holford (2003) *Optimum Nutrition for the Mind.* Basic Health Publications.

5

WHY PEOPLE KILL THEMSELVES:

THE MEDICAL VIEW

Within medicine, it is generally accepted that over 70 per cent of suicides are caused by depression, 15 per cent by schizophrenia, and most of the remaining 15 per cent by psychiatric conditions such as alcohol and drug abuse, anorexia and anxiety.

Theory as fact; non-science as science

In medicine as in life in general, when a theory is repeated often enough, it eventually becomes accepted as fact. This is especially likely when the theory is one which is beneficial to the medical profession, compatible with the profession's beliefs and practices. Many doctors look at the problem of suicide through the lens of psychiatric illness. The resulting tunnel vision impedes the growth of a broader, more holistic approach to suicide.

Doctors increasingly believe that the most likely fundamental underlying cause of suicide is an imbalance of chemicals in the brain. While many psychiatrists believe that 90 per cent of suicides are due to 'mental illness', this does not mean they are right. Modern medicine bases this belief on psychological autopsies, which the profession rate highly. But these autopsies are no more than a psychiatric interpretation of the events preceding the suicide. If the psychiatrist is biased, albeit unintentionally, the psychological autopsy will also be biased.

Medical experts instinctively look for evidence of 'psychiatric illness' following a suicide rather than seek to understand the human pain and despair which brought that person to the point where no other option held great attraction for them. As a group, psychiatrists do not sufficiently consider the possibility that social, emotional, psychological and relationship problems provide sufficient cause for a person to take their own life. The medical explanation of suicide is rarely complete without reference to the central role of 'psychiatric illness'. I believe this view does not accurately reflect the reasons people choose to take their own lives.

Certainly, many people who take their lives are depressed. There is a great deal of depression, anguish and despair in our society. What I am questioning is the labelling of this emotional turmoil as 'mental illness'. Working as a medical doctor for over twenty years, I have come to realise that emotional distress is understandable and appropriate in the context of how that person's life has unfolded for them. I believe it is erroneous to presume that one must be 'mentally ill' to contemplate ending one's life. Unfortunately, such an approach does not sit well with modern psychiatry's preoccupation with 'mental illness' — with diagnosing, labelling and prescribing.

Doctors tend to believe so much in their theories that they become convinced of their validity, even when there is little solid evidence to back them up. Once theories compatible with medical philosophy and practice become accepted as fact, there are many benefits for the medical profession:

- Theories are questionable, facts are not. In discussions and arguments either with the general public or groups who question medical practice, theories will always have to be vigorously shown to be better than other possible theories. Not so with facts. Facts have already passed through the questioning stage.
- Psychiatrists become society's experts on suicide since they are the experts on 'mental illness', because they are in possession of the 'facts'.

267

- Those who believe that psychiatry's approach to suicide is seriously misguided can be easily dismissed. Having 'established' that 'mental illness' is the key issue in suicide, psychiatrists can easily dismiss dissenters who question their beliefs and practices.

Governments, the media and the public alike take their lead from medical experts. Consequently, newspaper articles on depression and suicide fall into this 'presenting theory as fact' trap. We have now reached the point where medical theories on mental illness and suicide have become widely accepted as established fact. Hardly a week goes by without this sort of misinformation appearing in the national media. There is rarely a rush from within the medical profession to correct the misinformation via the 'Letters to the Editor' column the following week. I believe this may be because the misinformation strengthens the position of the medical profession, conveying the impression that doctors understand more about these issues than they actually do.

Is the prevailing medical view right?

When expert doctors speak about health matters, few people feel confident and knowledgeable enough to publicly challenge them. It is not easy for non-medical people to question doctors. The medical profession quickly responds to such challenge with complex language and statistics which confuse even the most tenacious and persistent questioner, putting him or her in their place. But it is vitally important that the pronouncements of the medical profession are challenged, to test whether they are as valid as they seem.

Journalist John Waters is not impressed by the 'mental illness' theory as the cause of suicide. In *The Irish Times* of 13 January 1998 he wrote:

One of the traditional cop-outs about suicide has been that

it is the consequence of mental illness. The purpose of emphasising this connection has been to spare the families of suicide victims but also society at large from the guilt arising from the accusation that a suicide might otherwise represent. There have been strenuous attempts of late to create a causal link between suicide and what is called depression. Indeed, in a recent interview, psychiatrist Dr Patrick McKeon reiterated the conventional view that the vast majority of suicide victims have been suffering from 'some underlying psychiatric problem, mainly depression or mood disorders'.

Later in the same interview Dr McKeon spoke more specifically about the nature of what is called depression. Dr McKeon said that 'human beings, to live with themselves, have a natural infusion of positive perspectives on things, that enables us to keep going in life. When that's taken away, that's actually called depression.' This suggests to me that depression is not simply a clinical condition that descends on the individual like a virus. It is inextricably related to the external conditions of that human being's life and his perceptions of these. To say that suicide victims are depressed is telling us nothing. Everyone gets depressed but not everyone commits suicide.

In my opinion, John Waters makes far more sense regarding suicide than many psychiatrists. When I read what psychiatrists say regarding why people end their own lives, I usually feel there is a serious lack of human understanding within their words and writings.

Psychological autopsies: a critique
When a person dies, and the cause of death is not clear, an autopsy is carried out. During this postmortem examination, the pathologist examines the body, searching for evidence of

the cause of death. Autopsies have been carried out for decades. They are an established part of modern medicine's efforts to identify the cause of death. If there is insufficient evidence regarding the cause of death following an autopsy, then the cause of death remains unknown.

Autopsies carried out on people who have taken their own lives do not give any clues as to why the person did so. There are no postmortem findings which point to underlying tissue or organ pathology, as would be found when death occurs due to a heart attack, cancer or diabetes, for example. Indeed, postmortems carried out on people diagnosed as having had 'mental illnesses' such as depression, manic depression or schizophrenia do not reveal anything regarding organ or tissue pathology which might point to a physical cause for these 'conditions'. This reality raises significant doubts regarding the medical belief that these 'conditions' are caused by physical brain abnormalities. Perhaps in response to consistently negative findings at postmortem, psychiatry has created the notion of a 'psychological autopsy' as a method of identifying why people end their lives.

The cerebrospinal fluid is the fluid which surrounds the brain. Some researchers have tenuously linked cerebrospinal fluid levels of serotonin to impulsivity. Extrapolating from this, many psychiatrists link serotonin and suicide, which is sometimes an impulsive act. There are many unknowns and uncertainties in this research; researchers must guard themselves from making premature conclusions. Serotonin naturally occurs in many areas of the body. Measuring the serotonin levels within the general blood stream reveals little about the complexities of serotonin function. It is widely accepted within all medical specialties that blood tests for serotonin, its precursors and derivatives shed little meaningful light on serotonin function. Similarly, serotonin is present throughout many parts of the human brain. Measuring the level of serotonin, its precursors and derivatives in the cerebrospinal fluid may tell very little regarding the complex function of serotonin within the human brain. As the late psychiatrist Dr Michael Kelleher commented (see p. 346) having become somewhat disillusioned with ambivalent serotonin result studies, 'the serotonin link with suicide may have been overstretched'.

In a psychological autopsy, the events prior to the suicide are examined by doctors for evidence of 'mental illness'. Psychiatrists try to get as much information as possible about the person's psychological state preceding the suicide. They attempt to piece together a psychological picture of the person which might provide some clues as to why that person took their own life. Typically, doctors apparently find enough information to make a postmortem diagnosis of a 'mental illness' in over 90 per cent of suicides, even if the person has never seen a doctor or psychiatrist.

Psychiatrists approach a psychological autopsy from the perspective of psychiatry. Psychiatrists may speak with family members and friends, looking for clues and signs, not of emotional distress, but of what psychiatrists believe to be psychiatric illnesses. Before they even begin the autopsy, they are heavily prejudiced in favour of making a psychiatric diagnosis.

A psychological autopsy is based on opinions, not facts. A psychological autopsy carried out by a psychologist or psychotherapist might come to a totally different conclusion to the one arrived at by a psychiatrist. What a psychiatrist decides is definite evidence of a 'diagnosable psychiatric disorder' might well be interpreted by an experienced psychologist or psychotherapist as evidence of severe emotional distress. But the psychiatrist's view will typically override other views, because psychiatrists are deemed to be *the* experts in the field.

I believe that modern medicine's belief in psychological

autopsies is open to question. Major conclusions are being drawn from these autopsies; conclusions which are being accepted as facts, upon which future health policies on suicide are based. Psychiatrists regularly quote psychological autopsies as proof that 'psychiatric illness' is the chief cause of suicide. But this is only one of several possible interpretations.

The purpose of an autopsy is to seek to establish the cause of death. If no physical evidence of physical illness, or of the illness that caused death, is found at autopsy, then the pathologist carrying out the autopsy will report accordingly. The pathologist will not come to a conclusion regarding cause of death without adequate physical evidence. In contrast, psychological autopsies represent a new, questionable departure from this practice; the conclusion of a psychological autopsy is arrived at in the absence of physical, demonstrable evidence at autopsy. The following tragic case demonstrates how potentially inaccurate psychological autopsies can be.

In his mid-twenties, John took his own life. His distraught family could not understand why, in the prime of his life, he had ended it all. John seemed to have everything going for him. He had just completed a university degree course. John was due to start his first job just three weeks before his suicide.

Kathy, John's sister, attended me two months after his death. She was desperate to come to some understanding of her brother's suicide. A friend of hers who had attended me previously recommended me to her in my capacity as a counsellor and doctor. Prior to meeting Kathy, I had not met John or any of the family. Kathy came to me because she was suffering the intense pain of losing a loved one through suicide. She was deeply confused and hurt. She could not understand why John did not come to her or the family for help. Why had he killed himself now, when things were really falling into place for him? John had his degree, his job, his independence, money. Why suicide? Why now? It just didn't make sense.

John did not leave a suicide note to explain his reasons.

The pain and loss experienced by people bereaved by suicide is so intense that words cannot describe it. The grieving process following the death of someone close to our hearts is always painful and prolonged. When the death occurs because the person has decided to end their own life, the grief and loss become even more unbearable. Kathy attended me for six months. She gave me a comprehensive history of the family life which she and John had experienced. Kathy also presented me with a detailed picture of John's external world, his life as she saw it. I attempted to feed back to her how John may have felt at various times in his life; what may have been going on inside his internal world, that crucially important part of each of us which we rarely feel safe enough to discuss with others. When our sessions concluded, we both felt we understood — to some degree at least — why John had ended his life.

To the outside world, John's life might have seemed quite normal and ordinary. John was the youngest of four children. Kathy was second-youngest in the family, two years older than John. John and Kathy and had always been close. Kathy recalled that their father was an aggressive, unpredictable man. Their mother was very quiet. Most days, their father would become aggressive at home. Their mother, being very passive, did not intervene. She was scared to stand up either for herself or for the children. Communication between their parents deteriorated steadily through the years of marriage. As a result, the younger children (Kathy and especially John) bore the brunt of their father's frustration and aggression. By the time he first went to school, John was already shy and timid. His experiences at school heightened John's sense of fear and isolation. For years he screamed and did everything possible to avoid going to school.

Kathy said that neither parent acted on John's pleas regarding school — quite the opposite. John was regularly physically punished by his father for trying to avoid going to school. John's mother did not have the courage either to tackle the problems at school or to stop her husband from beating John when he kicked up every morning before school.

Life seemed to improve for John between the ages of ten and thirteen. A talented soccer player, he played with the local football team. He was popular, and was getting attention and affirmation from the team, the coaches and the supporters. Consequently, some of his emotional needs were being met. However, this stopped when he entered the teenage years, as he withdrew from sports after a minor row with his team-mates.

John finished school and qualified some years later with a university degree. Kathy recalled that while at university, he had seemed happy. John had a hectic social life and seemed to have plenty of friends. Soon after he received his degree, the time came to take up his first job. The family noticed that during the three months preceding his suicide, he became increasingly withdrawn. John stayed at home virtually all the time, often staying in bed most of the day, not wanting to meet people, even his own family. He appeared very anxious and frightened. The least thing would greatly increase his anxiety. Then John decided to end it all and he took his own life.

To understand the potential for misinterpretation when relying on psychological autopsies carried out by modern medicine, here is an account of how a psychological autopsy on John's suicide might be interpreted, followed by what I believe is a far more accurate assessment of why he took his own life. In John's case, psychiatrists would likely conclude that John ended it all because he had a 'psychiatric illness'. They would interpret his staying in bed during the day, his withdrawal, his depressed mood to be sure signs of a severe clinical depression. Psychiatrists would confidently state that he fulfilled the criteria for depression which are widely accepted within psychiatry.

As discussed earlier, (p. 102 ff.) the *Diagnostic and*

Statistical Manual of Psychiatric Disorders-IV (*DSM-IV*) is the 'bible' of psychiatry. A psychological autopsy on John's life would find that at least six of the criteria outlined in the *DSM-IV* as evidence of a 'Major Depressive Episode' were present before his death:

Criterion A1: He was depressed, sad, hopeless and discouraged for two to three months prior to his suicide.

Criterion A2: John clearly had lost interest in many things, and there was virtually no pleasure in his life during his final months.

Criterion A3: His appetite was much reduced in the final months. He frequently skipped meals. He had lost interest in food.

Criterion A4: His sleep was disturbed for several weeks before his death. At times he would sleep most of the day as well as night (hypersomnia). At other times, he was very agitated at night, and could not sleep (insomnia).

Criterion A5: At times, John was very agitated and restless. At other times he was the opposite, and would gaze absently for hours at the television.

Criterion A9: John's suicide took a considerable amount of pre-planning given how he ended his life (in order to protect confidentiality I will not go into the method he used). John must therefore have had suicidal ideas in the hours, days or possibly weeks before his suicide.

John met these six criteria. Only five criteria need to be met in order to diagnose a 'Major Depressive Episode'. From a psychiatrist's perspective, the result of John's psychological autopsy is conclusive; John took his life because he was suffering from a 'Major Depressive Episode'. He is entered as another statistic, further proof that 'psychiatric illness' is the underlying cause of suicide.

I believe that psychological autopsies miss the point, due

to the unintentional prejudice of the psychiatrists who carry them out. They should really be called 'psychiatric autopsies', because they are carried out under the supervision of psychiatrists. We do not need labels or psychiatric diagnoses to understand why people kill themselves. They end their lives for human reasons. They feel desperately distressed in this world. They have lost hope that their great distress can be relieved; in order to kill the pain, they resort to killing themselves.

Young children need love, acceptance, freedom from abuse, freedom of expression. If children feel loved and accepted as they are growing up, they are more likely to develop high self-esteem. And people with high self-esteem tend not to take their own lives. However, if the growing child does not feel that he is loved and accepted unconditionally in his life, he may begin to feel threatened, unsafe. Children have a deep need to create as much safety as possible for themselves in their lives. They may develop strategies — protectors — to help them cope in a family or a life which to them does not feel safe.

Avoidance is one of the most common protectors human beings use when feeling threatened. If something scares the daylights out of us, often our first impulse may be to run away. John's tendency to avoid people or situations when feeling unsafe began at a very young age, though it went unnoticed within the family. Children have a natural tendency to reach out to their parents for hugs and physical comforting. John's father was an unpredictable man. He was not comfortable showing any affection to anyone. John soon learned that if he reached out to his father, his father might well ignore him. By the time John was four years of age, he was cautious about reaching out to his father. Painful as it was for John not to reach out to the father he loved, it was better than reaching out and being ignored — better than having his approval-seeking gesture rejected. Rejection is painful at any age. To a small child it can be devastating.

From a young age, school was tough going for John. For many years, he cried every morning, begging his parents not to send him to school. John was having great difficulty coping with his teachers. John told his parents this, but they did not act on it. His parents became sick and tired of his behaviour every school morning. They regularly lost their temper with John, lifting him into the car against his will and bringing him to school. John was regularly humiliated, beaten, ridiculed and criticised in school.

John's father was rarely at home. When he was, he was unpredictable and often aggressive. Being a passive person, John's mother felt unable to stand up for him. Traumatised and feeling unsafe, John increasingly withdrew into himself, even in his childhood years. John's quietness and shyness was commented on at school. Perhaps John chose the strategies of avoidance and quietness as a means of survival. If he did not take any risks and kept his mouth shut, there was less chance of him being criticised, ridiculed, rejected, laughed at, humiliated or beaten, at home or at school.

As a young teenager, John was emotionally vulnerable. He had to protect himself from further hurt, criticism and rejection in any way he could. Sport was one of the few things he felt confident about during his teenage years. John knew he was good at soccer. Through sport he got approval, praise and social contact. But he remained emotionally fragile during these adolescent years. Being so easily hurt and needing to avoid rejection so badly, John suddenly gave up soccer after a minor disagreement with his team-mates and never played again. He lost all the friends he had through sport. His withdrawal from people and from life gathered momentum during his teenage years.

John did well enough in his school exams to go to university. According to friends he made there, he was popular and well-liked. His sister told me that his time at university was good for him. But when he finished his final exams, his tendency to avoid situations or people resurfaced. He stayed at home all day. John withdrew from his friends. He also withdrew emotionally from his family, even from Kathy, to whom he had previously been close. Suicide was his final act of avoidance. John could not take any more pain.

In every case I have encountered, emotional, social, psychological, self-esteem or relationship issues lie at the heart of suicide. I believe that parents do the best they can for their children, in accordance with their own level of self-esteem and their own experience of life. It is inappropriate to blame parents or the family when loved ones take their own lives. As long as society in general — including the medical profession — continues to underestimate the role of self-esteem, relationships, emotional, psychological and social issues, I believe that medical intervention will not reduce the suicide rate. The public, particularly those who are at risk of suicide, deserve better.

A 1998 study on attitudes to suicide among thirteen- and fourteen-year old Irish schoolchildren by Dr M. O'Sullivan and Prof. M. Fitzgerald was published in the *Journal for the Association of Professionals in Services for Adolescents*. The researchers found that these teenagers looked on suicide as solving a problem. The acceptance of suicide as a problem-solving exercise among schoolchildren was described as a 'striking feature' by the authors of this study. Dr O'Sullivan and Professor Fitzgerald concluded that society needs to address the social nature of suicide.

Most medical experts do not accept that suicide can be explained by understanding how people see and interpret themselves, their life, relationships, and experiences. Given how central, how vital such issues are to our existence, common sense would suggest that they should receive appropriate consideration in any evaluation of possible causes of suicide.

6

WHY PEOPLE KILL
THEMSELVES:
AN ALTERNATIVE VIEW

The overall suicide rate in Britain has been declining slowly over the past twenty years. Nevertheless, suicide figures are twice those of road traffic accident fatalities in the UK. It is estimated that the true suicide rate is fifty to sixty per cent higher than the official figures. Many key factors regarding suicide point to social, emotional, psychological and relationship issues.

Why do people take their own lives?
I believe that many of the following apply to the majority of people who take their own lives:

- Very low self-esteem
- Feeling very unsafe, vulnerable and insecure within themselves
- Having a major conflict within themselves: conflict between the human need to be accepted by others as they really are on the one hand; but on the other hand, the fear of being rejected, of not being good enough, so they put on a front, an outward show. People are often astounded when people who were 'the life and soul of the party' or people who outwardly had 'everything to live for' take their own life. The greater the distance between the image a person presents to the world — their 'mask'— and their real self; the more lonely they feel; the more convinced they are that things can never

improve, the more likely they are to take their own life, seeing no other way out of their pain

- A lack of intimacy in their lives. They may well have people in their life who really love them. But many people are terrified of opening up even to the people they love and who love them, terrified of being seen to be vulnerable, perhaps also terrified that they may not be able to handle their own grief and sadness. 'I'm afraid that if I start crying I may never stop' is a comment I have heard on many occasions from people in deep distress.

- A lack of unconditionally loving, supportive relationships with people who will accept them as they are, or being afraid to reveal their true selves even to those who do love and support them unconditionally.

- Having been abused either sexually, physically and emotionally, or have had troubled relationships in their family of origin

- Having experienced losses which are too painful to endure

- Finding themselves ostracised in some way from important people in their life or from society in general

- Finding themselves faced with what seem to be intolerable obstacles in their lives, obstacles which seem impossible to surmount.

While modern medicine concentrates almost all its suicide research on establishing that suicide is primarily a 'psychiatric' problem, the human factors which bring people to the point of suicide are calling for attention. Much current suicide research is focusing on 'the suicidal brain'. I would much prefer to see the focus on 'the suicidal mind', 'the suicidal person' or indeed the 'suicide-inducing society' which we appear to have created.

The dramatic male and female patterns of suicide over the

past 30 years are a stark reminder of the central role of social, emotional, psychological, relationship and cultural issues in suicide. Across all age groups, the suicide rate in men exceeds that of females. Three-quarters of suicides in Britain are by males. While suicide rates for woman in Britain have almost halved in the past 30 years, the suicide rate for men in Britain has almost doubled during the same period. The highest rate of suicide occurs in young men aged from fifteen to twenty-four. In this group, the suicide rate in 2003 was 67 per cent higher than in 1982. In the 25–44 age group in Britain, men are almost four times more likely than women to end their own lives.

These dramatic changes in male and female suicidal rates argue against the theory that suicide is prompted by biological factors. It is stretching the imagination to suggest that, in the past thirty years, changes have occurred within the brains or genes of males — but not in females — which account for the dramatic rise in male suicides.

What follows are some of the social, emotional, psychological, relationship and cultural issues which can drive people to take their own lives.

Loneliness

So common is loneliness nowadays that it is akin to an epidemic. Tragically, it is a silent epidemic. In a society which expects us to be successful and upbeat about life, there are few people to whom we can express our loneliness. The degree of loneliness may vary from mild, infrequent loneliness to an ever-present torrent of emotion whose depth words cannot describe. Most people who take their lives have reached a point of unbearable loneliness. For some, the pain which deep loneliness brings can become too much to live with.

The majority of people who are suffering from 'mental illnesses' which doctors say are the underlying cause of most suicides — depression, schizophrenia, alcohol and drug abuse and other conditions such as eating disorders and anxiety — have one thing in common. They are very lonely. The degree of loneliness a person experiences in their life can sometimes be traced back to their childhood. Sometimes the child felt the loneliness at the time, but often the depth of the pain of loneliness is so overwhelming that the child suppresses it rather than feel such emotional distress. Suppressed feelings remain with the person. Later in life, the pain may resurface, resulting in anxiety, depression or other forms of emotional distress which doctors label and treat as 'mental illness'.

Families particularly likely to create lonely children are those where one or both parents have a drink problem; where one parent is aggressive and the other is passive and does not confront the aggressor; where parents are unhappy and unfulfilled in their relationship; where children are not given the freedom to express how they feel freely, for fear of upsetting their father or hurting their mother or vice versa. Children of parents who have had a so-called 'psychiatric illness' for many years often experience deep loneliness. Their distressed parent may have become so preoccupied with themselves and their own survival that they are unable to meet the emotional needs of their children. Families where one or both parents are away a lot, or preoccupied with work and other activities are in my opinion more likely to produce lonely children. So are homes where there is little or no expression of love. Children need to be repeatedly told by their parents that they are loved and they need bagfuls of hugs to prove it. Sometimes there is a major imbalance; one parent being emotionally remote from the children and not communicating love to them, while the second parent is at the other extreme, almost smothering the children with love.

People hide their loneliness because it is not publicly acceptable to be lonely. You do not have to be alone to be lonely. I have met many lonely individuals who always have people around them. But it is not enough to be surrounded by people, even family and friends, unless you feel you can be yourself with them. We all wear a mask. We reveal to others only what we feel safe to reveal. The more of ourselves we need to conceal, the more lonely we will be.

Everyone who knows Marie thinks of her as a bubbly, cheerful person. She came to see me in my capacity as a counsellor wanting to talk to someone about her deep loneliness and distress. If Marie had a penny for every time people have said to her 'Honest to God, you're a tonic!', she would be a rich woman. Marie knows different. Behind that mask of humour and frivolity lies much loneliness and sadness. Marie knows that her humour is a front. She recently showed me a piece she wrote, as if talking to this cheerful mask. I was so touched, I asked her if I could include it in this book. She calls her humorous mask 'Coco the Clown':

Hi Coco,

I am so glad you are part of my life. I know the going must be difficult for you at times. You are called upon almost daily. I never realised before now what you mean to me. I feel safe when you're around. Maybe I even overuse you. I certainly hide behind you, some people know only you. I feel really lost and abandoned when you're not around or when people don't quite get your drift. You first came into my life when I was a lonely child. I was so careful to keep you to myself until I realised that other people enjoyed you. I know I probably depend on you too much, but then again you are my best friend. Thank you for all the support and shelter you have provided. I don't know where we go from here, but I hope you will always be a part of my life.

Marie recently became aware that she goes into this humorous mode when she feels threatened in social situations, or in situations likely to evoke great sadness. The greater the likelihood that she will experience great despair and loss, the stronger the urge to laugh her way around the situation. This desire to behave in the opposite way to how one is feeling is an understandable human response to overwhelming despair, a way of protecting oneself from fully experiencing sadness and loss.

In her work with me, I have attempted to create a safe space for Marie to explore, express and release the pent-up sadness and distress she has felt for decades. Ours is the first relationship in her life where she felt safe enough not to pretend, to wear that mask. As a result, she has released a great deal of her distress. My total acceptance of her tears, her anger, her regrets and losses — her vulnerable side — has helped her accept these aspects of herself. She now feels less need to resort to Coco the Clown, though we both agree that she should never lose her wonderful sense of humour, of which Coco is an important part.

Loss and hurt
The loss of what is cherished can be devastating. The pain and emotional hurt is sometimes so great that suicide seems the only way to kill the pain. There are countless examples, depending on the person's life circumstances and experiences — loss of love and intimacy following the ending of a relationship or the death of a loved one; the loss of status and usefulness which occurs when people retire or when the kids fly the nest. The loss of what might have been — the woman who desperately wants children but cannot have them; the man who desperately wanted promotion but was passed over. The loss of one's health can lead to depression and suicide.

There is also the loss of hope for the future — losing hope that anyone will ever love them or be there. A person's decision to end their life in reaction to a particular loss or trauma may seem excessive to others, but the final trigger is often the straw that broke the camel's back. The person has reached a state of such despondency that it does not take much to send them over the edge. There have been too many losses and broken dreams, too many hurts and rejections, creating a depth of despair where every possible solution looks hopeless. In such a state, like the fighter pulverised by an opponent, the final blow may seem light enough. By then they have thrown in the towel. There is no fight left in them.

Public humiliation with the accompanying loss of face and status can be devastating enough to trigger suicide. Both the fear and the experience of losing face can be very difficult to deal with. The successful businessman who goes bankrupt. The previously successful student who flunks an exam. A dark secret which suddenly surfaces to the cold light of day for all to see and judge. Facing people can be very difficult when you feel that you have let yourself or others down. Losing face is linked to self-esteem. The lower a person's self-esteem, the more painful it becomes to be seen to fail in public. Sometimes it seems less painful to end one's life than to live with the pain of losing face.

Many people believe that suicide is a selfish act; that the suicidal person should get a grip on themselves and remember the loss their loved ones will suffer if they take their own lives. In reality, most suicidal persons believe they are such a burden that those people around them would be better off without them.

Social upheaval and change

Suicide rates are affected by changes in society. Social changes which unite people and communities tend to reduce the suicide rate. When a country is at war, you might think that more people would be inclined to take their own lives; actually, the suicide rate tends to drop. This is possibly because the national sense of unity, pride and purpose bring people closer together, creating a powerful community spirit. On the other hand, the suicide rate increases when social changes isolate people, reducing people's sense of hope, identity and belonging.

The dramatic increase in the suicide rate of young men reflects how enormously the lives of men have changed during the past thirty years. Five decades ago, men earned the family income and women stayed at home to look after the family. Both sexes had a sense of who they were and what was expected of them. The role and identity of women in society have expanded dramatically, as have the possibilities open to women. In contrast, the role of men is less clear than it used to be. Many men struggle to cope with this.

Superficially, the young male lives the life of Riley compared to his counterparts of thirty years ago — sex, freedom, alcohol, drugs, no religious oppression, no corporal punishment at school. But inside, many young men are unsure of themselves and their role in modern society. From an early age, boys tend to be conditioned — at home, at school, among their friends and in the media — not to show their feelings. In the process, young men are given the message that they must hide away a core part of who they are: their feelings, their vulnerability, their fear of not being good enough, of not meeting the expectations they believe others have of them.

Men become increasingly afraid of — and therefore avoid — intimacy, true closeness with others, even loved ones. They play a dangerous game called 'big boys don't cry'. Sometimes men reach a point of utter desperation, at which point the game of life may become too painful to endure any longer. For men conditioned not to ask for help, not to show vulnerability, suicide becomes a real option; a way to end their pain without losing face.

Nowadays, the role of women has expanded greatly. As well as their historical role as the child-bearer and home-maker, women can do virtually everything that was traditionally the domain of men. For some young woman who feel there is no purpose to their lives, there is one option which young men do not have; they can have a child. Suddenly life has a purpose. The mother is important; she has a child; someone to love, to look after — a child who will love her in return. People who used to ignore her now come over to her and admire the baby. In general, society rallies around her. She may receive some assistance from the State. In contrast, men are becoming less and less essential to the everyday life of society. There are many families where women are now rearing children with little or no input from the father. Many men argue that this sense of feeling ostracised is enhanced by the court's approach to separation, divorce and access to children following relationship breakdown.

A record number of suicide victims were found during 1998 in a forest at the foot of Japan's Mount Fuji. Had there been a massive outbreak of psychiatric illness in Japan, which would explain, in psychiatry's language, why Japan experienced a dramatic suicide-rate increase? Hardly. However there *was* a major social crisis in Japan in 1998. Their economy virtually collapsed. Japanese authorities suspect that the increased rate of suicide was linked to increased fear, uncertainty and hopelessness experienced by Japanese citizens as a consequence of the economic collapse.

Relationship issues

Research suggests that suicide is closely linked to how human beings bond with each other in relationships. For every human being, their first and most powerful experience of bonding occurs in their own home. How people bond with others in their adult life will therefore be influenced by how safe they felt within the key relationships of their childhood.

According to the Samaritans, relationship difficulties are the reason most cited by those who attempt suicide. The enormous changes in a person's life created by the break-up of a relationship or a marital separation can be overwhelming. Add to this the immense guilt and loss which separating or divorcing parents experience towards their children. The end result can be a tidal wave of emotional pain and social alienation which, in the words of one client of mine who went through a marriage break-up, 'makes three feet of rope sound attractive'.

Psychological research suggests that when parents break up, boys do not cope as well as girls, and they suffer much more psychological stress. Usually the mother gets custody of the children. Mothers and daughters tend to become closer to each other and develop a mutually supportive relationship. Boys, however, feel themselves being rigidly controlled by their mothers and find it more difficult to form a mutually supportive relationship with their mothers.

The number of suicide attempts increases around St Valentine's day and Christmas day. Dr J. Birtle and his colleagues noticed that an unusually high number of people had taken an overdose of drugs and presented to casualty departments on St Valentine's day. They carried out a study to evaluate this link in more detail. It involved three health districts in the Birmingham area over five years. The researchers concluded that there was an association between St Valentine's day and suicide attempts, particularly in suicide attempts by adolescents. They also found that there was a link between suicide attempts and Christmas day.

The researchers concluded that:

Those in contact with adolescents should be particularly vigilant during emotionally charged festivals such as Christmas day and St Valentine's day. Previous studies have shown an association between suicide attempts and stressful events such as an unsuccessful relationship, unemployment, and physical illness. The festival of St Valentine's day may induce stress due to unrequited love.[1]

A few weeks ago, a man I am working with was telling me about his life. Among other things, he mentioned that he had planned to end his life on Christmas day two years ago. He was alone that Christmas day, very lonely and without any sense of hope that things would improve for him. The pain was too much. He hung a rope from the ceiling, and was about to end his life. His phone rang. It was his favourite niece, who rang to say 'Happy Christmas'. His niece said 'I love you'. On hanging up the phone, he burst into tears, and took the rope down. Hearing that he was loved, that he did actually mean something to another human being, got him through the day.

There is no evidence that a massive outbreak of 'mental illness' occurs every year on St Valentine's day and Christmas day. The triggers for suicide attempts are human issues, not 'psychiatric illness'. People who feel isolated within their family, culture or community are far more likely to end their lives than people who feel they belong.

Sexuality

There is substantial evidence that young homosexual men are much more likely to take their lives than heterosexual males. This cannot be put down to psychiatric illness. Homosexuality is not currently viewed as a mental illness, though it is only a few decades since it was viewed as such by the medical profession and society in general.

Gay men and lesbians encounter many psychosocial problems which their heterosexual counterparts never have to deal with:

> The psychosocial problems of gay and lesbian adolescents
> are primarily the result of societal stigma, hostility, hatred,
> and isolation.[2]

Journalist Cathal Kelly questioned the continuing silence around suicides among gay youth:

The figures for gay youth suicide are stark. Twelve different studies in North America between 1972 and 1994 show that an average of one-third of young gay men attempted suicide, with nearly 40 per cent of these making repeated attempts. The rate of suicide attempts among young gay men was found to be ten times higher than the attempt rate for young men generally. Two further studies published earlier this year (1998) confirmed that young gay men are seven to thirteen times more likely to commit suicide than heterosexual men.[3]

Issues around sexuality can be deeply threatening for young people. There is a great deal of peer and advertising pressure on young people around sex and sexuality. Struggling to come to terms with sex and relationships, some teenagers find themselves without the support and understanding of key people in their lives. Many parents avoid discussing sexual issues with their children. Many teenagers are equally reluctant to discuss sexual issues with their parents. When parents are open to discussing sexual matters, their children have that option open to them if they wish to avail themselves of it. The issue of sexuality needs to discussed and explored far more openly in our society.

Hopelessness
Modern medicine accepts that when people feel they have no hope for the future, they are more likely to end their life. Medical experts say that hopelessness occurs as a result of depression. The next step in the medical scheme of things is to treat the depression with antidepressants in order to lift the depressive illness. The theory is that the hopelessness will also improve as a consequence. But hopelessness is not a 'mental illness'; it is a human reaction when life becomes overwhelming. A person becomes hopeless when they see no

way out of their crisis, believing that things will never improve. At that moment, no option other than suicide may appear to end their torment. Many people will take their own lives rather than acknowledge their excruciatingly painful emotional vulnerability. Given that our society does not provide appropriate acceptance, understanding and support structures, perhaps this is not surprising.

People with serious illnesses sometimes reach the point of complete hopelessness and decide to end it all. Any serious medical condition where the person experiences constant pain and loss (of mobility, independence, hope) may drive sufferers to the point of suicide. Illnesses that seriously undermine quality of life and are not likely to improve may bring people to the point of despair where suicide becomes a way out of their misery. It is well known and accepted that prolonged physical pain may trigger suicide. Is it all that surprising that prolonged emotional pain may similarly bring up suicide as a way to kill the pain?

Marital status

Modern medicine has long recognised that marital status has a bearing on an individual's suicide risk. Happily married people have the lowest suicide rates, followed by single people, widowed, divorced and separated people (especially those recently separated) in that order. Unhappily married men and women are more likely to end their lives than those whose marital relationships are happy and fulfilling. Married people have a partner with whom they share their lives. While many single people are perfectly happy either to be in relationships or not, as suits the individual, others do feel the lack of an intimate relationship in their lives. The three groups of people most likely to take their lives — the widowed, the divorced and the separated — have one thing in common. Their marital relationship has ended, leaving them without their most intimate relationship, which had been so important in their lives.

Research suggests that the rate of suicide soon after divorce or separation is substantially higher in men than in women. Following divorce or separation, men's access to their children may be considerably restricted. In disputes over custody of the children, the courts tend to favour the mother as the principal custodian. Consequently, men may find themselves deprived of close, frequent contact with their children. On Christmas day 2003, separated men held a demonstration in Dublin to highlight their lack of access to their children on Christmas day. The contact separated fathers do have with their children may no longer be within the familiar surroundings of the family home and environment. With the intention of minimising the children's upheaval, the man is more likely to have to leave the family home than his partner, often having to set up home away from friends and neighbours. Consequently, men may find themselves disconnected from important relationships and social networks. The evidence suggests that women are more likely to have more supportive social networks than men following divorce or separation.

Religion
Many researchers point out that the increase in the rate of suicide is partly due to the decline in the popularity of religion. In the past, when religion had a much stronger influence on society, suicide was considered a major sin against God. People would not risk attracting the wrath of God by ending their own lives. They suffered on in silence, or took consolation in alcohol or whatever else they could find, to escape from their feelings of misery and despair. In addition, religion can give people a sense of belonging, a link with God, meaning and purpose in their lives, light at the end of life's dark tunnels.

Cultural and other factors
Medical research on emigrants from different European

countries to both America and Australia has shown that for the next two generations, the suicide rates of the emigrants remained consistent with their country of origin. As the influence of the old culture diminished within these families, as they adopted the lifestyle of the country to which they had emigrated, the suicide rates within these families changed to the rates of their adopted country.

Unemployment

The rate of suicide is higher in people without jobs. This is especially true for men; the suicide rate amongst unemployed men is 2–3 times that of the general population. Among other things, society values people according to their job, their status, their income. Not having a job — especially for men — can be a severe blow. There are other knock-on effects of unemployment which create great strain for the unemployed person and their family, not least the financial implications of not having a steady income. Unemployment is associated with loss of face and prestige. What is often not taken into account is that sometimes the fundamental problem is more than the lack of employment. The person's emotional vulnerability may make it too threatening to seek or to hold down a job. It seems to me that employment status is an important factor, one among many important human concerns which together add up to make a person feel that life is worth living or not.

A study of teenagers aged thirteen and fourteen looked at what factors these teenagers felt might push them or their peers to suicide. Virtually all the answers were important social factors, rather than psychiatric illness:

> 49 per cent felt that the commonest reason for suicide was linked to schools, examination pressures, bullying and intimidation.
>
> 35 per cent mentioned issues relating to their home life and family.

13 per cent felt that social isolation was an important trigger.

20 per cent said that depression was an important factor.

Young people — the age group most likely to take their own lives — have a great deal more stress in their lives than perhaps we realise. A 1998 British survey commissioned by the *Bread for Life* campaign confirmed this. The range of issues young people have to deal with as they are growing up has greatly increased; peer group pressure, friendship, parental expectation, family conflict, marital separation and divorce, bullying, sex, sexual orientation, eating disorders, alcohol, drugs, image, teenage pregnancy, and finding suitable employment all exert pressure on these young people. The choices and possibilities open to teenagers these days greatly exceed those available even ten years ago. For many young people, increased choices enhance their options. However, for some, increased choices and possibilities increase their anxiety. This is especially true for young people who have lost confidence in themselves, who doubt their ability to cope with the considerable choices and expectations of modern living.

Teenagers are searching for their identity as human beings in their own right. The behaviour of teenagers is often motivated by a deep need to be accepted, to fit in with peers and create some sense of independence from their family. In many homes, teenage behaviour is interpreted as rebellion, and results in punishment and criticism. With the best will in the world, these parents may have misinterpreted the situation. And in so doing, they may have unwittingly heightened their child's sense of vulnerability and insecurity.

If we are really serious about reducing the suicide rate, we must concentrate our efforts on the needs of individuals. I believe that as long as psychiatry dominates the 'expert' platform, the issues explored above will remain sidelined in favour of multi-million pound 'Defeat Depression' (with drugs) campaigns which have never been shown to reduce the suicide rate. It sometimes seems that modern medicine is presuming that the quality of a person's key relationships has little or no bearing on a person's suicide risk, or at most just exacerbates or ameliorates the underlying 'illness'. Given how intense relationships can be, how central they are to life, this is perhaps a dangerous presumption.

Suicide: a sane act

To people contemplating suicide, ending their own life makes a great deal of sense. Suicide is not an act of insanity. The decision to end one's life is not the result of a sudden flick of a switch in the brain. At that moment of utter despair, suicide seems the only way to kill the pain. Even when, to the outside world, the person's decision to kill themselves is inexplicable, I believe that the person knows precisely why, at that moment in their life, suicide seemed the right action. Until modern medicine wakes up to this, I believe that doctors will make little progress in their efforts to reduce the suicide rate.

According to the late GP and coroner Dr Bartley Sheehan:

Suicide is a response to the individual's perception of their circumstances and their experience. All of the perceptions that lead people to suicide are internal to the person. They are proper and appropriate perceptions. They are the individual standing in their own experience of their own lives. It may make no sense to you or to me or to anybody else, but it is their experience.[4]

In my work with clients, I have found that by getting in touch with people about their experience, hearing and knowing what that experience is, and I do get an understanding of why a person wishes to end their life. I have also found that connecting with people in this way can itself be a healing experience for the person. Being really met in this place of utter despair can sometimes be enough to bring the person back from the brink of suicide.

Dr Sheehan's views make sense to me. I believe he is accurately reflecting the inner world of people who take their own lives. Every individual who makes a serious suicide attempt is clear about one thing. They want their inner pain and turmoil to end. As they plan their suicide, they can see no other way out of their despair and hopelessness.

As the following case histories show, the determination of the majority of those who take their lives to proceed with the act strongly suggests that these individuals are very clear regarding what they are about to do.

Mary (p. 324) carefully planned her suicide attempt in advance. She travelled from Dublin to Galway so that she could throw herself into the river Corrib. Before jumping into the river, she calmly went for one last cup of coffee. She was very clear that she had had enough pain in her life. She saw suicide as her only way out.

Anne (p. 309) described what a sane act suicide is. When she reached the depths of despair, suicide entered her mind as a realistic way of ending her desperate emotional pain and suffering.

In the 1997 *Late Late Show* (a very popular TV programme broadcast in Ireland) dedicated to suicide, several examples of carefully planned suicides were shared. A prison officer describes the suicide of a prison inmate:

> *He was in a cell, and what amazed me was the ingenuity of how he actually committed suicide. He was in a padded cell for his own protection; there was just a mattress and a blanket in it. Unfortunately the glass was missing from a spy-hole. He tore the cover off the mattress and made a knot. He shoved the knot out through the spy-hole. There was a flap on the outside of the spy-hole. The flap came*

*across, caught the knot and jammed it. He apparently just
sat down behind the door, and that's the way he committed
suicide. I had actually just checked on him myself, and a
couple of minutes later it was brought to my attention that
there was a knot sticking out through the spy-hole. We went
to check it out. We pushed the knot in, and we opened the
door, and the poor chap fell out on top of us.*

A study of suicides in Sweden found that four out of five people
who end their lives make some sort of communication to one
or more people about their intentions. Given their depth of
despair, this communication may not be clear; its significance
may be understood only after the person has ended their life.
It therefore seems as if most people who take their own lives
have pondered over this decision for some time. The decision
is not an insane choice. They have had enough. They have to
end their pain. Suicide, the ultimate act of avoidance, is the
option which makes most sense. It seems most appropriate at
that moment in their lives.

Relationships and families

No man develops by himself: a person develops always in
relationship with others. The relationships that most matter
are those that occur within the family. It is now known that
one person's ability to cope with life and another person's
limited ability or inability to cope with life can be traced
back to the pattern of relationships that operated within
his family.[5]

According to Virginia Satir, American family therapist and
author of *Peoplemaking*,[6] a five-year-old child has already had
about a billion interactions with other people, principally his
or her parents, carers and family. People who enter relationships
or get married are expected to know how to handle difficulties

and conflicts which frequently arise in their relationships. Parents are expected to know instinctively how best to rear their children.

But parenting is the most difficult profession on earth. Parents receive little training or guidance. Many do not have support when the going gets tough. How we relate to other people is fundamentally important to our happiness and well-being. Yet we do not have a structured and easily accessible service to help people understand themselves, others, and improve our ability to communicate with others.

Because they usually look after the medical care of several members of the family, general practitioners are also known as 'family doctors'. Ironically, GPs receive little training in relationships and interpersonal communication. In my opinion, the medical profession does not sufficiently understand how relationships can hurt — and heal. For the first fifteen to eighteen years of every person's life, the relationships within the family are critically important. Relationships do make lasting impressions. Yet modern medicine does not devote any time or research to deepening its understanding of relationships. Here is a brief summary of the main relationships in a young person's life and how important they are to every human being:

The family of origin

Every person shares their early life with other people. We all had a father, a mother and perhaps brothers and sisters. Their presence — or absence — plays a central part in our lives. Most children live at home until their late teens. Powerful and intense relationships between the child and the various members of the family have a huge influence on how they emerge from being a dependent child into adulthood. After a young adult leaves home to create their own life, relationships with parents and siblings usually remain important.

Children need to feel safe, secure and supported at home.

They need to know that their parents' love for them will not be withdrawn under any circumstances. If a young person leaves their home of origin with high self-esteem, feeling safe enough to shape and create their new life, they will usually want to maintain contact with their family of origin. The bond of love usually ensures that keeping in touch with family remains high on their priority list, while at the same time they continue to carve out their own life, in their own way.

Young adults with low self-esteem may need to rely heavily on the family for support in a world which appears threatening. Conversely, they may rebel and have little to do with their family. Often, young adults do not feel they can communicate their true feelings and vulnerabilities within their family. Experience may have taught them that their family cannot or will not hear what they need to say, cannot give them the emotional safety and support they need.

I believe that in general parents do their best for their children, given the parents' own self-esteem, experience and sense of safety in the world. But I have come across many cases where the parents have been unable to meet the needs of their children. Parents are human beings, after all. Many parents were themselves reared in home environments where their emotional needs for safety, security, unconditional love and acceptance were not met. Consequently, many parents do not feel safe in their lives. Feeling unsafe, many parents react to life and to their children by protecting themselves. They feel they have to. Their emotional survival depends on it.

The critical relationships for a child are obviously those within the family of origin, in particular with parents. Parents' own needs to protect themselves from hurt or criticism may prompt them to deal with the child in such a way that the child feels the parents' love has been withdrawn. The more often this happens, the more unsafe children feel, and the more coping mechanisms they develop — avoidance, overcompensating, not speaking their mind, competitiveness, anxiety, rebelling, aggression, passivity and perfectionism, to name just a few. It is important that young adults be encouraged to create their own life, to leave the nest. I have seen many families where the parents, owing to their own emotional vulnerabilities, have held on to their children well into their adult life. This situation can create huge emotional conflict and greatly reduce their offspring's ability to create a fulfilling life for themselves.

Low self-esteem is known to be linked with virtually every so-called 'mental illness' including depression, schizophrenia, alcohol abuse, and drug abuse, the conditions most likely to precipitate suicide. Many researchers have found that low self-esteem is directly related to suicide. I believe that developing high self-esteem in our children is one of the most important preventative steps society can take to reduce the suicide rate. Relationships — within the family but also in the child's wider world of school, neighbourhood and extended family — have a significant influence on a child's level of self-esteem.

The extended family
Ideally, relationships with members of the extended family should feel safe and supportive. They should affirm and reinforce the child's sense of self-esteem and self-worth. Such extended family relationships are wonderful, a real blessing. Unfortunately, extended family relationships can have the opposite effect, undermining a person's sense of self-worth. Sometimes emotional, physical and sexual abuse occurs in relationships with extended family members, as well as within immediate family members. These relationships can have a devastating effect on a young person's life. Such invasion of the young person's life by an extended family member may occur when the parents do not see — or choose not to see — what is going on. They are too stressed to hear or act on the appeals of their children to put a stop to the abuse. Not believing

a disclosure of sexual abuse has been shown to be a important factor regarding later psychological distress in victims.

Other important relationships in our early lives

Young children have many important relationships outside of their own family. Many preschool children spend a good deal of time in crèches or with minders. At four or five years of age, children begin their relationship with school and all that goes with it — relationships with teachers, other children, peer pressure, belonging, fitting in, rules and regulations, school or work, expectations. As children grow older, they enter more relationships. Many social activities involve new relationships and new challenges. These new relationships and expectations can be far more threatening to young people than we adults sometimes realise.

The quality of the child–parent relationship affects relationships and situations outside the home. Some parents may not have sufficient self-esteem to stand up for the rights and feelings of their children — at school, with friends, with extended family members. If a child has a problem with a teacher, or is being bullied, or has an aunt who is very critical, they depend on the parent to resolve this conflict for them. Of course, there are times when children need to act on their own behalf. But they need to know that their parents will act on their behalf when they are unable to deal with the situation on their own.

If the parents do not hear the child's cry for help; if the parents do not or cannot take the necessary steps to find out precisely what the problem is and act to resolve it without delay; if the bullying continues; if the problem with the teacher continues; if the child's bombardment by a judgmental aunt, uncle, grandparent or other important person in their life continues, the child's self-esteem may be seriously undermined. The child may sense that those to whom they turn for safety are not providing enough protection. The child may then have to develop other protective strategies, designed to decrease the threat they feel: protective mechanisms such as anxiety, avoidance and withdrawal.

Relationships and the family are discussed in greater detail in other books. My intention here is to emphasise their importance and relevance to any discussion about emotional distress, 'mental illness' and suicide. Any assessment of the tragedy of suicide is incomplete without a thorough study of the family and relationships. Children need to receive clear messages from their parents about how unique and priceless they are. Unfortunately, some children are reared on a diet of criticism, judgement, put-down messages, and comparison with siblings or other young people. Because parents themselves need to protect themselves from showing their own vulnerability, many teenagers do not feel close to their parents.

Many young people will choose not to discuss at home issues which dominate their thoughts and their conversations with friends — sex, contraception, love, the transition into adulthood, drugs, alcohol — but may appreciate knowing that they can if they choose to, if their parents are open to such issues. Whatever intimacy children had with their parents in their earlier years tends to diminish during the teenage years. Many parents who fully believe they have a good relationship with their children do not realise that their children may be afraid to tell them things. Children sense what they can tell their parents and what they cannot.

If children feel safe and loved unconditionally in their relationship with their parents, they are more likely to feel comfortable about bringing up whatever is bothering them. If they know they will get an open and compassionate hearing, they are more likely to discuss issues with their parents. The parent will often not need to even ask — children will ask for help if they feel will get the response they need. If the parent does ask questions, children will open up only if they know from previous experience of this relationship that it is safe to open up without fear of rejection, judgement or ridicule. Perhaps too often, parents offer advice from their own perspective, rather than tuning in to their child's perspective of the situation or problem.

It is important that children are reared to deal with the reality of the world as it is. This world can be a tough place to be; a place where others will intrude upon us and invade our space. Children need to learn how to cope with these realities, how to assert themselves. To deal with this complicated world, young people need to believe that they can shape their own destiny; that they can deal effectively with the challenges they meet on a daily basis; that if plan A doesn't seem to be working out for them, they have the confidence and support to adjust, adapt or change to a plan B as appropriate. We can send men to the moon. We can send a spacecraft to Mars. But we have not set about creating a systematic way of raising self-esteem and assertiveness in our people. This is some reflection of the society we have created.

We find it difficult to cope and we survive by pretending that everything is all right. This came across strongly in *Boys Don't Cry*, a programme about suicide in young men broadcast on *Panorama*, BBC 1 on 14 December 1998. A young man who had taken his own life was described by his male friends as a poser, a prankster, full of laughs. The interviewer asked his friends if he confided in them or spoke about his fears, his distress. From the bar-counter, pints in hands, they replied that he kept everything to himself. Appearing shocked by the very idea of confiding in others, his friends said that talking about yourself was not something you did with your mates, 'not with the lads'.

If people cannot talk about their feelings with their friends and they do not feel comfortable showing vulnerability with their families, to whom can they turn? Speaking about the family of one young man who had taken his life, the presenter said:

Like so many parents, this young man's parents thought they knew their son, but there were obviously things he felt he could not share with his parents.

I remember Philip, an eighteen year old who had been quiet and withdrawn throughout his teenage years. He lived within a loving family, but I felt that the dynamics of the interpersonal relationships within the family provided some clue. Philip's father was a dynamic, high-achieving businessman, to whom no problem was insurmountable. The home was run like a business venture. When Philip went to his father with problems, his father quickly responded with solutions and ideas. Unwittingly, Philip's father did not give Philip the chance to air his worries, explore them with his father, and find his own solutions. Being insecure, Philip was intimidated by his father's apparent self-assuredness and decisiveness, and over the years responded by rarely going to his father with his problems. People can become isolated and withdrawn even when they live within a loving family.

The public and the medical profession need to realise that every person's own reality is valid for them. Whether it is hearing voices, becoming withdrawn, depressed, or highly anxious, what the person is experiencing must be accepted as valid for that person. A respectful exploration of that reality will frequently lead to a deeper understanding of what is going on for the person.

The stories of Eileen and Anne are two case histories of middle-aged women who found themselves on the brink of suicide. For these women, the central role relationships played in bringing them both to the point of self-destruction is self-evident in their stories, as is the failure of the medical profession to offer meaningful help.

Eileen's story

Eileen's life story demonstrates the devastating effects troubled family relationships can have on people: effects which can permeate into the person's adult life. Eileen contacted me having heard me speak on radio regarding my desire for a more person-centred health service. She has felt lonely and unloved throughout her life. When she sought help from the medical profession for her emotional distress, the 'help' she received actually pushed her closer to suicide. Given how typical her story is of the lives of countless thousands, I asked her to write her story in her own words:

I am a forty-year-old married woman and mother of two wonderful children. A few years ago, I could have been lost to them forever. I tried to take my own life with a cocktail of pills that were supposed to cure all my problems. From my experience, GPs who are too busy or who don't take time to listen and just dish out pills to get rid of you have a lot to answer for. They treat the symptoms and ignore the real cause.

I had contemplated ending my life many times. Five years ago I almost succeeded in taking my life when the behaviour of one family member finally drove me over the edge. I was once again reduced to tears, and I decided I couldn't take any more of this life. I had lost my identity as a human being and I just couldn't cope any more. It was as if I was on a merry-go-round and couldn't get off. I had absolutely no quality of life and — it seemed to me then — no hope of regaining any. It wasn't an attention-seeking gesture, as my GP later told my son — I was furious when I heard that. I took enough tablets to make sure I wouldn't survive and locked my door to prevent anyone finding me in time.

I didn't leave any notes. I didn't show any hints that I am aware of to anyone about what I was going to do. As it happened, one of my sons came home unexpectedly and came looking for me. Otherwise I would have died. People say that suicide is a coward's way out, but I believe it takes courage to do what I did. At that moment, I felt I was doing my family a favour. People also say that suicide is a selfish act. I certainly didn't feel selfish at that moment. I felt the complete opposite. I felt they'd all be better off without a useless and dysfunctional mother.

I'm a middle-aged woman now, and my life has been made up of losses, rejections, being used and abused physically and mentally. I realised at a very young age that my parents were bad-tempered and violent. I tried to protect my siblings by always taking the blame and being severely punished for the little incidents of childhood, like breaking a cup. No matter who did the wrong I took the blame to save them from being battered until pain was experienced or blood was drawn, usually from the legs. So the pattern developed that I either got blamed for every wrong, or I took the blame myself.

I was raped when I was 16 years old by a family friend, a well-known and respected member of the community. Because I didn't feel loved by my parents, I couldn't tell them. For years after the rape, I was burdened with guilt, believing I was somehow to blame for it. When your self-esteem is so low and your need to be loved is so great, you cling to anyone for affection and don't realise until it is too late that you are being used — not loved. I'm not a bad person. All my life I have loved too much, given of myself too much, both emotionally and physically. I have been over-generous with my time and dedication to family and others.

By my late thirties, I was well and truly burnt out. I had nothing left to give, but I was still expected to keep on giving because there was no one to step into my shoes. Looking back now, I moved from an abused, traumatic and fearful childhood into marriage at a very young age. I married young to escape from home. But unfortunately, I married a man who was very insecure and immature, who was and still is suffering the effects of a neglected, insecure childhood, which he will not acknowledge. We both carried baggage into our marriage which was a disaster from day one. That was twenty years ago and I'm literally crying inside ever since.

By the time I was thirty-one years old, I had lost six people who were close and dear to me, five of whom died young — three very close friends, my favourite uncle, my sister, and my grandfather whom I loved very much. My husband never really married me in the true sense of the word. He always remained tied to his mother's apron strings. He was rarely there for me when I needed him but he was always there for his mother. I raised my children on my own and during the many bereavements I had in my life, he was never there for me. When I miscarried two pregnancies, one after the other, he screamed at me to shut up whimpering so that he could get to sleep. He spent his life either in the pubs or in bed sleeping off the effect of the drink.

As the mother of young children, I had to go out to work when the children were very small to pay off the huge debts incurred by my husband's total lack of responsibility to his wife and children. Because we lived in relative poverty and had huge debts, I was constantly trying to work outside the home and still be home enough hours to rear my children and keep the house clean. This left me working eighteen to twenty hours a day with little or no time to eat properly, and certainly no time for me.

My GP didn't have time to listen to the real cause of my problems and just kept throwing more and more pills at me. He stopped listening to me, and treated me as if I was a hypochondriac. I became very aware that I was being ignored by my GP and I became very frustrated and depressed because I was feeling worse rather than better.

307

The medication I was on made me feel like a zombie. I was taking diazepam [a tranquilliser], Prozac [an antidepressant], Prothiadin [another antidepressant], and Rohypnol [a sleeping tablet] all at the same time, along with other medication. I was like a walking chemist shop. As a result of all this medication, my speech became slurred and I was incoherent. My concentration was gone and my memory was seriously impaired.

Getting worse, I just couldn't cope any more. I felt so empty inside, I couldn't see any future. Everything seemed so hopeless, so black, no way out. That was when I attempted suicide. I believe the medication I was on which was supposed to improve how I felt — the antidepressants, tranquillisers and sleeping tablets — actually contributed to my reaching the point of suicide, because I felt like a zombie. And because the best that the doctors could offer was actually making me worse, I lost all hope of improvement. Psychiatrists may say what they like, but let any one of them be subjected to all I was subjected to all my life and see if they wouldn't crack under unrelenting torture of many kinds.

After my suicide attempt, I decided to take control of my own health. I changed doctors and insisted on getting the proper tests and treatments which were necessary for my medical conditions. I'm no longer a pushover in the doctor's surgery. I haven't swallowed a pill for two years — which makes me wonder if I ever really needed the seven different medications I was taking every day for years before my suicide attempt. I jumped off the medication roller coaster. I dumped all the pills down the loo and I started to live again. I am and always have been sane, and at last I am enjoying my children. I am just a human being whose emotional needs were never met — not in my childhood and certainly not in my marriage.

Contrary to the prevailing medical view, 'mental illness' was not the cause of Eileen's suicide attempt. Eileen became distraught because her emotional needs were not met in her life — her need to feel loved, to feel close to her parents in her early life and later to her husband. The failure of these relationships to meet her needs for love, support and affirmation left her feeling very insecure and consumed with self-doubt. I believe it is a travesty of natural justice that people such as Eileen are labelled 'mentally ill'. Having lived a series of disappointments and put-downs, Eileen was again put down by the medical profession to whom she turned for help.

Children's development into self-assured and confident adulthood is facilitated if the important adults in their lives—parents particularly — demonstrate in word and deed that they love their children deeply. Since children often see themselves as they think their parents see them, parents need to communicate to their children that they matter; that the parents believe in, respect and trust their children. Children need to be affirmed as important, unique human beings. Parents frequently presume that their children know they love and believe in them. This love and belief needs to be expressed and demonstrated to children. Otherwise, they may have to try to read their parents' minds.

Anne's story

Now 40 years old, Anne has felt suicidal on many occasions. The eldest of five children, she grew up in the suburbs of Limerick city. She was reared in a family which to the outside world was normal, caring and respectable, a high-profile family in the community. But within the four walls of the family home, it was a different story. Love was rarely shown. The children were emotionally and physically abused by parents who were themselves in great distress. Anne never felt close to anyone during her childhood. When Anne was only three years old, she sensed her mother's deep emotional frailty. She felt, even at that tender age, that her mother could not be there for her.

When Anne was eight years old, she was sent by her parents to live with elderly relations. Anne was the only child in that house. She did not get on with her surrogate parents. She became intensely lonely and felt abandoned by her parents. She begged her parents to take her back, but they refused. Hers was not a family where feelings were discussed; Anne kept her intense emotional pain to herself. So intense was her pain that for years she had to suppress any awareness of how seriously dysfunctional her family was.

In her own words, Anne describes her experience of anxiety and depression, and how close she came to taking her own life. Anne's suicidal feelings were not caused by 'mental illness' but by loneliness, relationship conflicts, overwhelming anxiety and low self-esteem. Her life experiences resemble those of many people who are labelled 'mentally ill.' I felt that people who have gone through similar life experiences would identify with Anne's, so I asked Anne to write her own story:

Some experiences defy accurate description. I believe that being in a suicidal state within yourself is one of those places. The pain is so deep, it occurs at a level where words don't apply. Words such as hopelessness, despair, black, and abyss all come to mind, but they only touch at the edges of this awful place. For me, no words come close to reaching the core of this profound and unbearable pain. Having said that, I will try as best I can to describe what was going on for me at those times, and what brought me on many occasions to the point of self-destruction.

Having come from a highly neglectful, painful and deeply rejecting childhood, I came into adulthood hating myself, and with a deep sense of feeling inferior to everyone. I felt worthless and invisible, unloved and totally unlovable. I felt it was even wrong to allow myself to be loved. I was deeply insecure and dependent on others. How I saw myself fed into every area of my life — my family, my workplace, my relationships, and my social life. In order to protect myself from feeling the pain of hurt, rejection and abandonment, and deep, deep sadness, I spent all my time avoiding situations where I might be hurt or rejected. Instead I spent my life caring for others. I went into extreme perfectionism in my life and in my job.

I was breaking up inside, while outside I kept smiling and pretending that all was well. That I felt it absolutely necessary to keep all this pain to myself and hide what was really going on inside me from my family and friends brought me into a place of great loneliness and emotional isolation. Eventually my body broke down and I became seriously ill. I felt that my family were totally unable to cope with my life-threatening illness. They couldn't even talk about what was happening for me. I don't blame them for this. I am now coming to a place of compassion and understanding for them. I know they had to react in this way in order to cope with my illness.

But the pressure of bottling up what I was feeling any longer — and hiding the terror of a life-threatening illness — was becoming too much to bear. I experienced acute anxiety symptoms on a daily basis and my health continued to deteriorate. I wanted to die. Everything I did took an enormous amount of energy out of me. My anxiety became chronic and was accompanied by terror, daily panic attacks and depression.

My life had by now lost all sense of meaning and normality. I had become addicted to tranquillisers and sleeping tablets. I had lost my health and my sense of independence. I was still struggling with many painful emotional issues. Worst of all, I had lost all peace of mind. There were times I felt I was going mad. I craved *understanding for the pain I was in, but emotionally, I felt I was in a desert. To talk from the heart, to feel, to trust, to be real in our family could not be faced or even discussed within our family. That was how we lived. But for me the pressure of pretence had become too great. There is a point of emotional pain beyond which a person cannot endure, and I had reached that point. I became hopeless. I saw no hope that things could ever change. I woke every morning into a nightmare of hopelessness, oppression and terror about how I would cope with my pain, and the aloneness and pressure I felt trying to hide it constantly from those around me.*

I was in a black hole of total darkness within myself. It was too painful to stay in that black hole of despair, but I couldn't see any way out. I couldn't see any future. Many times, I did not live from day to day. I just held on from hour to hour, not knowing for how long more I could endure the pain. Now I knew what despair was. I wanted to kill myself. It was the only way out. On more than one occasion, when I planned out how I would take my life, I silently said 'goodbye' to a young niece of mine whom I dearly loved. Nothing can describe the utter isolation I felt on those occasions. But to reach out and say what was going on for me risked more rejection, more abandonment. And that was more than I could take. The only way left for me was to end it all. Suicide is tragic, yes, but it is a wise and sane action — the ultimate act of avoidance of any further pain.

What the medical profession offered didn't work for me. I attended seven doctors: three GPs, one psychiatrist and three other specialists. Without listening to what was going on for me at a deep emotional level, the three GPs, the psychiatrist, and most of the other specialists were telling me that there was a 'biochemical abnormality' in my brain which was causing my depression and that I needed antidepressants. I was carrying such a great weight of pain and I had reached such a low point in my life that I wanted to end it all. The last thing I needed was to be told that there was something 'wrong' with my brain. That drove me deeper into hopelessness. I remember clearly rushing home to ring my therapist after one such consultation with a doctor just to hear her tell me that there was nothing 'wrong' with me. I felt so distressed that evening that if I hadn't had my therapist's reassurance, the preceding consultation with a doctor could well have been the last straw that might have broken me.

As I already mentioned, I attended a psychiatrist on one occasion. That consultation lasted 30 minutes. I remember feeling during our conversation — 'he doesn't really know what emotional pain is like.' I desperately needed to feel empathy from that psychiatrist, but I didn't feel any. I knew halfway through our interaction what the outcome would be, and I was right. He spoke of chemical disorders in my brain, and the need for antidepressant drug treatment. Once again I felt misunderstood, flawed and hopeless at hearing that a chemical in my brain was the cause of my deep feelings of pain, loss and emotional isolation. But I would have tried anything to ease the pain, so I started taking antidepressants.

Then began a further nightmare of trying one antidepressant after another. Each produced intolerable side effects, from intense agitation and feelings of unreality to violent headaches. Yet, none of these drugs gave me any sense of well-being or peace. Antidepressants, my last resort, the thrust of the recommended treatment by the medical experts, had failed.

The medical profession and psychiatry need to look seriously at how they view the people who come to them with deep emotional issues. These are life-and-death situations. These are people who are fragile and very vulnerable at that moment in their life. To merely look at a set of symptoms and not look behind them to see what is causing them is not good enough. To send people away after a ten- or twenty-minute consultation with a box of tablets and a message about a chemical disorder can mean the end of the road for some people, the last straw. I know that if I had not gone on a different road, to seek another way of healing, I would not be here today. On many occasions, I left my family home not knowing whether I would ever return. I remember one Sunday evening, I knew I had to get out of my home. I told my family I was going to Mass. Somewhere in me, I felt that if I got into the car, I wouldn't ever come back. As I left my home, something made me turn left, instead of the usual right turn onto the main road. I went to visit Joan, an acquaintance who lived nearby. At that time we barely knew each other.

I poured out my heart to her and instantly I knew she understood. She spent more than three hours hearing me, and being with me, in my deep suicidal distress. That was two years ago, and since then Joan's love, her empathy, caring and support have known no bounds. I have indeed been inspired and healed by her. I now know that only love heals. In recent years I have been blessed to have a deeply compassionate therapist in my life. She is the person who has saved my life, and has changed it forever. Without her enduring unconditional loving acceptance of me over the past number of years, I feel I would either have wasted away — because I didn't care whether I lived or died — or I would have ended my agony by suicide.

I knew her love for me was always there. But sometimes I would lose sight of that love, and these were the blackest moments of all. These were the times I came closest to ending up in the river. During those 'nightmares' I would sometimes get a fleeting glimpse of that unconditional compassionate love. And that would be the turning point for me. I would break down and cry uncontrollably, thanking God that I had not ended it all. For I had felt again the depth of my therapist's understanding love, and that had stopped me going over the brink.

In fact, I have been thrice blessed, because fifteen months ago, Terry Lynch, my present GP, came into my life. He has a deep understanding of human behaviour and healing. His caring and support for me have known no limits. There were many days when before a consultation with Terry, I wanted to end it all. But after the consultation, because I knew he had heard me, cared for me, and connected with me in my place of total despair, my aloneness would lift. I would again feel it was worth hanging on in there.

Some time ago, when I was going through a particularly bleak and despairing time, what held me in there over the weekend was knowing that both for Saturday and Sunday Terry had given me a time at which I could ring him and talk. On both those days, I clearly remember that the only thing which gave me hope and kept me from giving up was knowing that at some stage during the day I could connect with someone who cared about me, who deeply understood my pain. That proves to me that love saves lives.

The love I have experienced in these three relationships is a love that has no strings attached. It is a love that loves me for myself unconditionally, no matter what I do, say or feel. It is a love that meets me in my pain, and understands me in my loneliness. It is a love that sees and hears me. When I am in deep despair, I cannot see beyond the pain. What helps me during those awful times is not tablets or solutions, but to be met by another person in that painful place, and to feel they understand what that place is like.

315

Then the despair lifts, and I can move on. It is also a love that sees the 'rightness' of where I am, at that moment in my life. It is a love that believes in me and empowers me and is helping me to see myself as a person worthy of receiving and giving love. I would like to finish with a few lines from Brendan Kennelly:

> *Though we live in a world that dreams of ending,*
> *That always seems about to give in,*
> *'Something' that will not acknowledge conclusion,*
> *Insists that we forever begin, begin, begin . . .*

For me, that 'something' is hope, for without hope we cannot feel, and without feeling, we cannot feel love. Without the love I have received in these three relationships, I would not be here today to tell my story.

Within her own family, Anne had always felt desperately alone. Like many a family, hers was one where family members could talk about many things — the weather, the match, the neighbours, politics, TV programmes, but not about feelings, worries, human fears and vulnerabilities. If she did talk about these sensitive issues, she was quickly silenced. She learned to keep her feelings and her thoughts to herself. She has often said to me that she feels far closer to her five-year-old niece than to either her parents or her five siblings. Prior to meeting me, Anne had attended seven doctors. Each doctor diagnosed depression and recommended antidepressants. None of them explored her childhood, family life, low self-esteem, feelings, or her distress. Not one of these seven doctors connected with her in her despair.

Anne says that the most important healing force in her recovery was not antidepressants, not tranquillisers, not a diagnosis. It was love — the love she felt from her therapist, from me, and from one wonderful friend. In these three relationships, Anne knew she mattered. Her uniqueness and pricelessness as a human being was repeatedly affirmed in these relationships. Consequently, she has gradually begun to reconnect with society, to create a life for herself which has meaning and fulfilment. This is really not so surprising. Love does heal, yet few doctors understand the immense healing power of compassion and caring. Love as a healing force doesn't get much mention in medical textbooks. Yet if doctors were more compassionate, and better listeners, I believe there would be far less need for prescription drugs such as antidepressants and tranquillisers — and possibly far fewer suicides.

What was the 'love' which was so central to Anne's recovery? It was all the things she desperately needed as a child in her own home, but which her parents were themselves too vulnerable and hurt to give to her — unconditional acceptance; permission to express herself; safe relationships where she would not be judged, criticised, rejected, ridiculed or abandoned.

Many doctors become uncomfortable when patients show their feelings. Crying is an important release of emotions that need to be expressed. But when patients cry in doctors' surgeries, the doctor's response is often to reach for the prescription pad. Whatever one thinks about the patient needing a prescription, the doctor frequently has a need to write one. The prescription is a swift way to stop the expression of emotion and end the consultation. Many service users have told me that they soon learned not to tell their psychiatrists and GPs how they really were feeling or to show emotion, since this often resulted in an immediate medication increase.

Doctors greatly underestimate the impact on some people when they tell patients that their depression is a biochemical brain disorder. That no proof exists to back this up makes this all the more disconcerting. For Anne, being told she was suffering from a biochemical brain imbalance drove her even further into despair, and close to taking her own life.

On the other hand, some people — and some families — are relieved to be told that their distress is caused by an abnormality in their brain. This absolves people from the guilt of believing that it is 'their fault'. For some people, believing that one's medication is correcting a supposed chemical abnormality removes any personal responsibility for or involvement in one's recovery, which some people find comforting. Nevertheless, telling people that their brains are not functioning properly in the absence of supporting laboratory evidence clearly constitutes misinformation, and there are other ways of helping people understand that it is not their fault. In my experience, recovery is usually more complete and long-lasting when the person — with appropriate support, affirmation and encouragement — becomes actively involved in their recovery journey.

As Anne says, I have been her GP for the past year and a half. However, I have not been providing Anne with a typical GP-type service. Most GPs would have treated Anne as the previous three GPs did — with a diagnosis and a prescription. I took a different approach. I focused on creating a deep, trusting relationship with Anne, where she felt important and cared for. Our relationship became much more like a deep friendship between two human beings than a typical doctor–patient relationship. Perhaps the medical profession has underestimated the most important part of the doctor–patient interaction — the relationship itself.

Frequently, when people attend both a therapist and a GP, they get conflicting messages. The therapist says the emotional distress is caused by emotional, psychological or relationship issues, while the doctor says the cause is a brain chemical imbalance. The therapist believes that listening and talking is the best therapy. The doctor advises that drug therapy is best. These confusing messages create doubt in the patient's mind, often undermining their recovery. This did not happen in Anne's

318

case, because I adopted the same approach as her therapist. I believe that Anne's recovery was enhanced because she was getting the same consistent message from me and from her therapist.

It is sad and unnecessary that in our society there is still such stigma around 'mental illness' and suicide. I have heard many stories from people recently discharged from psychiatric hospitals of how people avoid them, often crossing the street to escape meeting them. It is also sad and unhealthy that it is still not okay to talk openly about attempted suicide. When Michael attempted to take his life, his family gathered into a huddle to discuss what they would say to neighbours and friends. They agreed to say that Michael had an accident. His family did not want the shame of an attempted suicide visited upon them within the community. Such defensiveness is common, and reflects the judgmental and prying attitude which still pervades modern society. And given how eager people can be to rush to judgement, I could see their point.

Self-esteem: a key issue

How people feel about themselves has a huge bearing on their lives, including their likelihood of suicide. I believe that doctors greatly underestimate the importance of low self-esteem, mistakenly see it as the result — rather than a possible cause or trigger — of the 'psychiatric illness' they are in the process of diagnosing.

Psychiatrist Dr J. Overholser and his colleagues outlined their research paper which highlighted the link between low self-esteem and suicide:

Self-esteem can have a profound influence on a person's thinking, emotions, and responses to stressful life events. Both suicidal ideation [thinking about suicide] and suicide attempts may be related to persistent negative views of the self. A negative view of the self may involve seeing the

319

self as worthless, and the future as hopeless. The adolescent with low self-esteem may see life as not worth living and may perceive everyday stressors as overwhelming. Thus, self-esteem deficits appear to be directly related to suicidal tendencies in adolescents.

Low self-esteem has been found to be closely related to depression in child psychiatric patients, adult psychiatric patients, and college student samples. Also, a strong association has been found between depression severity and low self-esteem in adolescent psychiatric inpatients, with improvement in depression coinciding with increases in self-esteem.[7]

The authors of this paper highlight how little research has been done by psychiatry in the area of self-esteem:

Despite the potentially important role of self-esteem in suicide risk among adolescents, few studies have directly examined the role of self-esteem in depression and suicidal behaviour among adolescents. Most research on self-esteem defects has been limited to larger studies of depression that includes self-esteem as a minor part of the study.

The researchers concluded:

Treatment of depressed and suicidal adolescents should address the self-esteem deficits that may underlie these emotional problems.

Here is a psychiatrist stating that both depression and suicide are emotional rather than psychiatric problems. Yet, mainstream psychiatry seeks to establish that these are primarily psychiatric problems, which in the eyes of the medical profession means physical, brain defects. Why? Because psychiatry's very survival may well depend on perpetuating the notion that so-called 'psychiatric illness' has a physical explanation, be it genetic or biochemical.

For years I have noticed a strong link between low self-esteem and depression. I believe that low self-esteem is a key issue in depression and in all 'psychiatric illnesses'. Dr Oalosaari, Dr Aro and Dr Laippala of the University of Tampere in Finland published their study on parental divorce and depression in young adults in the medical journal *Acta Psychiatr Scandinavia* in 1996. Low self-esteem was shown to be a predictor of subsequent depression in young adults, regardless of their family background or gender.

In recent years, parents have become aware of the key importance of fostering self-esteem in their children. But parents receive little guidance in this regard. This is partly because psychiatry — rather than psychology — dominates the field of mental health, and psychiatrists underestimate how important self-esteem really is. No suicide prevention programme will be successful unless self-esteem is a key topic within that programme.

A central feature of suicide is that the person decides that they cannot continue living as they are. Many people who reach the point of suicide feel stuck in the life and the situation they find themselves in; that there are only two choices — to carry on in their current intolerable life situation, or to escape from it through suicide. In many respects, our society does not allow, encourage or support people to change identities, lives or roles which have become intolerable or soul-destroying for the person.

Notes

1. Dr J Birtle et al. (1990) *British Medical Journal*, 24 March.
2. American Academy of Paediatrics (1993) *Statement on Homosexuality and Adolescence*, October.
3. Cathal Kelly (1998) *Gay Community News*, October.
4. Dr Bartley Sheehan (1991) *The Irish Times*, 8 January.

5. Dr Tony Humphreys (1996) *The Family: Love it and leave it*. Dublin: Gill & Macmillan.
6. Virginia Satir (1978) *Peoplemaking*. London: Souvenier Press.
7. Dr J. Overholser (1995) *Journal of American Academic Child and Adolescent Psychiatry*, July.

7

THE MEDICAL PROFESSION'S
APPROACH TO SUICIDE

In 1992, the British government set out to reduce the suicide rate by 33 per cent in those with psychiatric illness and by 15 per cent in the general population by the year 2000. Neither of these goals have been achieved.

Does modern medicine prevent suicide?
Medical experts believe that suicide is almost always caused by psychiatric illness. Despite the supposed expertise of modern medicine, little evidence exists to demonstrate that the interventions of the medical profession reduce the suicide rate.

People who have been in-patients in psychiatric hospitals have received the best that psychiatry has to offer. Yet they are more likely — and not less, as you might expect — to kill themselves after discharge. Another group with a particularly high risk of taking their own lives are those who have previously attempted suicide. Most hospitals in westernised countries have a policy regarding people who attempt suicide. Once out of danger of dying from their suicide attempt, they are assessed by a doctor, usually a psychiatrist. Appropriate follow-up psychiatric care is arranged once they are discharged. This is now standard practice. Psychiatry has established contact with both of these high-suicide-risk groups. Both receive the best treatments that psychiatry has to offer. But their treatments are not working — indeed, they may be counter-productive.

Some people treated with drugs for depression in hospital take their own life within weeks of the commencement of treatment. Psychiatrists say this occurs because, as they improve, they gain enough energy to go about ending it all. This view ignores other explanations which are unpalatable to the medical profession:

- The social stigma of having been admitted to a psychiatric ward causes upheaval in the person's life.
- The increased hopelessness and isolation people feel when they are not listened to, when instead they are told to keep taking the tablets.
- The humiliating experience of a psychiatric admission creating within the person the conviction that they would rather die than risk having to go through that trauma again. Many recently discharged patients feel that they are sent home with insufficient meaningful follow-up. They are sent home to pick up the pieces pretty much on their own.

Mary's story

The following is the transcript of a live interview broadcast on Radio Eireann on 26 June 1998. Suicide was highly topical at the time. Mary was interviewed by Emer Woodful, referred to hereafter as EW:

EW: *We have had many, many calls about suicide over the past few days and Mary is one of those. Good morning to you, Mary.*

M: *Good morning, Emer.*

EW: *What would you like to say to us?*

M: *It's twenty years this year since I was first admitted to a psychiatric hospital, and I have been admitted countless times to psychiatric hospitals, and I have made a few attempts on my life, and one very serious one, and therefore I think I am qualified to say something on the topic. And what strikes me is that every time there's a programme done, or a feature on suicide, an eminent psychiatrist is wheeled out to speak expertly on the subject. And in my experience psychiatry in its present form — even though there are good things about it, and there are good psychiatrists — psychiatry in general, in its present form contributes to suicide instead of lowering the rate. That's my own opinion.*

EW: *In what way, Mary?*

M: *Well, the most important quality that I would look for in a psychiatrist is a willingness to listen, to understand, to empathise, and not, not an over-readiness to diagnose, categorise, and reduce the person to a label, which is stamped on them, and once it is stamped on them, reduces if not eliminates their possibilities of employment or social life thereafter, and once labelled and categorised and put on disability benefit (if they've no other income) then they have the added stress of living on approximately £70 a week plus perhaps rent allowance, suffering the scorn of community welfare officers, psychiatric nurses, and everybody in general. Because once you are reduced to that state, you have no social standing. You have no money, and you are known to be 'mental'. Then everybody heaps scorn upon you and what you are. And what you were is completely lost forever unless somebody remarkable realises it.*

EW: *What was your life like, Mary, that you felt so bad about your life that you wanted to die?*

M: *Well, at the time that I jumped twenty feet into a raging torrent — it was in March, and it was after midnight, and it was on a cold night, and it was completely dark except for a moon out, and there was nobody about, and I stood for two hours, and I had to talk myself into jumping into that river, and by God knows what — providence — I was washed up against a weir, and I chose to climb out. And this is another point — I'll go into the question you asked me in a minute — but this a point*

325

I'd like to make. A researcher who was on the Late Late Show, and he was talking about a study he had done in Cork on suicide, and he noted that people who commit suicide, if at a certain point after they've taken the poison, or kicked the chair from under them, or jumped into the water, if they could turn the clock back, inevitably, they all would.

And the point is that, it is not that people want to die — and I'm not glamorising suicide by saying this — it takes immense courage to take your own life. It's not that a person wants to die, it's that they cannot cope with life. And I suppose what made me take that jump was the utter belief that my life as it was then, packing meals in an industrial therapy unit, and living in a group home where every moment of your life was accounted for, and being totally cut off from everyday life, from — as they say — normal society and that. The absolute and utter belief that nothing would ever change. I remember saying to myself; 'nobody will ever love me, I will never have children, I will never work'. And I kept repeating those things to myself until I made myself jump in.

EW*: So you were looking down a really dark tunnel.*

M: *Yes. And as I jumped into the water I cried out 'God forgive me, God forgive me!' because I knew that what I was doing was wrong.*

EW: *And what age were you, Mary, when you did this?*

M: *That was 11 years ago, so I would have been twenty-seven, twenty-eight.*

EW: *And what was your life like up to that point that you had fallen so low in your own life, and in your own feelings of worthlessness?*

M: *Well, my first admission to a [psychiatric] hospital was prior to my going to university, and while I was at university I had several admissions to hospital, and despite that I struggled on. But in the first job, which wasn't actually a job, it was really a temporary placement, I again became 'ill' in inverted commas and was admitted to hospital. And then the following year I got on to a publishing course in Dublin and again became 'ill'. And the following year I just sort of 'slid' through. And the following year I fell madly in love — with somebody who fell madly in love with me — for the first time in my life, and became 'ill' and he just, virtually, didn't want to know me any more.*

And then I found myself living in a group home. And that's when I . . . it was quite a calm, almost a casual decision, you know. It just kind of occurred to me one day as I was going down to meet one of these people who reviews your entitlement to your disability. And I thought 'there will be a bus to Galway at such-and-such a time, and I could get on it, and I could go to Galway and drown myself in the river Corrib'. Because I thought 'well, if I'm going to do it, I'd better make sure that I do it properly, otherwise they [the psychiatrists] will lock me up for good'.

And that's what I did, and I got on the bus, and all the way to Galway I kept repeating to myself, I said 'I have to do this, I have to do this, I have to do this'. And then when I got to Galway I even went into a coffee shop and sat down and had a cup of coffee. And then I walked over and went down past the cathedral, and down by Nun's Bridge, and into a spot which I had actually often chosen when I was a student, you know, tried to convince myself to jump in before that. And I stood there for two hours. And then I thought, well, in case they don't find my body, I'd better leave a note, so I left some of my belongings and a note there. And then I just stepped up on the railings and jumped in.

EW: *And then, what made you grab on to that weir?*

M: *Well, I didn't grab on to it, I actually . . . when I was in the water, I went right down and I was so relaxed, I wasn't frightened at all. I was just so peaceful and I was waiting to die, and I thought 'in a few seconds it'll all be over'. And I felt* completely at ease, and perhaps that's what saved my life, because they say if you struggle in the water, you'll drown quicker. And I just sunk in to the water, and I heard this roaring in my ears, and I thought, 'Oh, that must be what people who are dying experience'. And then I felt something like metal against my neck, then a sort-of-a-fern brushed my cheek.

And then suddenly my head was above the water and I was looking at the moon, and I was confused. I thought 'I'm not dead yet' and I was puzzled for a while. Then I realised my skirt was so saturated with water that it was pinning me against . . . I don't understand it, it's where they change the level of water. I was pinned against this weir, or whatever it is that adjusts the water level, and I looked about me for a while, and I thought 'will I wait here until the water rises to the level to cover my head, or will I get up and jump in again?'

Then I thought sort-of half-heartedly 'well maybe its not so bad after all' and then there were some bars there so I just pulled myself up. I got up and got on to the bank — and this is the funny part actually, because I went to the nearest house and knocked on the door. And when the woman opened, because it was rag week that week, she thought it was a prank by some student, and she slammed the door in my face!! [laughing].

EW: *Oh dear!*

M: *I suppose I can afford to laugh now, because I feel safe, I feel safe, I feel as if I've distanced myself sufficiently from it that I can look back now and even though I can realise the horror of it, I can see the funny parts as well.*

EW: *And, Mary, what has helped you move into a space that you feel is obviously a much safer one?*

M: *Well, the single factor is a relationship with a man whom I met in a psychiatric hospital, and I don't know why, but he understands me as well or even better than I understand myself, and despite . . . I mean he has seen me ill, he has seen me in all my varying moods and whatever, and he loves me. I mean, that's the only word I can use, and accepts me for what I am, and sees the potential in me because — that's another point — a lot of the potential of psychiatric patients is completely lost and smothered by the concentration on their illness. I don't know who said it about 'great men and madness do near a-lie, and thin partitions do them divide'. And there are a lot of immensely talented people whose talent is completely burnt up and wasted in psychiatric hospitals. And it has not been a smooth path by any manner of means. We've had a terrible, terrible struggle together. And we're still struggling but we're still together — touch wood. If you're in adverse circumstances together, if you're thrown together early, in adverse circumstances, then that proves a relationship, really.*

EW: *Definitely. And what is your life like now, Mary?*

M: *Well, by most people's standards its very dull, it would seem very dull. I cannot work because I'm classed as disabled because of all the years of illness. I live in a rented house which we did up ourselves, and I take great pleasure in just the whole idea of having a place that you can paint your own colours and hang your own pictures, and that sort of thing, and I actually enjoy life probably more than if I was slotted into a job. I still have huge ambitions, and I think that's what keeps me going.*

EW: *Well, listen, thanks very much for calling us this morning, and look after yourselves!*

M: *Oh don't worry, I'm well looked after!*

EW: *Good! All right, Mary, Thanks very much for that, thank you. All right. Bye-bye . . .*

When it comes to understanding suicide, perhaps Mary has the edge on the psychiatric experts. Unlike most psychiatrists, Mary has personal experience of reaching such a level of despair and hopelessness that suicide seemed the only way out. It is clear from the interview that Mary has been on the receiving end of psychiatric care for many years of her life. She has a pretty thorough understanding of the psychiatric system, and what it is like to be a psychiatric patient.

Might modern medicine contribute to suicide?

Psychiatry does not emerge well from this interview with Mary. As she said, every time suicide is featured in the media, an eminent psychiatrist is wheeled out to speak expertly on the topic. This practice reinforces the view that psychiatrists are the experts when it comes to suicide, that psychiatry is the field of study most likely to solve the tragedy of suicide. Mary was clearly not happy about this. It is the first point she makes and may well be why she contacted the programme in the first place. Mary believes that, rather than helping to lower the rate of suicide, psychiatry in its present form actually contributes to suicide. Not only was Mary speaking from years of personal experience of and exposure to psychiatry, but through her years of attending psychiatric hospitals she would have come to know many other psychiatric patients and would have seen how they were treated.

I too believe that psychiatry contributes to suicide. The last thing a person in the depths of despair needs is a system which labels rather than listens. In the interview, Mary speaks about the qualities she believes psychiatrists should possess:

a willingness to listen, to understand, to empathise, and not, not an over-readiness to diagnose, to categorise, to reduce a person to a label.

It appears that she frequently felt her psychiatrists did not listen, did not understand or empathise with her but were over-ready to diagnose, to categorise her. Perhaps Mary's experience gives us a clue why people discharged from psychiatric wards are at a greatly increased risk of suicide.

Mary eloquently describes the stigma of psychiatric labelling: reduced or eliminated social life and employment opportunities; poverty; increased social isolation and public scorn, including at times the scorn of those who are part of the psychiatric care team. She makes many points that should be studied very carefully by those involved in the care of the hurt and the vulnerable, none more important than the following:

It is not that people want to die, its that they cannot cope with life.

People take their lives because they have reached the point where the only way they see to end their despair and pain is to end their existence.

When the person reaches such a low point in life that they are seriously thinking of taking their own life, it may have become almost impossible for them to reach out for help. If they do reach out one more time, it is crucial that they are — as Mary said — listened to, empathised with and understood. But doctors instinctively focus on other things — making a diagnosis, and prescribing medication. In my experience, regarding emotional distress, many doctors are not good listeners. Many do not empathise well with their patients.

The average consultation with a GP lasts between seven and ten minutes. When you subtract the time taken up by the doctor taking a medical history, carrying out physical examinations, doing and arranging tests, writing prescriptions and letters, informing the patient about the prescribed medication, arranging referrals, making and taking phone calls, writing in and going through the chart, patients will be lucky to get three-to-five minutes in which to express themselves to the doctor. Patients will be aware that the doctor does not have enough time to give them a full and proper hearing.

GPs may argue that, through many consultations over the years, they get to know their patients well. However, this cannot be said with regard to young men, the group with the highest risk of suicide. Young men do not attend doctors frequently enough for GPs to get to know them well. Over the years, a person may indeed visit their GP many times. However, how the doctor approaches each meeting with a person is influenced by past consultations. Once a GP had diagnosed 'depression', this will significantly influence what happens in subsequent consultations. Although GPs may have many consultations over the years with their patients who have been diagnosed as having a 'mental illness', the content of these consultations is very much determined and defined by the medical history of the person. So, when a person who has been diagnosed as having a 'mental illness' attends their GP in distress, the doctor is likely to see the distress as a symptom of their 'mental illness'. The doctor then focuses on the supposed 'mental illness', assessing how best to treat it. If such a person tells their GP that they are suicidal, this is likely to be seen as a worsening of their 'mental illness' requiring urgent medical intervention — admission to a psychiatric hospital, or a medication increase, for example.

Many patients know this; rather than risk being cut short by the doctor, many people decide not to open up. They keep their pain to themselves. Without realising it, the doctor has confirmed their worst fears — that no one will listen to their story. Such an approach by a doctor or psychiatrist can be the last straw, reinforcing their belief that no one understands their pain. Thus, the person's isolation and hopelessness is heightened — final confirmation that suicide is the only way to end the pain of living.

Many people who attempt suicide attend their general practitioners a few weeks prior to the attempt to end their life. Psychiatrists maintain that GPs are failing to diagnose and treat depression (with antidepressant drugs). But there are other possible reasons why the visit to the GP might not ease the distress these people were experiencing. For people who are considering suicide, the process of withdrawing from life and people begins a long time before that last visit to the GP. By the time of this final consultation, they may have withdrawn within themselves in a desperate attempt to protect themselves from further hurt and pain. They are close to complete withdrawal from reaching out to anyone.

The visit to the GP may become the patient's last hope. In the eyes of the patient, this can quite literally be a life-or-death consultation. If the meeting goes very well, the patient leaves the surgery feeling heard and understood. They feel that this doctor really cares. The hope engendered by that consultation may bring them back from the brink of suicide. But if the visit does not go well — in the eyes of the patient — the suicidal person may leave the surgery with their suicidal inclination reinforced. This person needs an unhurried consultation.

They are aching to be understood. Instead they are likely to be diagnosed, probably as having depression, and prescribed antidepressant drugs. They want someone to listen. But the doctor does not really listen. The GP treats the 'underlying diagnosis' with drugs, or refers them to a psychiatrist who is even more expert at diagnosing and prescribing than the GP. Once a person tells their GP that they are seriously suicidal, the GP's focus changes, as they then attempt to convince the person to be admitted to a psychiatric hospital. The patient needs the doctor to be with them. Instead, the doctor may talk at them, albeit with sympathy. They desperately need to connect with the doctor, but the doctor wants to treat the 'mental illness'. The consultation ends. The patient does not feel heard. Not feeling heard is a form of rejection. When this rejection comes from a doctor — the expert — the doctor has confirmed the patient's worst fears. There is no hope. They are beyond help. No one will ever listen.

Rejection always hurts. But when you are close to suicide,

the pain of rejection is unbearable. The patient may not reach out to anyone again. More than tablets or a diagnosis, people who are depressed or close to suicide need a lifeline, a close trusting relationship with their doctor or therapist, a relationship which gives them hope. For a person in the throes of emotional turmoil, knowing that someone connects with them in their pain frequently gives the person the will to hold on to their life. This understanding is a crucial part of the doctor–patient relationship. This was clearly not the sort of relationship Mary had with her psychiatrists. Speaking of how she planned her suicide, she said:

If I'm going to do it, I'd better make sure I do it properly, otherwise they [the psychiatrists] will lock me up for good.

Rather than offer her the lifeline she desperately needed, Mary felt very threatened and intimidated by her psychiatrists, as do many people who find themselves attending psychiatrists. After years of contact with the mental health services, she speaks of psychiatrists as if they were more like enemies to be avoided than the caring professionals they are expected to be.

The interviewer asked Mary what had helped her to recover. Mary's reply speaks volumes. The single most important factor was a loving relationship, which had given her a sense of safety and understanding in her life that had been missing for years, if indeed she ever possessed it. She does not mention psychiatry as being a help in her recovery — quite the opposite. She points out the damage that psychiatry can do:

A lot of the potential of psychiatric patients is completely lost and smothered by the concentration on their illness. There are a lot of immensely talented people whose talent is completely burnt up and wasted in psychiatric hospitals.

Doctors do concentrate on the 'illnesses' they have decided these people have, rather than on the enormous potential that lies within each human being.

Mary has come a long way from that time of utter despair and hopelessness which drove her to jump into the river Corrib. She found the strength within herself to move away from her terror and turmoil. She recovered through having her human needs met; through a loving relationship, companionship, sharing, safety, security, and having a place to paint her own colours and hang her own pictures.

When Barbara first attended me, she felt stigmatised by her previous doctor's approach to her depression. Five minutes into her first visit to her GP regarding her emotional distress, the doctor told her she was suffering from depression, which was caused by a biochemical abnormality. Barbara came to see me as a GP for a second opinion. Being told that her depression was a mental illness caused by a biochemical imbalance in her brain offered Barbara no hope. She was extremely angry with the previous GP; so much so that I asked her to express her anger in writing:

It is probably the patient's belief that they are mentally ill that actually contributes to suicide and the hopelessness and despair. Unless that mental illness label is removed, not only will medical intervention be ineffective, it will contribute to suicide. I would not be alive today if I did not have the absolute love, understanding and encouragement of one priceless friend. What kept me alive was his belief in me. He could explain to me what was happening — that was what I needed most. An explanation of what depression was and facing up to and feeling the reality of my childhood. That pain almost killed me — in ways it would have been so much easier to die.

Depressed people feel it their time to die because they have lost themselves. We feel that we ourselves have died. There is no greater loss than that. So why can't the medical

335

*profession see that we are not mentally ill? We are very hurt
human beings. We have tried so hard to be human to other
people in our lives. It is our humanness that is our greatest
strength, and probably it is also what causes us so much
pain. I think that my humanness is the last thing I have held
on to. I still feel other people's sadness and pain and I try to
help. When that humanness goes from me I'll give up.*

Barbara had experienced many painful losses in her life. Her
depression made sense, given how her life had unfolded. Her
life story was complex, as are all life stories. Yet her previous
GP, who hardly knew her, presumed to know that her depression
was caused by a biochemical abnormality.

There is no public currency or language for depression,
for mental health problems. If you break a leg, your cast is
obvious to everyone, evoking instant reactions of caring and
understanding from family and strangers alike. Not so with
depression or other 'mental illnesses'. The reactions from
family, friends, strangers, workmates on hearing that someone
is depressed can compound the person's isolation and
loneliness. Some people still cross the road to avoid meeting
their neighbour who has just been discharged from the local
psychiatric hospital.

Why is the risk of suicide greatly increased following psychiatric admission?

Research shows that there is a greatly increased risk that
patients who have been discharged from psychiatric hospitals
will take their own lives. Dr David Gunnell is a senior lecturer
in epidemiology and public health medicine at the department
of social medicine at Bristol University. At the annual conference
of the *Irish Association of Suicidology* in 1998, Dr Gunnell spoke
about groups with an increased risk of suicide.

According to Dr Gunnell, alcoholics, drug misusers,

Samaritan clients and people with a history of deliberate self-harm are twenty times more likely to take their own life than the general population, while current and ex-psychiatric patients are ten times more likely to take their own lives than the general population. But one group are in a different league in terms of their suicide risk. Within four weeks of discharge from psychiatric hospitals, psychiatric patients are ten to twenty times more likely to kill themselves than current or ex-psychiatric patients generally. Extrapolating from Dr Gunnell's finding that current and ex-psychiatric patients are ten times more likely to take their own lives than the general population, this means that patients discharged from psychiatric hospitals are 100 to 200 times more likely to kill themselves than the general population within four weeks of their discharge.

These figures tally with those of Goldacre and Seagroatt. Theirs was a large-scale British research project. The records of 14,240 people were assessed for twelve months after they had been discharged following a psychiatric admission to hospital. The researchers found that the suicide rate was greatly increased for the whole twelve months during which the study was conducted. But the risk was particularly high during the first 28 days following discharge from hospital:

> Deaths with a coroner's verdict of suicide in the first twenty-eight days after discharge were 213 times more common for male and 134 times more common for female patients than would be expected during 28 days in the general population.[1]

Diabetic patients, stabilised on their treatment, do not leave hospital with a greatly increased risk of a diabetic coma. If it were found that people admitted to hospital with an asthma attack, stabilised on treatment while in hospital, were greatly at risk of dying from another asthma attack shortly after their discharge, there would be a public outcry.

337

In discharging a person from hospital, the psychiatrist is in effect stating that this person recovered sufficiently from their 'illness' to be discharged home. Given that suicide is seen within the medical profession as evidence of serious 'mental illness', one might reasonably expect that a person deemed well enough to be discharged from a psychiatric unit might have a lessened risk of suicide rather than raised, as seems to be the case.

Perhaps psychiatrists do not know their patients well enough. When people spend seven to ten days in a psychiatric ward, they may have little contact with the consultant psychiatrist under whose care they were admitted to hospital. Rather than give the person time and safety to open up, the consultant typically concentrates on the diagnosis rather than on the person. The psychiatrist focuses on the (drug) treatment, rather than establishing a therapeutic and healing relationship between patient and doctor. Once the patient has been admitted, it is unusual for the psychiatrists to spend more than five or ten minutes a day with their patients. Some may feel that they don't need to. The 'diagnosis' has been made, and 'treatment' commenced. The psychiatrist feels he has carried out his duties successfully in accordance with the job specifications.

But this is not good enough, and often patients and their families know that. The patient frequently leaves hospital feeling worse than when they were admitted, although they may not reveal this to their doctors. Patients know that if they say they are not getting better, they will be kept in hospital longer. They will probably be put on stronger medication than they are already on, with worse side effects. They might be given ECT (shock therapy). To survive within the psychiatric system, many patients learn to lie to their psychiatrists. Many hospital patients learn how to play the game of 'becoming the good and obedient psychiatric patient'.

Goldacre and Seagroatt concluded:

When an individual commits suicide after discharge from hospital, especially soon afterwards, the appropriateness of the discharge and the adequacy of supporting services in the community may be questioned.

The many psychiatrists involved in this study — and there were many, given how large this study was; 14,240 patients, who between them had a total of 26,864 psychiatric admissions in six British health districts — were apparently not very good at identifying people with high suicide intent.

According to research published in 2000 by the National Schizophrenia Fellowship, as many as one in three suicides by people with a 'mental illness' occurs while they are still a hospital in-patient. Many of these suicides occurred outside hospital, while the patients were still registered as in-patients.[2]

GPs and other mental health care workers may feel pressured to refer people who voice suicidal tendencies to a psychiatrist. This is frequently done out of fear that if the person does end their life, they may be blamed for not referring the person to a psychiatrist. This scenario exists because psychiatrists are seen as *the* experts in mental health care, as *the* group most likely to bring about recovery in the person, a perception which in my opinion is highly questionable.

Jim went through a difficult time when his marriage hit a rocky patch. He came to see me as a GP. Between us, we decided that Jim be admitted to a psychiatric hospital for his own safety, since he had become preoccupied with taking his own life. However, the experience was so dreadful that Jim discharged himself after five days. Doctors and nurses asked him many questions, but they showed little willingness to listen to him. Jim desperately wanted someone to talk through his problems with him, but when he asked for counselling he was told that it would not help him. The two medications prescribed for him made him feel strange. In five days, his consultant psychiatrist spoke with him for about ten minutes in total. Jim neither liked nor trusted this psychiatrist, who seemed more interested in figuring out what was 'wrong' with Jim than in relating to him.

Jim did learn something from his psychiatric admission. The shock of his experience in hospital catapulted him to a realisation that either he would work through his crisis outside of hospital or he would kill himself. Thankfully, he has come through his crisis. We continued to meet weekly, and sometimes twice weekly, for months after his discharge. In contrast, many psychiatric in-patients have little effective, person-centred, supportive follow-up after discharge. Jim was sure of one thing; come hell or high water he would never again be admitted to a psychiatric hospital. Thankfully, with counselling Jim has come to terms with his marital problems. But his hospital experience illustrates how the trauma of being a psychiatric in-patient can push one towards suicide, rather than pull one back from it.

In Britain, community mental health teams function within the community. These teams normally consist of social workers and community nurses as well as a designated psychiatrist and sometimes an occupational therapist and clinical psychologist and other nonprofessional workers. People in the team visit people usually at home, monitor them, talk with them and family members, discuss medication, help if they can with social and housing problems and benefits, liaise with GPs and other services. They tend to concentrate on people with the most severe mental health difficulties, including people who might be, or previously have been, admitted to psychiatric hospital. Each member of the community mental health team will have their own particular understanding and perspective regarding the nature of people's mental health problems and their needs. However, as with most mental health service workers, the community mental health team will be significantly infused and influenced by the dominant belief system within mental health — the medical /psychiatric model.

In many areas, the need for such community-based services greatly outweighs the supply, diluting the potential benefits of the community health care team. While many people find their help useful, the need for such support structures massively outweighs the capacity of the service.

Young people and the medical profession

There is disturbing evidence that young people do not see the medical profession as being approachable in a time of crisis. A 1998 study by Dr M. O'Sullivan and Professor M. Fitzgerald was published in the *Journal for the Association of Professionals in Services for Adolescents*. The study focused on teenage attitudes to suicide. The researchers found that only 15 per cent of those interviewed would recommend psychiatric help to someone who spoke about killing themselves. In another study carried out by the National Suicide Research Foundation in 1998, 100 university students were interviewed. Not one of these students mentioned GPs as a possible route to getting help if they were thinking of harming themselves or ending their life. According to this study, GPs are probably the last recourse for young people who are seriously depressed and considering suicide. The researchers concluded that: 'The youth don't see doctors as people they can turn to for help.'

A 1994 survey of the attitudes of teenagers to health and health care was carried out by Dr Jones and colleagues.[3] The survey revealed some alarming information concerning how teenagers view the general practice medical care system. Nine out of ten teenagers would prefer to visit a special teenage clinic than their own GP. More than nine out of ten did not want their own GP to run these clinics.

I have heard psychiatrists attributing this reluctance to attend the medical profession as a reflection of young people's inability to ask for help. While this may partly explain why young people do not seek medical help, there is another possible explanation which is less palatable to the medical profession. Perhaps part of the reason young people are not reached by doctors is because they do not trust the medical healthcare system.

Perhaps teenagers believe that their pain and isolation will not be fully understood by doctors; that GP consultations rarely last more than seven-to-ten minutes — not nearly enough time for them to express what they really need to say. Perhaps they feel that doctors are part of a powerful establishment which scares them; that doctors are far more likely to concentrate on prescribing a drug rather than hearing their deep anguish. They may fear that what they tell the GP will get back to their parents. And most frightening of all, if they tell the GP how badly they really feel, they may quickly end up in a psychiatric hospital possibly against their will, labelled as 'mentally ill', with all the stigma and humiliation that goes with a psychiatric hospital admission.

For the sake of our young people, the medical profession must face up to a painful truth. Regarding mental health issues, the medical service is being largely rejected by adolescents and young adults. 'Expert' views will make no impression on suicide rates if this critical issue is not addressed. It is time that modern medicine stopped telling people what is good for them and started listening to the views of ordinary people .

Aidy, my son

Brian, the father of a young man who took his life over a year ago, obtained a copy of the Irish edition of this book, published in 2001. Since then Brian, who lives in Britain, and I have been in regular communication. What follows are some of Brian's thoughts and reflections on the life and death of his beloved son Aidy:

Aidy was a very happy little boy when he lived with his mum, dad and his sister. He was very upset when his parents separated when he was seven years old. However, he seemed to recover with the knowledge that both his parents loved him and he had his own room at both his mum's and dad's houses. Both Aidy and his sister came to stay with me on a regular basis along with their friends at my house. Aidy and I became very close and although we lived over 150 miles apart, we saw each other every week. Aidy did very well at school and was good at football, representing both his school and district, he was also very popular with both sexes. It wasn't until he left school at 16 that he noticed any change, though none of his friends or family noticed any change until he was 19 and at university.

Aidy had always believed his problems started with anxiety which led to him becoming depressed in 1993 and being prescribed Prozac which Aidy has always believed caused him to go manic. When we were told in 1995 that if Aidy took Lithium he would be alright, we believed that this was the answer. Whilst Aidy took Lithium for eight years, he felt the medication was just masking the problem and he couldn't let his emotions out. Aidy was told by another psychiatrist in 1999 that he was not manic depressive and he should have had counselling in 1993 before he was told to take medication. He believed Aidy's problems commenced when his parents were divorced when he was ten and other personal problems, when at college and university had resulted in his breakdown in 1993.

Whilst Aidy was in hospital in May 2002, I read Terry Lynch's book which completely changed my views and confirmed everything Aidy had been saying. We thought what the psychiatrists were saying was gospel, they certainly gave that impression when he was alive and within twenty minutes each had labelled him manic depressive for the rest of his life. When Aidy was in hospital two months before he died, he read this out on a ward round:

'It seems to me that my problems stem from anxiety, which led to the highs, and lows I have had. I believe that the only way I can stop these highs and lows is to address this anxiety. It is as though I will do anything to avoid this anxiety and the reality of it. It has really messed up my life. It must stem from somewhere and I personally do not believe I will ever move forward unless the root of it is found and dealt with. The anxiety has stopped me from enjoying life, work, and relationships and led to my suicide attempt last year. How can I overcome my fears and be myself. Can counselling help?

I do not believe the medication I am on is the right stuff for me at this time (Lustral, as SSRI antidepressant). I am very low and it is only the anti anxiety tablets (lorazepam) that have helped me. Yesterday for example I felt I could not face anyone on the ward, my mind was blocked with all the old anxiety feelings from before and I felt a right mess.

This is a feeling I have had for a very long time and is the result of continuous worrying when I was a kid through my teens and resulted in my depressive breakdown when I was 19.'

The psychiatrist asked Aidy if he felt suicidal, he said yes. The psychiatrist said we cannot stop you doing that; a percentage of the population do commit suicide we can only try and prevent it. He added that lorazepam was addictive which we already knew and we also believed that Lustral was more addictive. Having seen Aidy in this frame of mind before, I knew that he needed a sedative type of medication, a benzodiazapine such as lorazepam, that would have helped him through the early stages of recovery. Past experience had shown that he would start to recover six weeks after the onset of the depression. He was in the first week of that recovery stage when he felt physically strong enough to take his own life but did not have the sedating effect he needed at that time to prevent it.

When he left hospital, he saw another psychiatrist six days before he died and again we asked for his medication to be changed only to be told to increase the dosage of the SSRI Lustral that has no sedating effect and in all probability did nothing to prevent his suicide.

I am only a layman and I am not advocating the use or non-use of medication. But I am a dad who loved his son with all his heart and could see what he needed. Terry [Lynch] actually backs up what Aidy was saying in his book and I quote:

'Tranquilliser drugs can sometimes be helpful in a crisis situation. By sedating the person, they may give them some breathing space, a break from the intense emotional experience they are going through. They may calm a person to a point where carers may be able to get through to them.'

We just wanted Aidy to be on a sedative for a few weeks. Since Aidy died, I've been back to see four of the psychiatrists who treated Aidy and questioned as a layman their diagnosis of him. To my amazement, to a man they agreed they should have listened more to what Adrian was trying to tell them. What appeared to be an exact science when he was alive was suddenly no more after his death. Sadly medication has done nothing for Adrian over 10 years and did not solve the anxiety problems that he had which tragically lead to his untimely death at the age of 29.

At Aidy's inquest, I read out the last 3 paragraphs of Terry's book, which made a great impression on me. I spoke with much emotion to a hushed audience, adding that parents whose children are having emotional problems at school, college or university seek the help of a psychotherapist who would give their children counselling

345

before taking the route of medication that could well mask the problem rather than solve it.

Fortunately we have some lovely memories of Aidy and we as a family can also remember all the happy times Aidy had over the past ten years when he wasn't low and how he made us all laugh and was so kind and thoughtful. I miss and love Aidy very much as does his mum, his sister, the rest of the family and all his friends.

We console ourselves in the knowledge that he is no longer in pain.

Suicide and 'psychiatric illness': informing the public

Medical correspondent, Dr Muiris Houston[4] claimed that there is now a definite biological explanation for suicide. Throughout his article, Dr Houston linked suicide to low levels of serotonin in the brain. Medical preoccupation with establishing a link between serotonin levels and suicide is not new. Until his death in 1998, Cork psychiatrist Dr Michael Kelleher was highly regarded within the British Isles as an expert on suicide. In an interview with John Waters, Dr Kelleher expresses considerable enthusiasm for a link between low serotonin and suicide:

> There is now strong evidence that biochemical levels may be a strong factor in the new wave of young suicides. This research indicates that people with low levels of a substance called serotonin are more likely to commit suicide.[5]

Four years later, however, Dr Kelleher's enthusiasm for a link between serotonin and suicide had apparently waned considerably:

> Only a minority of suicide attempters show the relevant changes in serotonin metabolism. It is possible that the connection between suicide and serotonin has been overstretched.[6]

Perhaps disillusioned with the lack of real progress in linking serotonin to suicide, in this article Dr Kelleher shifted his attention towards another biological notion, to possible links between suicide and the immune system.

Dr Patricia Casey cautioned that the serotonin–suicide link remained unproven:

> Recently there has been a growth of interest in the biology of suicide, and the role of serotonin in suicidal behaviour has been investigated, as has that of noradrenaline and adrenaline. The results are as yet inconclusive.[7]

The link between serotonin levels and suicide is far from established. To claim that there is now definite biological evidence for suicidal behaviour is, I believe, quite premature and potentially very confusing for the public who read such confident statements. Dr Houston's article was part of a major *Irish Times* investigation into suicide. Only one article of three days of reports articulated the views of people who had themselves made serious suicide attempts. This article, written by Padraig O'Morain and published on 28 March 2001, presented the personal accounts of three people who had been deeply suicidal earlier in their lives. Ironically, since this three-day investigation predominantly highlighted the benefits of the medical approach to suicide, none of the three people reported that their recovery was as a result of medication, or the medical/psychiatric system. Rather, each attributed their recovery to sharing problems with others, friendship, receiving support and affirmation through support groups and learning to express their feelings and work through their problems.

One man whose story was featured said that he did not get better, despite psychiatric help. His recovery began when he became involved with GROW, a mental health support group which provided him with support and friendship:

> *The enormous outpouring of welcome and the*
> *understanding and acceptance on these peoples' faces —*
> *that was really the first step on my journey to recovery.*

A second man reported that he spent more than five months in a psychiatric hospital and more than six months 'on medication, going around like a zombie'. He said:

> *I kept things to myself. You couldn't admit you weren't good, that was one of the biggest problems. Big boys don't cry. People need to talk about it. A trouble shared is a trouble halved. You realise then that other people have the same problem as yourself.*

The third person featured in the article described her experience:

> *I was put on medication which was to take over my life for seven years. I became totally addicted.*

Reflecting the sense of hopelessness and the absence of a vision of recovery among her caregivers that many psychiatric patients pick up from their doctors, she said that 'nobody told me in the six or seven years I had been going through the system that I could be well'. In the only part of the entire article which was in any way positive towards the psychiatric system, this woman's first admission to a psychiatric hospital seems to have helped her. But rather than attributing her improvement to psychiatric treatment, the biggest relief was not having to hide her distress anymore:

> *The secret was out. Everyone knew I was sick, and for me that was the greatest relief of my life.*

For these people, it seems that not having to hide their distress any more, together with having their human needs met through human contact, support and understanding benefited them far more than medication for a hypothetical serotonin or other brain chemical imbalance. Are the medical experts hearing what their patients are telling them?

In my opinion, the lack of logical thought shared by many doctors regarding the cause of depression and other so-called 'psychiatric illnesses' revealed itself in the book by psychiatrist Andrew Slaby. In his book, Dr Slaby takes an in-depth look at eight young people who attempted suicide, some of whom did not survive the attempt. While I am not doubting the author's compassion and sincerity, I believe that some of his conclusions lack common sense, being heavily influenced by traditional psychiatric beliefs and practices. He wrote:

Today [1994], depression is better understood than before. It is a biological vulnerability that surfaces when sufficient disturbing life experiences occur.[8]

The author shares with most of his psychiatrist colleagues the belief that depression is primarily a biological disorder. He presents his belief to the general public as if it were an established fact — 'depression is a biological vulnerability'. But since there is no proof that the cause of depression is a biological defect, he is — albeit unintentionally — misinforming the public. Yet the stories of these eight young people, as told by Dr Slaby, point to emotional, psychological, social and relationship problems within their lives rather than a biological defect:

Were their cries not heard? No, something was heard: Chad's silence, Sarah's continuous crying, Carly's rage, Tim's reactions to an abusive father, Kent's mental illness, David's drug use, and John's anxiety about his sexuality.

The 'mental illness' which one of the eight young people (Kent) suffered from is stated to be schizophrenia. It is clear from the book that emotional distress and troubled relationships were central to Kent's so-called 'mental illness'. After Kent's suicide,

349

his mother said:

> I can never forgive Tom [Kent's father] for not meeting Kent's needs. But what can I say? I wasn't there for him either.

The author acknowledges that the enormous focus within medicine on depression is not having any effect on the suicide rate:

> Adolescent depression is recognised, diagnosed and treated more frequently than even five years ago. And yet the escalating statistics of adolescent suicide seem to nullify any serious progress.

Dr Slaby's book was published in 1994; in the intervening years, the medical profession has put enormous energy and publicity into diagnosing and treating depression. Yet, the suicide rate in many countries including Britain remains stubbornly high. As a traditional psychiatrist, Dr Slaby believes that antidepressant medication is central to recovery from depression. He stated that depression is a very treatable illness. Here we have a paradox which surfaces repeatedly in psychiatry; if depression is now recognised, diagnosed and better treated, and if depression is the most common cause of suicide, why is there not an equivalent reduction in the suicide rate?

When something is repeated often enough, it becomes widely accepted as gospel truth. Modern medicine's repeated assertion that the cause of depression is biochemical has become widely accepted as a fact. In *The Teenage Years*, jointly written by broadcaster Fergal Keane and psychologist M. Murray, the authors discuss the causes of depression in the traditional psychiatric fashion; two main groups, reactive and endogenous. Reactive depression is described as depression for which there is an understandable cause. It is their comment on the second group — endogenous depression — that caught my eye:

Endogenous/biological depression: This form of depression normally has more biological origins and less immediate environmental triggers. As a result, there is often no discernible or apparent cause.[9]

This statement is factually incorrect and therefore misleading, albeit unwittingly. This book is written for the general public. When the authors make a statement which implies that what is said is a known fact, the general public will accept it as such. When they write that 'this form of depression normally has more biological origins and less environmental triggers', the public will naturally accept this on face value. But no proof exists that the cause of *any* form of depression is biological in origin.

The authors' use of the term 'endogenous/biological depression' is most unfortunate, though relatively common. It implies that endogenous and biological are interchangeable terms, compounding the misinformation. They are not interchangeable because it has not been established that depression has a biological cause. Medicine is filled with elitist words, a language which mystifies the subject and prevents the public from understanding medical terminology. Endogenous depression is an elitist term. To anyone in the street, this title sounds impressive. But the real meaning of the term 'endogenous depression' is that 'we doctors don't know what is causing this, so we assume it originates within the person'. Doctors frequently label people as suffering from endogenous depression because many doctors are not skilled enough to identify subtle triggers for the depression.

Other examples of medical misinformation on depression, mental illness and suicide are commonplace in the media. It is understandable that journalists take what the medical experts claim with such authority to be established fact:

The fact that up to 90 per cent of suicide deaths are linked with some form of psychiatric illness (usually depression).

351

Endogenous depression is primarily a biological complaint caused by an imbalance in the brain. It is frequently hereditary.[10]

Here is another example of medical theories presented to the public as if they are established facts. Three statements are here stated as fact when they are merely theories. It is not a fact that 90 per cent of suicides are due to psychiatric illness. Nor is it true to say that endogenous depression is a 'biological complaint'. And there is no solid evidence that depression is hereditary. While depression is more common in families where parents are depressed, this may equally be due to the emotional impact of a depressed parent on children.

Do antidepressants prevent suicide?

Most doctors (and consequently the public) believe that antidepressant drugs are very successful at treating depression. Depression is stated to be the major cause of suicide. Since most doctors believe that antidepressants prevent suicide, one might reasonably expect that antidepressant treatment is known to be effective in reducing the suicide rate. No such evidence exists. According to Irish psychiatrist Dr J. F. Connolly:

For many years, in spite of the fact that antidepressants were widely available and widely prescribed, it did not appear that they had any effect on the suicide rates for depressed patients.[11]

Antidepressants have become increasingly prescribed during the past twenty-five years. More than one in twelve women and one in twenty-eight men in Britain are currently on antidepressants, but there is little evidence of a reduction in suicide rates. When doctors speak in public on the prevention of suicide through antidepressant drugs, they do not inform the public that this is an unproven hypothesis. They usually convey the impression that this has already been established.

As is candidly outlined by a leading psychiatrist, this is not the case:

> No clinical trials have been conducted to indicate treatment efficacy of pharmacotherapy [in preventing suicide]. It is a failure of modern psychiatry that we still cannot say to patients with suicidal depression: 'treatment X has been scientifically proven to significantly reduce your risk for suicide'.[12]

Over four years on, Dr Malone's comments are as true now as they were in 1999. According to the 1998 Aware report on suicide, there is evidence that antidepressant drugs may actually increase the risk of suicide:

> A review conceded that the effectiveness of individual psychiatric and psychotherapeutic treatment remains unproven for suicide prevention. There is some suggestion that maintenance treatment with antidepressant drugs to prevent recurrences of depression may increase the suicide rate. This risk is considered to be small, but it points to the fact that long-term antidepressant use may precipitate a cycling instability of mood, while still having an antidepressant effect.[13]

In my opinion, this is an example of how — perhaps without realising it — doctors come up with explanations which do not undermine their own beliefs or their treatments. I believe that to say that antidepressants may produce mood instability while still working as effective antidepressants is contradictory. If the antidepressants were working, patients would not have these unstable mood swings. But the experts need some way of explaining this without undermining the 'effectiveness' of their treatments.

Notes

1. Goldacre and Seagroatt (1993) *The Lancet*, 31 July.

2. G Hogman (2000) *One in Ten*, 3rd ed., National Schizophrenia Fellowship.

3. Dr Jones, Dr Finlay, Dr Simpson and Dr Tricia Kreitman BSc. The study was published in the *British Journal of General Practice* in October 1997.

4. Dr Muiris Houston (2001) *The Irish Times*, 27 March.

5. Dr Michael Kelleher, in an interview with John Waters in *The Irish Times,* 8 January 1991.

6. Dr Michael Kelleher and Dr Fergus Shanahan (1995) Psycho-immunology and Suicidal Behaviour, in *The Irish Medical Journal,* Jan/Feb.

7. Dr Patricia Casey (1997) *A Guide to Psychiatry in Primary Care.*

8. Andrew Slaby (1994) *No One Saw My Pain.*

9. Fergal Keane and M. Murray (1998) *The Teenage Years*, p. 181

10. For example, Christopher Russell wrote in *The Sunday Independent* of 13 September 1998.

11. According to Irish psychiatrist Dr J. F. Connolly in the *Irish Medical News* of 7 September 1998.

12. Dr Kevin Malone, 1999, Mater Hospital, *Irish Medical News, 27* September.

13. According to *Suicide in Ireland: A Global Perspective and a National Strategy,* 1998, p. 11.

8

PREVENTING SUICIDE

In keeping with trends throughout most developed countries, there is a concerted drive within the British Isles to treat depression with antidepressant drugs. The experts (psychiatrists mainly) explain why: psychiatry has 'established' that those who take their lives are 'psychiatrically ill'. The most commonly found illness is depression. Therefore, if we blitz the nation, searching for cases of depression and treat them, the suicide rate should be reduced dramatically. A major driving force behind this international blitz is the pharmaceutical industry, which makes billions from this approach. These medical experts come across as if they know they are doing the right thing, and I do not doubt that they believe they are doing the right thing. However, these experts rarely mention that suicidal people were excluded from the drug trials of SSRI antidepressants.

Prevention policies based on presumption

Dr D. J. Gunnell is a senior British lecturer in Public Health. He does not appear convinced that the current health strategy on suicide is known to be effective. In 1998 he said that the effectiveness of health service efforts to prevent suicide is based on speculation:

> GP education programmes, and antidepressant and lithium prescribing require further investigation, as do the role played by telephone counselling services [such as the Samaritans].[1]

355

Dr Gunnell makes a valid point. The effectiveness of psychiatry's attempts to reduce suicide *is* unproven, but that is not how psychiatry portrays the situation to the general public. Through the media, psychiatrists repeatedly inform the public that effective drug treatments are now available for depression, and that by treating depression we will reduce the suicide rate. They do not say that their approach is speculative.

Recent research suggests that lithium may reduce the risk of suicide in people diagnosed as having manic depression, and that the major tranquilliser clozapine may reduce the suicide risk of people diagnosed as having schizophrenia. It remains to be seen just how significant is the believed suicide-preventing action of these two drugs.

Understanding suicidal behaviour is not enough

The phrase 'suicidal behaviour' is quite popular within modern medicine. Medical experts repeatedly emphasise that in order to reduce the suicide rate, doctors must develop a better understanding of suicidal behaviour. I do not believe that psychiatry has a deep understanding of the human condition. I do not see how doctors can develop a thorough understanding of suicidal behaviour unless they adopt a much broader approach to people in emotional and life crises.

Suicidal behaviour cannot be understood without looking at the deeper issues. The reason why modern medicine is not getting very far on the suicide issue can be traced back to how the medical profession sees a human being. Doctors are trained to look almost exclusively at the physical aspect of people — the human body and how the various organs and systems in the body function and interact with one other. Many doctors know little about other aspects of the human being, such as the emotional and psychological aspects of human existence. Doctors focus on suicidal behaviour as if suicide can be tackled by understanding this behaviour. But it cannot. Behaviour of any sort will only be understood when:

- The feelings which prompted the behaviour are understood — feelings of fear, overwhelm, anger, worthlessness, hopelessness, deep insecurity and vulnerability, for example.
- The emotional needs, which the person is trying to meet through their behaviour, are recognised and understood. Suicide is one way of ensuring that there will be no more rejection and abandonment. Suicide is the ultimate act of avoidance when the pain of living has become too overwhelming. Suicidal behaviour is often a cry for help. Because of the distressed state of the person, the signs may be subtle and go unnoticed. On the other hand, the cry for help may be heard and acted upon. Emotionally vulnerable people rarely feel safe enough to ask for the real help they need. They will rarely say 'I feel deeply distressed and emotionally vulnerable, I cannot cope any more, please help me', especially if they are men. Through suicidal behaviour, they may drop hints to those around them that they really need help. But the clues may be heavily disguised. By disguising the cries for help, people protect themselves from further hurt and rejection they might experience by exposing their deep vulnerability and not receiving the support, love and acceptance which they crave. By disguising the cries for help, they also prevent themselves from feeling the full impact of their emotions, since in expressing the depth of one's distress to another, one comes directly in touch with the pain of one's distress. Many of us human beings 'will not go there', since we are not sure that we can handle and survive such pain and distress.

If we are to understand and prevent suicide, we need to see suicide and suicidal behaviour as it truly is; a protective act of

357

avoidance. It is protective because by ending their life, the person guarantees that their pain, their deep emotional vulnerability, their isolation, loneliness, and desperate fear of hurt, rejection and abandonment are over — forever. Suicide also puts an end to the pain of guilt, self-hatred and self-rejection, constant torments for people in emotional turmoil.

What kind of carer?

What kind of carer works most effectively with people who are emotionally distressed? A GP? A psychiatrist? A psychologist? A psychotherapist? A counsellor? A friend? GPs do not give people enough time to express themselves or to explore the issues which are at the root of the problem. Nor do they have sufficient training in and understanding of the human emotions and behaviour. GPs are preoccupied with diagnosing so-called 'psychiatric illness'. Once there is any trace of depression or any 'mental illness', the prescription pad comes into play and the real listening stops. I believe that both GPs and psychiatrists prescribe antidepressant drugs and tranquillisers far too often and far too easily.

I do not believe that psychiatry in its present form should be the foundation stone upon which effective recovery strategies are built. Through its close relationship with the pharmaceutical industry, psychiatry has tied itself to a future where only selective medical research will be carried out.

Psychiatry is prepared to countenance one form of 'talk therapy' — cognitive-behavioural therapy, in which therapists attempt to create more positive patterns of thinking and behaving within the person. While this form of therapy does work for some people, in my opinion psychotherapy needs to encompass a broader, more comprehensive approach than that of cognitive-behavioural therapy.

One possible reason for psychiatry's acceptance of cognitive-behavioural therapy as opposed to other forms of psychotherapy might be that cognitive-behavioural therapy is less threatening to psychiatry. It can easily be brought into the medical model alongside drug treatments. While more comprehensive psychotherapy can — and sometimes should — also be used alongside medication, these therapies sometimes disagree with the medical profession's extensive use of medication for emotional problems. Therefore, psychotherapy in general represents a threat to psychiatry's dominant position in the treatment of 'mental illness'. Perhaps it is little wonder that most psychiatrists show little enthusiasm for psychotherapy.

A common misconception is that psychotherapy is still based on Sigmund Freud's approach. Increasingly over the past fifty years, Freud's views have lessened in importance. While many approaches to psychotherapy retain a varying proportion of his ideas, to describe psychotherapy as 'Freud's talk therapy' — as I have heard doctors and journalists do — is to display one's own ignorance of the enormous changes which have occurred within psychotherapy in the past fifty years. Personally, I see the therapy process as 'working through' rather than 'talking through' issues and problems.

I believe that in the majority of psychiatric research, the cart has been put before the horse. The outcome — that emotional and psychological problems are 'illnesses' caused by brain chemical imbalances or genetic defects — is presumed long before it has been established. Consequently, I believe that psychiatry's role in health care needs to be reformed significantly. But the momentum of modern psychiatry towards the 'mental illness' approach has gathered such pace that reform may be greatly resisted by mainstream psychiatry and its principal sponsors, the pharmaceutical industry.

Mental health carers must give people enough time to express themselves. They must have a deep understanding of what it means to be human. They need to be compassionate people who are balanced enough to show great caring and concern for their clients yet not become sucked into the person's problems. They must respect and care for their clients as equal human beings, not as inferior or less knowledgeable people than the service provider themselves. They must be superb listeners. They must know how to create a safe, therapeutic relationship with their clients, and how to gently encourage the person to reclaim responsibility for and confidence in themselves, their life and their decision-making.

Service providers must to be prepared to sit with their clients in their despair and pain. They should seek to help people solve their own difficulties rather than jump in with their own solutions. It is not always so much a question of how much the doctor or therapist knows. It is human understanding and compassion, and how well he or she communicates this caring that matters. If service providers lose sight of these fundamental qualities, they can do their clients more harm than good. While there are therapists who work to these standards, the counselling professions still have some way to go.

Service providers must be able to be ordinary. There is no need for airs and graces, for superiority complexes in this work. In my opinion, the most effective mental health care worker is one who does not forget their own humanness during meetings with clients.

There are many schools of therapy promoting different approaches. Some therapists strongly believe they must tell the client what to do. Others believe therapy should be non-directive — the therapist deliberately resists the temptation to tell clients what is best for them. Studies have shown that the most important factor in successful therapy is not what type of therapy is used; the important factors are the quality of the relationship between client and therapist, and the commitment of the client. One reason why the counselling professions have failed to break psychiatry's stronghold on 'mental illness' is their lack of a unified and co-ordinated approach to counselling. This makes it much easier for psychiatry to divide and conquer the counselling professions. But perhaps the willingness of counselling and psychotherapy to countenance different approaches is healthier than psychiatry's more tunnel-visioned approach.

A truly holistic approach to mental health care, provided by an empathic, understanding team, each of whom bring their own particular expertise, clearly has its merits, provided that the team do not lose sight of the real needs of mental health service users. Family and good friends can play a central role in supporting the person through their crisis. The more meaningful support people have, the better.

The views of an experienced counsellor

Jim Byrne is a senior counsellor at University College, Galway, who has been counselling students for many years. I am very grateful for his contribution, in which he outlines his own beliefs about the current suicide prevention policy, its limitations, and his views on how to help people who feel suicidal:

Suicide is a very complex phenomenon, and in many cases, the suicidal mind is not a sick mind. Social isolation, family disharmony, unemployment, relationships and other personal issues are commonly found in the treatment of those who are suicidal. These issues are rarely addressed when these people are admitted to the psychiatric services. However, what is even more important is that the psychological terrain of the mind of the would-be suicidal victim is often not even looked at. Unendurable psychological pain, feelings of helplessness and hopelessness, isolation and despair are always present in the lives of those who wish to end their lives. No one

361

commits suicide out of joy; the enemy of their life is pain. Pain is what the person committing suicide seeks to escape.

Suicide is not random. It is never done pointlessly or without purpose. Suicide is both a movement away from pain and a movement to end consciousness. This area, the emotional and psychological pain, must become the major focus in the management of suicide. These issues demand that skilled professionals and caring individuals be given the opportunity to work with those at risk. The incidence of suicide can be lowered and many young lives saved if those in daily contact with the individual can learn to recognize and intervene effectively when they hear that all-important cry for help. Not all cries for help receive the attention they need. Commitment to a psychiatric unit or a mandatory psychiatric interview while in hospital recovering from the suicide attempt will not suffice. If we, the professionals, don't address these early warning signs professionally, how can we expect society to do so?

In my own experience of counselling those at risk of suicide at university, I have very rarely found the need to involve the local psychiatric services. Most young people who are suffering from emotional or social problems are greatly relieved when they find someone who listens to them and who can identify with the mental anguish they are feeling at the time. Also, to have someone who will intervene in the areas that are causing them to be suicidal is a major factor in enabling them to look at the future, less burdened and more hopeful.

I have found, over the past twenty years of counselling, that if these inner psychological issues and needs are addressed in counselling, it is rare that suicide will occur. This form of management of those at risk of suicide is not the model used in the present-day psychiatric services. This is not a reflection of these services but, as they depend on

> *a medical/chemical solution to solve the emotional pain of*
> *those at risk, they have very little to offer. The psychiatric*
> *model of treatment does not address these important areas*
> *of the individual sufferer's life. Until our health services*
> *train and sensitise relevant professional staff to work in*
> *these areas, it is my opinion that our suicide rates will not*
> *be reduced.*

The views of Jim Byrne and others whose views differ somewhat from the approach of modern medicine need to be afforded the same attention as those of modern medicine itself. The prevailing view of the medical profession should no longer be accepted at face value. The time has come to find out what experts really mean when they say, 'We now know that...'. Far too often, it would be more correct for the expert to say, 'we now *believe* that...'. We must put an end to the practice of presenting theories as if they were established facts. We must bring together the best brains we have, the people with the deepest understanding of the human condition.

We must listen to leading and experienced psychologists, psychotherapists, counsellors, social workers, and others who have something valuable to contribute to the improvement of mental health services. We must listen to the views of service users and their families. We cannot allow modern medicine to monopolise the 'expert' position any longer. We must get beyond the presumption that people end their lives because they have a 'psychiatric illness'. Perhaps most importantly of all, the voice of service users must be heard far more than it has to date. We need to look at the real issues behind suicide. We must fully acknowledge the role of low self-esteem and low self-confidence, human vulnerability, stress, relationship conflicts, emotional, social and psychological issues, and develop appropriate responses. We must take an honest look at the society we have created, and the many ways in which society's values, expectations, censorship and coercion can cause people to become deeply distressed. We must take on board the reality than many people become hurt, ostracised, overwhelmed and marginalised within our society, and we must develop comprehensive responses to these realities.

Bullying is one such reality. According to a report[2], research suggests that bullying may be a factor in twenty per cent of suicides. This article referred to a study by the anti-bullying centre at Trinity College, Dublin. The findings of this study 'indicate that workplace bullying contributes to between 18 per cent and 22 per cent of suicides', according to Professor Mona O'Moore, the centre's co-ordinator. The findings were presented at an international conference.[3]

A 2003 study on bullying, undertaken at the University of California, found that bullying in schools is pervasive. According to the study carried out by UCLA Professor of Education Sandra Graham, depression, social anxiety, emotional distress, loneliness, social marginalisation and disengagement from school are common among victims of bullying.

Nelson Mandela once said that it is not our weakness that scares us, but our power. Some people feel so unsafe that they cannot believe in themselves, even when others do. To believe in oneself means taking action. If the action which needs to be taken is too overwhelming, the person may not yet be ready to develop their self-belief until they are at a better, more solid place within themselves.

A story of hope

When I first met Jean, she was overcome with anxiety. Her sister brought her to me in my capacity as a GP. As she entered my surgery, she was shaking uncontrollably, unable to put a sentence together. I had to get Jean's history from her sister who accompanied her. Then thirty years old, Jean had been dominated by anxiety since she was a child. In the three months before attending me, Jean's anxiety had become extremely severe, despite her taking five tranquillisers and two sleeping tablets every day on medical advice. She had become increasingly withdrawn and had stayed indoors at home for weeks. She had virtually stopped eating and was not sleeping, in spite of all the medication. I had not seen a more severe case of anxiety in my seventeen years working as a doctor. Jean was breaking down right in front of me. As it turned out this was the beginning of a breakthrough for Jean, the beginning of her healing journey.

I was not sure how I should deal with this severely agitated person whom I had never met before. Five years previously, I would have done the medically appropriate thing. I would have considered giving Jean an injection of a strong sedative. I would have carefully thought about admitting her to a psychiatric hospital, against her will if necessary. Five years previously, I would have known no other way.

I quickly realised that sending Jean to a psychiatric hospital was about the worst thing I could do for her. Because she was already consumed with terror, the emotional trauma that a psychiatric admission would create for Jean might be unbearable for her. I asked Jean to lie on my couch. She was rigid as a board, wide-eyed with panic, continuing to shake uncontrollably. I gently placed one hand on her stomach and one on her heart. I asked Jean to close her eyes and listen to my words. For thirty minutes, I quietly reassured her that she was safe now, that there was no threat to her.

Within five minutes, Jean stopped shaking. After thirty minutes, her eyes remained closed. She lay peacefully on the couch as if in a deep, peaceful sleep. Jean's sister Helen remained in the room throughout. Watching Jean change from a state of severe panic to one of peace moved Helen deeply.

365

Jean had relaxed so much that her limbs felt heavy and she was yawning. She could at last talk to me coherently. We arranged an appointment for a few days later. I did not prescribe any medication. I did not refer her to a psychiatrist. I could see that a central part of Jean's anxiety was that she felt very unsafe, threatened by the slightest thing. I felt that I could play an important role in her recovery by fostering a trusting and safe relationship with Jean over the coming months.

In the three years since our first meeting, Jean has attended me about every two to three weeks. She had made steady progress. As I had hoped, her relationship with me is a great source of safety and security for her. She looks forward to our meetings. Our relationship is built on respect and caring; she feels highly valued as an important and unique human being. As our relationship developed, Jean shared her life story with me. Before long, I could sense how her severe anxiety might have developed. Her mother died suddenly when she was six. Jean was the youngest of a large family. Her family felt that she should be protected as much as possible from the pain of her mother's illness and death, so Jean was not brought to visit her mother in hospital. When her mother died, Jean was kept away from the funeral. When she asked her family why her mummy was not at home any more, she received vague replies which further increased her confusion. It is important to say that at all times her family had her best interests at heart.

Within months of her mother's death, Jean became very anxious. She refused to go to school. She missed at least half of the following six school years. At thirteen years of age, she gave up school completely and got a job in a launderette. Four years later, she gave that up and she has not worked since. Over the past twelve years, Jean had become a recluse. She avoided all contact with people, only venturing out occasionally. She has never had a close relationship, or even a close friend. For ten years, Jean had been attending her local psychiatric hospital once a fortnight. The psychiatric doctors she attended moved on every six months to be replaced by a new batch. No sooner had she developed any degree of rapport with them that they disappeared from her life. Eventually she learned that there was little point in opening up to these doctors, since they would soon be moving on. She told me that her consultations with these doctors lasted no more than a few minutes. These doctors concentrated on reviewing her notes and assessing her medication.

I asked her whether her years attending the psychiatrists had helped her. The only positive comment she made was about the relaxation classes, which initially helped her a little, but the effect was not lasting. She did not feel that the psychiatrists had been much help to her. Three months before we met, she stopped attending the psychiatric hospital. After ten years of frequent attendances, she was still taking five tranquillisers a day, and getting nowhere. The psychiatrists did not seem to know what to do next. Jean saw no hope in what they had to offer so she stopped attending. She became a total recluse, rarely venturing out to the local shop. She spent most of her time in bed at home. Jean eventually reached a state of constant severe panic, as she was when she first attended me.

Jean, her sister and I all feel that she has made dramatic progress. Both the frequency and the severity of her anxiety is now a fraction of what it used to be. She goes out and about at will every day. Without pressure from me, she gradually reduced her tranquillisers. After years of taking seven tablets a day and still experiencing severe, ever-present anxiety, for the past two months she has not taken a single tablet. Jean's sister has told me that the family are amazed at Jean's improvement.

Psychiatry's approach to anxiety is quite simplistic. Anxiety is a 'disorder' which psychiatrists and doctors in general try to eliminate, usually with tranquillisers. In the eyes of psychiatry,

367

anxiety is an illness per se, requiring medical treatment. I do not believe that anxiety is an illness or a disorder. Anxiety is a natural human response to a situation which is perceived by the person as threatening to their safety, their security. Anxiety does not suddenly appear without reason like a bolt from the blue to be eliminated with tranquillisers or antidepressants. Anxiety is a protective reaction when life becomes very threatening. Severe anxiety is an unpleasant experience; people understandably attend doctors in order to seek relief. But the cause of the anxiety is that the person's sense of safety and security is threatened. If the person is helped to address the safety and security issues in their lives, the anxiety will usually diminish.

Working with people over the years, I have noticed that anxiety — sometimes severe — can surface as a protection from one's own distress. In this regard, anxiety is a bit like a sandstorm. In a sandstorm, a person can barely see two feet in front of them. With anxiety, the person becomes so preoccupied with the anxiety that they do not see, or get in touch with, the distress which may have triggered the anxiety. It is as if, at some level within themselves, they created a sandstorm of anxiety, as a defence from becoming aware of and fully experiencing their distress. With appropriate help, support, guidance, patience, understanding and empathy, people can come through their distress. Many people who have attended me with severe anxiety have improved through dealing with various unfinished business in their lives, often involving unresolved grief, loss, abuse and life changes.

The psychiatrists misinterpreted Jean's problem. They diagnosed Jean as having a severe anxiety disorder of unknown origin. In more than ten years, they did not focus on her vulnerability, her lack of inner safety and security. The seeds of Jean's anxiety problem were sown at six years of age, when her mother died. Every child builds their sense of safety and security around their parents. The psychiatrists treated the anxiety, as if the anxiety were the problem. Had they focused on the real issue — her total lack of any inner safety and security, her immense grief and sadness — they might have got somewhere. Jean's anxiety was not her problem, quite the opposite: it was her protector. Feeling constantly unsafe and under threat, her anxiety protected Jean from taking risks which would have left her open to further hurt and overwhelm. Even simple everyday things like going for a walk had become very threatening to her. While becoming a recluse was painful, it was less painful than taking risks and becoming further overwhelmed with terror as a consequence.

As a child, Jean had been very attached to her mother. Suddenly her mother was no longer there for her. Jean's safety net disappeared from her life. Her family's well-meaning decision not to discuss her mother's death with Jean unwittingly compounded the situation. Jean could not begin to understand what had happened. She was not given an explanation which made any sense to her. Jean's whole world was threatened. If her very own mother could suddenly vanish without warning or explanation, then anything could happen to Jean too. Her sense of safety and security in her life was pulled from under her.

Within weeks of her mother's death, Jean began to withdraw from life. She saw school as a highly threatening experience where she felt very exposed and vulnerable. Jean avoided school rather than endure extreme terror every day. Her response to life increasingly became one of avoidance and withdrawal. Jean's father drank heavily and was often aggressive at home. Jean did not have a close relationship with her father. Throughout her childhood, she had no one to turn to.

Now, for the first time in her life, she has a relationship with a doctor who she feels understands her. Every time I see her, I reassure her that there is nothing psychiatrically wrong with her. She now understands that her anxiety is the direct result of the immense lack of inner safety she has felt for years. She knows that the main thing I focus on in her sessions with me is for her to experience a deep sense of safety. A person can relax only when they feel safe, which is why the relaxation classes at the psychiatric hospital only gave her slight and temporary relief.

I did not concentrate on a diagnosis with Jean. I saw her as a normal healthy human being who had a major lack of safety in her life due largely to past events. I always concentrate on people's normality. Psychiatry always gave her the impression that she was abnormal. On many occasions, the psychiatrist she encountered had never met her before. The psychiatrists she had attended for years gave her about seven minutes per consultation. Take from this the time it took to review her charts and write her prescription — that left less than five minutes left for interaction between Jean and the psychiatrist. Little meaningful interaction can take place in five minutes. It is hardly surprising that Jean left those consultations with her loneliness and hopelessness increased.

Her consultations with me last an hour. I let Jean decide what direction she wanted our sessions to take. She gets immense safety and relaxation from our talks and relaxation sessions. I repeatedly emphasise to her that she is a unique and priceless human being. She knows that I hold her in high esteem and — unlike the psychiatric personnel, who moved on every six months — she knows that I will be here for her next week, next month, and in three years' time if needs be. She therefore has a great sense of safety, support and equality in her relationship with me. These qualities are important to the healing process, but they were absent from her relationship with the psychiatrists she attended.

For the first time in years, Jean has a sense of hope for the future. I'm not pushing Jean to do anything. To do so would be to threaten her, to undermine her now growing sense of safety. I've not recommended that she force herself to do anything she's not ready for. As we work together, Jean is coming out of her shell. Given the degree of anxiety and hopelessness she felt prior to attending me, I believe that Jean might have chosen to take her own life but for the hope, trust and understanding she has experienced in her relationship with me. Jean dreaded going to see the psychiatrists. Because she felt so threatened by the psychiatrists, her anxiety always increased when she attended them. The symptoms the psychiatrists were trying to eradicate were actually being increased by those consultations. It is hardly surprising that their treatments did not work.

An analogy may help to illustrate what it is like to live in a constant state of anxiety. When a hurricane is approaching, people sit up and take notice. They barricade their windows, doors, homes and workplaces. If people have enough warning, they will spend days preparing for the hurricane, protecting themselves, their loved ones and their property. As the hurricane arrives, everyone withdraws into a place of safety until the storm has blown over. There is hardly a soul on the streets. Our TV screens regularly show us how hurricane-prone places such as Florida prepare for an oncoming hurricane. We all agree that this is a 'normal' human response. The hurricane is a major threat, which requires a correspondingly major response from people living in the path of a hurricane.

For people whose anxiety, distress and overwhelm is intense and ever-present, life is like one big terrifying hurricane, from which they constantly feel the need to withdraw to protect themselves from emotional annihilation. The same is true for emotionally distressed and vulnerable people whose overwhelm is interpreted as evidence of 'mental illness'. They feel as if every day is a huge threat to their very survival, filled with the risk of further rejection and emotional pain. Understandably, they withdraw and put up the barricades,

371

closing themselves off from people and from life.

I work with many people like Jean who regularly experience terror, who attend psychiatrists and are treated with high doses of tranquillisers. Many of these people went to the psychiatrist with one problem and ended up with two: their anxiety, either not improved or heightened, and an addiction to tranquillisers — the 'treatment' prescribed by the 'experts'.

Relationships and the family revisited

Few things in life are as important to people as relationships. No man is an island. The relationships children develop within their families are the foundations of so many critically important factors which have a huge bearing on the rest of their lives, including self-esteem, inner safety and security. Yet there is no mechanism in society to help people understand and improve how they relate to others. Relationship issues and difficulties are often the real, underlying reason why many people attend doctors. But the relationship issue is rarely touched upon, let alone resolved. Consequently, thousands of people every year leave the doctors surgery with a diagnosis which is misguided and a prescription they do not need, usually either an antidepressant or a tranquilliser.

When there is a great human need, society has an obligation to do whatever is necessary to meet that need. People need protection, so society has created the defence forces and the legal system. People need health care: most countries responded to this need by creating a system of health care which is widely available to all. People need to put bread on the table. Social welfare systems have been developed as a response to this need.

The time has come for society to respond to the massive human need for emotional safety and security. The widespread occurrence of emotional distress, 'mental illness' and the tragedy of suicide is calling to us to put into place a system in society where people can get help to overcome relationship issues. The key importance of relationships and their immense impact on people's lives must receive appropriate recognition. A framework needs to be devised which offers people help and understanding, to help them overcome problems created by relationships without judgement or blame.

These measures must be undertaken in a spirit of compassion for all concerned. Parents do their best for their children, but frequently parents' own need to protect themselves from further distress and hurt reduces their ability to provide their children with what in my opinion is the greatest protection there is from 'mental illnesses' and suicide — high self-esteem, self-confidence, self-belief, adaptability, created and fostered by unconditionally loving relationships and open communication.

Critically important though they are, these issues are rarely discussed. They are brushed under the carpet. Yet those within troubled families often know the reality of the situation, that all is not well within the family. Fear of criticism, judgement and punishment often prevents the parents in many such families from seeking help. Yet if help were available to parents in emotional difficulty, help based on a non-judgemental approach in an understanding and compassionate society, I believe that parents would be much more willing to seek help and support. Parents would receive appropriate help to resolve their own emotional and relationship issues. The vicious cycle of dysfunctional family creating dysfunctional family, generation after generation, might finally be broken.

We must place greater emphasis on improving communication. Few of us communicate with others — even our loved ones — openly and from the heart. There are very few people to whom we can truly express our feelings and vulnerability without risk of being judged. How we relate to others in our lives is well summed up by an article in a women's magazine many years ago. A member of the social scene was asked for her definition of a boring person. She replied: 'Someone who, when you ask them how they are, they actually tell you'. How many people are there in your life with whom you feel safe and accepted enough to reveal your true feelings and your vulnerability? If you have even one or two, then count your blessings.

Many people live in an emotional desert, lacking the intimacy of a loving and unconditional relationship. We need to learn how to listen to those around us, to encourage people to communicate their feelings. This came across powerfully at the end of BBC's *Panorama* programme on suicide in young men about five years ago called *Boys Don't Cry*. Three people spoke of their deep regret that they didn't hear the pain of their loved one. A mother whose son took his own life said:

If only I could have reached out and told him that he could talk and still be a man.

A second mother whose son ended his own life spoke:

I have a lot of friends who have boys the same age as Mark. And I have certainly spoke to them and said 'Look, if things change, if the mood changes, listen to them, talk to them'.

A young man whose friend took his own life:

You know, my friend, he committed suicide a couple of years ago. I met him on the Wednesday at the post office. That Friday I was in the studios in London and I got a phone call from me mate. He says 'How are you?' I said 'All right'. And the next thing I knew he was dead. He just threw himself off the flat later that day. And I just wish I'd asked him if he was alright. But we don't, do we? No one asks any more 'Are you all right? No - are you really all right?'

A year ago, a middle-aged man who was going through an enormous emotional crisis came to see me, as a counsellor, for several months. One session was particularly intense. I have rarely seen a man express such emotional distress as that man did that day; wailing, sobbing, at time on all fours on the ground, needing to be hugged, choked with distress. That session was a turning point for him, a real cathartic experience. While that session is indelibly etched in my mind, one aspect stands out in my memory. As he left at the end of our meeting, drained, exhausted, barely able to stand, he happened to bump into a male acquaintance of his in my waiting room. The door was open, and I heard the brief interchange between the two men. The other man asked him how he was. He replied, 'I'm good, thanks'. Whatever else he felt at this time of crisis in his life and after our intense session, he did not feel 'good'. But in this world where emotional censorship rules and distress must be kept under wraps, he did not feel he could tell this person how he really felt. I felt that this brief exchange between these two men, which lasted less than a minute, spoke volumes about the subtle censorships which are rampant within this society which we have collectively created.

This type of subtle censorship was echoed in the experiences of a twenty-year-old woman currently coming to see me as a counsellor. She had experienced great terror and absent self-confidence for several years. A year prior to her attending me, her anxiety became so overwhelming that she took a year out from university. She did not feel she could tell even her friends the real reason why she was not attending college, for fear of being stigmatised and rejected. Instead, she invented what she felt was a plausible story. She felt sad and upset at having to lie, feeling further isolated and marginalised as a consequence. But she felt she had little option. When the time came to decide whether or not she would return to university the following year, the idea of telling her friends that she might be taking another year off college filled her with dread. What excuse would she give this time around? To take a year off college was reasonably acceptable socially. To justify — to others — taking a second year off would be much more difficult. This great dilemma was created by her understandable belief that if the true reasons why she was contemplating a second year off became public knowledge, her life would not be worth living.

Censorship of our human vulnerability, distress and overwhelm is alive and well throughout our society. I sometimes feel that an important facet of therapy work with people is to provide them with a safe space to express themselves without fear of judgement, since to do so elsewhere in their life may seem impossible. Questions need to be asked as to why the therapy room is one of the few places in life where people feel safe and accepted enough to risk being themselves.

Wider society

Society as a whole must look at the real issues involved in suicide. For too long we have given power and responsibility for emotional distress, 'mental illness' and suicide to the medical profession. In doing so, we have created experts who conveniently absolve society of any significant role in the cause and prevention of suicide. Medical experts are spreading the message society wants to hear, a message which might be paraphrased as follows:

> Society is not in any way responsible for the suicide of our people. The cause is mental illness and society is not responsible for the creation of mental illness.

I believe that society does play a major role in causing emotional distress, 'mental illness' and suicide, and therefore has the potential to play a central part in reducing these also.

Psychotherapist Ernesto Spinelli highlights society's responsibility:

376

So long as a society holds on to medical models of mental illness, no examination or criticism of that society need be considered since the origins of the problem are considered to be primarily biological or genetic in nature, thereby minimizing — and exculpating — any socio-environmental factors. [4]

We must provide a comprehensive network of caring and supportive mental health services for people in emotional distress. I believe that this would provide a much more effective service for emotionally distressed people than what is currently available. But providing an emergency service is not enough.

By neglecting to look at key issues around 'mental illness' and suicide — relationships, dysfunction within families, low self-esteem, for instance — society is sweeping difficult issues under the carpet. Many people, including those who take their lives every year, are paying a high price for our failure as a society to embrace the real issues.

Millions of people lead a double life. The outward image which many young men present to the world is of hardworking, successful, important people, unruffled and cool as a breeze. Apparently happy and cheerful, they do not reveal feelings of depression, fear, or emotional vulnerability. They rarely ask for support, certainly not for emotional or psychological help. They often have a hectic social life. They seem to have it all, and are the envy of many. But the reality behind that public image may be a different story altogether. Frequently in emotional turmoil, many young men bottle it up, terrified to reveal any weaknesses which might taint their image. They fear losing the approval and acceptance of their relatives and friends. They suppress their emotions in an attempt to cope with life, which comes at them in relentless waves.

Cut off from their feelings, many young men feel cut off from people. Even in their closest relationships they feel alone and lonely. The greater the gap — or the bigger the mask — between the public image people feel compelled to portray and the true inner world of the person, the more desperate they become. Suicide then becomes a real option which will once and for all remove them from their anguish. For years we have known that thousands of men are terrified of admitting that they have feelings — not to mention revealing them to others.

Thousands of women also live double lives; the mask they put on every day for their family, friends and others, and the person inside, often lonely, unhappy and unfulfilled. The person inside remains silent and unheard. When Jane became depressed in her late twenties, the hardest thing was the enormous isolation she experienced. There were so few people to whom she could express her real feelings. At work, and even with friends, she felt that nobody wanted to know. When people ask her how she is, she pretends. She says she is fine. She pretends most of the day. She feels so alone inside. Yet nobody at work or in her social circle knows there is anything wrong. She has learnt to become a great pretender.

Jane would love to open up about how she feels but is scared that she will be labelled as a nutcase by her friends and work-mates. She has good reason. She has seen how many of her friends speak about depressed people in a less than charitable fashion. Terms such as 'loony-bin' and 'nutter' are frequently exchanged at their coffee-break. Jane feels so inferior, wondering if her friends would disown her if they knew how she was really feeling. She has a loving relationship with her husband, but once she leaves home to go to work, the mask goes on. She forces a smile for eight hours a day, feeling lost and alone inside.

I have noticed a trend in peoples' lives, particularly in women. They get married and perhaps have children. As the years go by, the needs of family and work increasingly take precedence over their own needs. They learn to stop taking care of themselves, to stop doing things for themselves. This process can occur so gradually that it goes unnoticed, like a thief in the night. Eventually the person may reach the point where there is no colour, no joy in their life and they wonder why. This insidious process can be so developed in a person's life that they need a great deal of help and encouragement to reverse it. Many times, people have said to me 'I don't know where to begin' when I am exploring with them ways of increasing the joy, meaning and fulfilment in their life and having their own needs met. Little wonder that many such people become depressed. They are so busy looking after other people's needs that their own needs for love, challenge, growth, fun and colour go unmet.

Why we have created a society where people have to pretend so much? Why is helping people come to terms with emotional distress not a high priority within our society? Why have we not created mechanisms in society to help people understand themselves better? Mechanisms to help people feel safe enough to be themselves in this world?

Why have we not created a compassionate society based on tolerance, openness and respect? A society where people can be themselves and express themselves without the ever-present fear of criticism, judgement, rejection or ridicule? Where the rights of people to hold differing views, and to be different are enshrined in our society's value system? Is it really good enough that when we are greeted with 'How are you?' by people every day, we rarely feel comfortable enough to tell the truth. We say 'fine', 'great', 'never better', when we really feel like screaming. The double life dilemma rolls on.

With regard to emotional distress, 'mental illness' and suicide we need to go back to the drawing board. We must let go of the presumed link between suicide and 'psychiatric illness'. We can construct a system designed to create a deeper understanding of human rights, equality, respect, self-esteem,

379

relationships, self-worth, understanding, emotional expression, tolerance, communication within relationships, and freedom of expression. I believe that such a framework would be more acceptable and more effective than the current psychiatric service.

For years the medical profession has retained control over mental health policy decisions. I believe that when it comes to the issues dealt with in this book — emotional distress, 'mental illness', and suicide — the medical profession should not be given the power to veto measures simply because doctors disagree with them.

I feel that modern medicine may be too close to the issues, too emotionally involved, to be able to stand back and take stock of itself objectively. Modern medicine's vested interest in maintaining the status quo, in ensuring that the concept of 'mental illness' becomes more and more accepted by the public, may well impede the medical profession's ability to see the issues clearly and objectively.

Nor will modern medicine invite other groups — the counselling professions, social workers or other mental health workers, for instance — to share its pedestal of expertise. Therefore, those whom the public have entrusted with the power to create change for the better — the legislators — should take whatever steps are necessary to ensure that the medical profession's monopoly of emotional pain, 'mental illness' and suicide is thoroughly and independently examined. I believe that a fundamental re-examination of emotional distress, 'mental illness' and suicide is urgently needed. I believe there should be a public investigation into the practice of psychiatry and the influence of the pharmaceutical industry, which should include GPs, who deal with 90 per cent of 'psychiatric problems'. Given that millions of people use the mental health services each year, and that there is considerable disquiet amongst the public about the mental health services, such an inquiry is long overdue. Governments worldwide have for decades abdicated responsibility for psychiatric research and treatment to the medical profession and the pharmaceutical industry. This abdication has allowed psychiatry to create its own brand of caring without having to truly account for its beliefs and practices.

Intolerant attitudes are still widespread. Recently a depressed client of mine was having coffee in a hotel lobby. At the table adjacent to hers, a group of people were discussing depression. One particularly loud man pontificated his views on depression to the group. According to him, depressed people are a blight on society and should be locked up. He is not alone in that view. It seems that discrimination and prejudice against so-called 'mentally ill' people is common in society.

Emotional distress is a fact of life. We cannot wish it away just because it makes us feel uncomfortable. If we are to tackle the issue of suicide, we must take action. The vast sums of money currently invested in psychiatry could be used to fund a caring and supportive service helping people overcome emotional distress. Such a system must see all human beings as equal, unique and priceless. It must approach people who are emotionally distressed in a respectful way, from a viewpoint that the person's emotional distress is always valid and understandable. Only then will we begin to provide appropriate care for emotional distress, and in doing so, reduce the suicide rate.

The stigma attached to 'mental illness' will disappear only when we realise that there is no such thing as 'mental illness'; that deep emotional distress is a natural human response to emotional pain and life-related distress. Only then will the millions of people worldwide who have been labelled 'mentally ill' have a chance of a compassionate hearing from both the general public and the caring professions. Only then will the shame and sense of inferiority these people experience so

381

profoundly begin to disappear.

There may be a strong reaction against any such change by those with vested interests, including the pharmaceutical industry and the medical profession. Doctors and drug companies will come forward with arguments which sound so logical as to why psychiatry is the body we must entrust with care of emotional distress. Do not be fooled. Psychiatry's track record is nothing to write home about. Psychiatry has created a niche of expertise for itself, as if possessing a special mystique, a unique wisdom and authority. This mystique limits the public's ability to thoroughly examine the true value of psychiatry's beliefs and practices. Only by demystifying psychiatry can the public identify the true value of the medical profession's approach to emotional distress, 'mental illness' and suicide. Only then can we begin to build a society and a health care system designed to meet the real needs of its people.

Notes

1. Dr D J Gunnell, in his presentation to the national conference of the Irish Association of Suicidology, 1998.

2. *The Sunday Times,* 19 October 2003.

3. Conference 'Workplace Bullying, Stress and Suicide' held at Trinity College, Dublin on 18 October 2003.

4. Ernesto Spinelli, (1989) *The Interpreted World: An introduction to phenomenological psychology*, p. 137. London: Sage Publications.

FURTHER READING

American Psychiatric Association (2000) *Diagnostic and Statistical Manual of Mental Disorders, Fourth Edition, Text Revision*. Washington DC: American Psychiatric Association.

Beeken, C. with Greenstreet, R. (1997) *My Body, My Enemy*. London: HarperCollins.

Boyle, M. (2002) *Schizophrenia: A scientific delusion?* London: Routledge

Breggin, P. (1993) *Toxic Psychiatry*. London: HarperCollins.

Breggin, P. (1994) *Talking Back to Prozac*. New York: St. Martin's Press.

Breggin, P. (2001) *The Antidepressant Fact Book*. Cambridge, MA: Perseus Publishing.

Breggin, P. (1997) *The Heart of Being Helpful: Empathy and the creation of a healing presence*. New York: Springer Publishing Company.

Breggin, P. and Cohen, D. (2000) *Your Drug may be your Problem: How and why to stop taking psychiatric medications*. Cambridge, MA: Perseus Publishing.

Breggin, P. and Stern, M. (Eds.) (1996) *Psychosocial Approaches to Deeply Disturbed Person.*, New York: The Haworth Press.

Chadwick, P. (1997) *Schizophrenia: The positive perspective*. London: Routledge.

Dethlefsen, T. and Dahlke, R. (1990) *The Healing Power of Illness: The meaning of symptoms and how to interpret them*. Shaftesbury: Element Books Ltd.

Duncan, B., Miller. S., and Sparks, J. (2004) *The Heroic Client: A revolutionary way to improve effectiveness through client directed, outcome informed therapy*. San Francisco: Jossey Bass.

Fisher, S. and Greenberg, P. (1997) *From Placebo to Panacea: Putting psychiatric drugs to the test*. London: John Wiley.

Glasser, W. (2003) *Warning: Psychiatry can be hazardous to your mental health*. New York: HarperCollins.

Glenmullen, J. (2001) *Prozac Backlash*. New York: Touchstone.

Godsen, R. (2001) *Punishing the Patient: How psychiatrists misunderstand and mistreat schizophrenia*. Melbourne, Australia: Scribe Publications.

Gould, D. (1985) *The Black and White Medicine Show: How doctors serve and fail their customers*. London: Hamish Hamilton.

Healy, D. (1997) *The Antidepressant Era*. Cambridge, MA: Harvard University Press.

Healy, D. (2002) *The Creation of Psychopharmacology*. Cambridge, MA: Harvard University Press.

Holford, P. (2003) *Optimum Nutrition for the Mind*. London: Piatkus.

383

Humphreys, T. (1996) *The Power of 'Negative' Thinking.* Dublin: Gill & Macmillan.

Humphreys, T. (1996) *Self-esteem: The key to your child's education.* Dublin: Gill & Macmillan.

Humphreys, T. (1996) *The Family: Love it and leave it.* Dublin: Gill & Macmillan.

Jamison, K. R. (1996) *An Unquiet Mind.* New York: Vintage Books.

Johnstone, L. (2000) *Users and Abusers of Psychiatry.* London: Brunner-Routledge.

Joseph, J. (2003) *The Gene Illusion.* Ross-on-Wye: PCCS Books.

Karon, B. and Vandenbos, G. (1981). *Psychotherapy of Schizophrenia: The treatment of choice.* New York: Jason Aronson.

Karon, B. and Widener, A. (1999) 'The tragedy of schizophrenia'. *The Ethical Human Sciences and Services Journal, 1*(4) New York: Springer Publishing Company.

Laing R. D. and Esterton, A. (1970) *Sanity, Madness and the Family.* London: Pelican.

Masson, J. (1997) *Against Therapy.* London: HarperCollins.

Medawar, C. (1992) *Power and Dependence.* London: Social Audit Ltd.

Medawar, C. *The Antidepressant Web,* http://www.socialaudit.org.uk

Mendelsohn, R. (1979) *Confessions of a Medical Heretic.* Chicago: Contemporary Books.

Newnes, C., Holmes, G. and Dunn C. (1999) *This is Madness: A critical look at psychiatry and the future of mental health services.* Ross-on-Wye: PCCS Books.

Newnes, C., Holmes, G. and Dunn C. (2001) *This is Madness Too: Critical perspectives on mental health services.* Ross-on-Wye: PCCS Books.

Rogers, C. R. (1995) *A Way of Being.* Boston: Houghton Mifflin.

Rowe, D. (2002) *Beyond Fear.* London: HarperCollins.

Rowe, D. (2003) *Depression: The way out of your prison.* Hove: Brunner-Routledge.

Satir, V. (1978) *Peoplemaking.* London: Souvenir Press.

Shaw, F. (1997) *Out of Me: The story of a postnatal breakdown.* London: Viking.

Shelley, R. (Ed.) (1997) *Anorexics on Anorexia.* London: Jessica Kingsley.

Skrabanek, P. and McCormick, J. (1998). *Follies and Fallacies in Medicine.* Whithorn: Tarragon Press.

Spinelli, E. (1995). *Demystifying Therapy.* London: Constable & Robinson.

Spinelli, E. (1989). *The Interpreted World.* London: Sage Publications.

Warner, R. (1994) *Recovery from Schizophrenia.* London: Routledge.

Whitaker, R. (2002) *Mad in America.* Cambridge, MA: Perseus Publishing.

What Doctors Don't Tell You, newsletter available from What Doctors Don't Tell You, 4 Wallace Road, London, N1 2PG, UK.

384

INDEX

This is Madness
A critical look at psychiatry and the future of mental health services
Edited by **Craig Newnes**, **Guy Holmes** and **Cailzie Dunn**
ISBN 1 898059 25 X 1999

This is Madness Too
Critical perspectives on mental health services
Edited by **Craig Newnes**, **Guy Holmes** and **Cailzie Dunn**
ISBN 1 898059 37 3 2001

Personality as Art:
Artistic approaches in psychology
Peter Chadwick
ISBN 1898059 35 7 2001

Spirituality and Psychotherapy
Edited by **Simon King-Spooner** and **Craig Newnes**
ISBN 1898059 39 X 2001

Violence and Society
Making sense of madness and badness
Elie Godsi
ISBN 1 898059 62 4 2004

Beyond Prozac
Healing mental suffering
Dr Terry Lynch
ISBN 1 898059 63 2 2004

www.pccs-books.co.uk